Globalization and Inequality

NEOLIBERALISM'S DOWNWARD SPIRAL

John Rapley

LYNNE
RIENNER
PUBLISHERS

BOULDER
LONDON

Published in the United States of America in 2004 by
Lynne Rienner Publishers, Inc.
1800 30th Street, Boulder, Colorado 80301
www.rienner.com

and in the United Kingdom by
Lynne Rienner Publishers, Inc.
3 Henrietta Street, Covent Garden, London WC2E 8LU

Library of Congress Cataloging-in-Publication Data
Rapley, John, 1963–
   Globalization and inequality : neoliberalism's downward spiral / John Rapley.
     p. cm.
   ISBN 1-58826-245-6 (alk. paper)—ISBN 1-58826-220-0 (pbk. : alk. paper)
    1. Political stability—Economic aspects. 2. Liberalism. 3. Globalization. 4. Economic
policy. I. Title.
   JC330.2.R36 2004
   303.48'2—dc22

                  2003023327

British Cataloguing in Publication Data
A Cataloguing in Publication record for this book
is available from the British Library.

Printed and bound in the United States of America

    The paper used in this publication meets the requirements
    of the American National Standard for Permanence of
    Paper for Printed Library Materials Z39.48-1992.

   5 4 3 2 1

Contents

Acknowledgments

The writer's life can be a lonely one. Yet, even in the deepest solitude, he or she depends on the support and input of many others. This book was many years in the making and went through several stages of development before it reached this final version. I have to thank many people for helping me during the long journey.

At different stages in the development of various parts of the book, I drew on the comments of Ian Boyne, Gavin Williams, Barbara Harriss-White, Lawrence Powell, Lindsay Stirton, Lincoln Williams, Vin Connolly, Damien King, Roger Tangri, Wariboko Waibinte, Frances Stewart, Elizabeth Rapley, and Judy Hellman. The librarians at the University of the West Indies (UWI) Mona were as helpful and charming as ever, always finding ways to circumvent the obstacles faced by a Third World university in helping me to find resources. I also want to thank my department head, Brian Meeks, who arranged to give me a semester's leave from teaching to finish the manuscript's first draft. During that time I made my home at the Institut d'Études Politiques of the Université d'Aix-Marseille III and was warmly hosted by the director of its Latin American and Caribbean Centre, Daniel Van Eeuwen. I would like to think I was as inspired as Cezanne was by the view of Mont Sainte-Victoire that greeted me each morning as I walked to the café to pen my day's thoughts. The Research and Publications Grant Committee at UWI Mona and the French embassy attaché in Kingston covered the expenses of this minisabbatical.

For the next couple of years, as I beheld what I considered a dramatic chain of events in the unraveling of neoliberalism, I patiently revised my manuscript. When it came time to finally wrap up the project, I was fortunate to be offered a fellowship at Georgetown University, where the Jesuits at the Woodstock Center—committed as they are to justice and development—took an interest in my work and hosted me most graciously. But my stay in Washington would probably not have come to pass had it not been for the support and friendship of Terence and Joanne Cooney, who received me and looked after me as a member of their family during my year away from home.

Finally, I wish to thank those at Lynne Rienner Publishers who helped bring this project to fruition, including Lynne Rienner, Shena Redmond, and Jason Cook.

Globalization
and Inequality

1

Inequality and Instability

"The palace is not safe when the cottage is not happy," wrote Benjamin Disraeli in the nineteenth century. If expressed in a pithy manner, the idea was hardly original. More than two millennia before, Confucius had written that the ruler

> is not concerned lest his people should be poor,
> But only lest what they have should be ill-apportioned.
> He is not concerned lest they should be few,
> But only lest they should be discontented.
> And indeed, if all is well-apportioned, there will be no poverty; if they
> are not divided against one another, there will be no lack of men, and
> if there is contentment there will be no upheavals.[1]

Among contemporary political scientists, it has become almost axiomatic that material inequality and political instability go together. The belief embodied in Disraeli's adage became an object of research among political scientists in the 1960s. James C. Davies argued that revolutions were provoked not by indigence, but by rising prosperity, if and when that prosperity ended abruptly, causing the citizenry to feel that they were being shortchanged by their political leaders. Around the same time, Samuel Huntington argued that since rapid economic growth tended, at least in the short term, to coexist with a widening pattern of income distribution—a rule of thumb among economists known as the Kuznets curve—it led not to rising contentment but to greater discontent.[2]

The theory of "relative deprivation" was developed by Ted Robert Gurr in his classic book *Why Men Rebel*.[3] However, Gurr borrowed the

1

concept from W. G. Runciman, who in turn, in his book *Relative Deprivation and Social Justice,*[4] had drawn upon a 1949 study of the U.S. Army that located discontent in comparisons to more successful reference groups. The concept therefore originated in social psychology, finding its way afterward into political science. Yet political observers had long been aware of the phenomenon. In *The Ancien Regime and the French Revolution,* Alexis de Tocqueville had noted that it was in those parts of France that had experienced the greatest economic improvement in the period leading up to the revolution that discontent ran highest. "Patiently endured so long as it seemed beyond redress," he had written, "a grievance comes to appear intolerable once the possibility of removing it crosses men's minds."[5]

From such insights, Gurr came to define relative deprivation as "a perceived discrepancy between men's value expectations and their value capabilities." He went on to add that "societal conditions that increase the average level or intensity of expectations without increasing capabilities increase the intensity of discontent. Among the general conditions that have such effects are the value gains of other groups and the promise of new opportunities."[6] Therefore, exposure to a new reference group could well induce discontent and a search for radical change, even in the midst of rising prosperity. This point is worth bearing in mind throughout this book, in light of the discrepancy that has arisen between the expectations created by cultural globalization and the opportunities made possible by economic globalization. The essential point that emerged from Gurr's study was that in contrast to the conventional belief that contentment rises with prosperity—which happens to underpin most economic theorizing—in fact the opposite relationship frequently occurs: economic growth may actually induce social discontent.

In the 1970s, some political scientists and sociologists developed a theoretical explanation for this fact. It was to be called the theory of the moral economy. The basic thinking was that subordinate classes consented to the domination of an elite, provided that the elite was seen to be observing certain responsibilities to those they governed. Once these norms collapsed, usually in times of rapid economic growth that coincided with institutional changes—creating a more atomized society—instability resulted.[7] And if the moral economy school was to be criticized, it was more for its economic reasoning—in particular its assumptions about the rationality of peasants and their purported resistance to change—than for its political theory.[8]

In a 1987 article, Edward N. Muller and Mitchell A. Seligson gave the inequality-instability nexus what was to be perhaps its most systematic treatment when they showed that increased income inequality led to a substantial increase in the probability of domestic political violence.[9] Subsequently, further treatment revealed that policy changes that induced greater income inequality and withdrew state protections for the poor in Third World countries had begun a wave of political protest, originating in the 1970s and continuing since;[10] similarly, it now seems to be an accepted position among criminologists that widening inequality leads to a rise in crime.[11] In the 1990s a stream of primary studies lent credence to these claims, suggesting that structural adjustment policies had fed political instability because of the way they removed protections for the poor and widened income distribution.[12] Indeed, so widespread was the agreement on this point that even the World Bank, by the late 1990s, had come to accept that adjustment programs had to do a better job of sheltering the poor or assisting their transition to a new economy: whatever the economic viability of adjustment programs, they were proving to be politically unsustainable.[13]

What is interesting to note is that in recent years, support for the inequality-instability hypothesis has come from an unlikely source, namely neoclassical economics. At one time, virtually all neoclassical economists accepted the thesis that income inequality was functional to growth because it raised the savings rate—rich people typically have a lower marginal propensity to consume than poor people—and therefore accelerated investment. Friedrich Hayek added the further nuance that since demand for new products almost always emerges from among the rich, who alone can afford the cost embodied in research and development expenditures, the rate of innovation is also augmented by income inequality.[14] In the United States, such thinking had a great impact among politicians and policymakers from the 1980s onward, providing justification for taxation and fiscal policies that favored the rich over the poor, in both Republican and Democratic administrations.[15] Yet many neoclassical economists have in recent years been expressing doubts about the validity of the thesis that inequality is good for growth. They have pointed out that in poor societies, it may speed physical capital formation but inhibit human capital formation, which is an essential precursor to growth in poor countries. More important to this discussion, though, recent research suggests that it creates an uncertain policy environment and political instability, inhibiting fixed capital formation.[16] Some of the basis for the shift in economic thought may be found in the research of those few economists, like Richard Easterlin, who try to ascertain the roots of human happiness and the role played in this by material prosperity. Based on his comparison of income changes and surveys of contentment over time, Easterlin concludes that what drives human happiness is not absolute but relative levels of prosperity.[17] In other words, it is better to be a rich man in a poor society than a poor man in a rich society, even if the latter individual's absolute level of prosperity is higher than that of the first. This is really not surprising. Relative wealth affords one power over other individuals, and a good many philosophers would argue, in keeping with Friedrich Nietzsche, that humans derive more satisfaction from gaining power over the lives of themselves and others than they do from gaining power over material objects (by way of greater purchasing power). The obverse side to this is that a diminution in relative power, brought on by a widening pattern of material distribution, will augment dissatisfaction in that share of the population experiencing the decline.

To date, though, research on this subject has been confined essentially to national or regional case studies.[18] Academics have correlated patterns of income and wealth distribution with the incidence of political instability within given countries, or sometimes within given regions. But inferences based on the global distribution of income and wealth have yet to be made. Accordingly, what this book seeks to do is import the insights from comparative politics on the inequality-instability nexus into the field of international political economy. It seeks to understand, in essence, the impact neoliberal globalization has had on income distribution patterns worldwide, and how the latter have affected political stability on both local and global scales (seeing the two as increasingly intertwined). To accomplish this, the book will borrow a concept from international relations theory—that of the regime—to apply within the theory of comparative politics. It will thereby make political regimes, rather than institutions, the object of study in assessing changes in political stability. In keeping with the way that globalization is changing the world in which we live, therefore, the theoretical approach of this book lowers the barrier separating comparative and international political economy, suggesting that with respect to at least some topics, the two disciplines are merging into one.

The neglect of the global causes and consequences of changes in income distribution and political stability among comparativists is perhaps a bit odd since, over the past decade, social scientists of all stripes have been preoccupied with the phenomenon of globalization. Among those who have written on this subject, a popular avenue of inquiry has been to focus on globalization's impact on the nation-state (which, of course, provides the contours of the national case studies in question). Opinion diverges, roughly, into two camps. Broadly, there are those who say that globalization has rendered the nation-state irrelevant, and those who say that it has not (about which more in Chapter 4). Those in the former camp are more likely to be found among neoclassical economists and management specialists. It can be argued that their conclusions are prejudiced by their disciplinary attitudes: tending to favor policies that minimize the role of the state in the economy, they are inclined to read into globalization a force that compels a retreat of the state. On the other hand, political scientists, particularly those with leftist leanings, are more inclined to put globalization in its historical context—something economists are more inclined to overlook—seeing it as not entirely novel. Of course, it is probably just as likely that their own disciplinary leanings prejudice them in favor of reading into globalization a force that reinforces or at least does not undermine one of their favorite objects of study (not to mention sources of employment)—namely the nation-state.

Nevertheless, hardly anyone would say that globalization is not altering the rules of the political "game." Though nation-states persist, and earlier reports of their demise have proved exaggerated, the way in which they operate has been greatly transformed. Military doctrines developed during the Cold War have been rendered largely irrelevant by the growth of the international drug trade, new brands of terrorism, and the possibilities of cyber-warfare. State firms almost everywhere have been privatized, and policymakers have shifted toward regulation as a means of using the state to influence economic policy. Financial liberalization and the emergence of a globalized capital market have compelled virtually all governments to become far more responsive to the signals that emanate from that market, not to mention those put out by increasingly independent monetary authorities. Fiscal policy thus operates within more confined boundaries. New communications technologies have posed challenges to authoritarian governments, while creating new opportunities for international criminal organizations. Tax policies have had to be redrafted in order to attract foreign investment or merely retain domestic investment, given the increased mobility of capital. Population movements have led to new forms of identity politics, which themselves pose new dilemmas for governing elites. The list goes on, and the importance accorded to each item varies with the disciplinary background or ideological predispositions of the discussant.

Returning to the question of the impact of material inequality on political stability, then, to date there has been a recognition of the global causes of the changing structure of income and wealth distribution. However, the context of the studies remains national. To cite one telling case, the documentary film *Life and Debt,* which encapsulates much of current radical thinking on globalization, attributes Jamaica's current ills to the downside of globalization, but lapses into the old habit of portraying Jamaica as victim rather than agent. The possibility that the instability resulting from Jamaica's woes at the hands of the global economy could itself reverberate on the global economy is scarcely allowed. Jamaica is portrayed in the otherwise excellent film as a recipient, not an exporter, of global forces. However, as I will argue in this book, if that reasoning was ever sufficient, it no longer is. Insufficient attention has been paid to the global *consequences* of this altered pattern of income and wealth distribution. This book seeks to remedy that lacuna by showing the ways in which what happens in one part of the new global regime affects all the other parts. If in a colonial world the flow of goods, services, and people was highly controlled by the mother country, today more resources travel in all directions, evading many of the controls the powerful countries attempt to place on the movement of these resources across their boundaries. It therefore follows that we have to move beyond the local and be prepared to find the effects of political-economic changes in one part of the globe showing up in an entirely different region.

I will therefore argue in this book that neoliberal policies have had the effect of raising aggregate income but skewing its distribution, thereby causing a rise in political instability and volatility, which, in turn, is undermining the viability of the neoliberal regime.

Regimes and Institutions

International relations theory makes use of the concept of the regime, which refers not to an institutional framework but to a prevailing way of doing things based on implicit and explicit norms. The concept has not really made its way into comparative politics. However, I will attempt such an adaptation in this book, arguing that we can best appreciate the impact of globalization in terms of the way it has altered or is altering not political institutions but political regimes. Most of the political literature on globalization tends to focus on the former, with the particular topic of debate being the future of the state. In the early 1990s, a popular topic in the academic literature was the crisis of the state—the supposed threats to the nation-state's hegemony posed by globalization—but in more recent years it has become apparent that "reconfiguration" rather than retreat has been the dominant trend. However, what this debate sometimes fails to capture is the profundity of the transformation that has taken place outside the formal sphere of politics. The focus on the state—which this book understands as an institution, or more properly a set of interconnected institutions, and not as a regime—has an obvious limitation, namely that it can blind one to these changes. Once one has proved that the state is not about to disappear—and it seems safe to say that this has now been established in the literature—it follows that globalization is not the paradigmatic change its early neoliberal proponents said it was.

Yet the change has indeed been paradigmatic. But the change does not manifest itself solely in institutional change, such as alterations in the organization of the state, but in social and political change as well. So far, sociologists and geographers have arguably done a better job capturing this evolving reality than have political scientists. With their studies of migration, cultural change—the globalization-localization and homogenization-hyperdifferentiation nexus—the deterritorialization of culture, and the emergence of the global city, they have touched upon a reality of profound change of which institutional decline or renewal is only a part, possibly no more than an epiphenomenon.

This book understands a regime to be the norms of reciprocity that govern relations between governors and governed, and between dominant and subordinate classes, presenting the argument that a stable regime corresponds to an implied contract that binds elites and masses in bonds of mutual obligation. Essential to a stable regime is a mass perception of distributive justice. This is not the same as equality. Distributive justice has historically been rooted in perceptions of not equal share, but just share, as Chapter 2 will proceed to elaborate. It is a contextual norm and therefore not an objective reality, being wholly and solely relevant to a given political system's environment. Regimes may change within a static institutional framework, and alternately the institutional framework may be changed without a regime being altered. Stable regimes, moreover, do not relate merely to material distribution, but have a cultural or spiritual component as well. Hence, regime stability tends to correspond to cultural stability, and regime crisis tends to correspond to cultural ferment and what Gramsci called hegemonic dissolution. When a regime breaks down—when, put simply, a party (usually the dominant one) is perceived to have broken its end of the bargain—political instability results as the regime enters into crisis. The word *crisis*, it is important to note, is employed not in the currently conventional sense to denote a time of catastrophe or severe difficulty (although a crisis may entail such), but rather in its original medical sense to mean a turning point or impasse at which a decision on future direction must be taken—that is to say, the point at which an existing regime can only be managed in an ad hoc manner but is no longer self-sustaining, resulting in a multiplication of symptoms of distress. Only by a restoration of the old regime or, more likely, the constitution of a new one will the crisis be resolved. When studied this way, politics is in all instances preoccupied with the role of the masses in the political system. Democracy may formalize this role, but mass consent is always essential to the power of the dominant. Regimes, I will argue, always depend on the approval of the governed.

In any event, a functional regime must contain two components: a distributive regime and an accumulation regime.[19] The logic is simple. To distribute resources, regimes must also generate them. Accumulation crises can sink a regime itself into crisis, as happened in the Soviet bloc states. But even with a viable accumulation regime, a political system with a malfunctioning distribution regime will still descend into crisis. Indeed, a political system can probably survive an accumulation crisis longer than it can a distribution crisis.

The presumption in many works and a great deal of popular discourse is that globalization is an independent variable. I will argue, however, that globalization is a descriptive but not a diagnostic term. That is to say, it describes a condition but does not identify its root causes. Instead, neoliberal policies have driven a certain type of globalization, one designed to strengthen the role of globalizing fractions of capital while eroding not only the state but also the regimes that operated to the benefit of the world's subordinate classes, thereby raising profit rates and accumulation. As such, neoliberal globalization has produced an eminently successful accumulation regime, and in the 1990s gave rise to what was one of history's most rapid phases of economic growth, particularly in the United States. However, in provoking a distributive crisis, the neoliberal regime has undermined and tipped itself into crisis. After several major but localized financial crises (Turkey in 1990, Mexico in 1994), the global regime entered into what would be a major crisis in 1997–1998, a crisis that began in Asia and reached its own logical culmination with the implosion of the U.S. stock markets beginning in the spring of 2000. Compounding this, of course, was the terrorist attack on the United States in September 2001, which led the world into a postmodern—not to mention costly—war, and whose causes, as we shall see, are closely related to those of the crisis that provoked the global recession. The regime is functioning badly, and while crises can be managed temporarily, they cannot be resolved within the context of the neoliberal regime. The result is that the severity of each subsequent crisis surpasses that of the previous, consigning the whole regime to permanent instability.

So far, this line of argument is neither terribly controversial nor particularly original. Journalists and academics, with an eye on the Third

World, have been pointing to outbreaks of antisystemic tendencies for at least a decade now. But what is original is the claim that, if these outbreaks of political instability and protest appear to manifest local causes and consequences, they are best understood as forming part of a global chain. The regime is global: while the extent and character of neoliberal adjustment varies from one setting to the next, shaped by local political conditions, most of the planet's inhabitants are increasingly integrated into a global political economy whose resource accumulation and distribution are increasingly governed by neoliberal principles. Thus this global regime can be studied as an organism in which problems in one part of the body will eventually, barring an amputation, metastasize throughout the entire being. Accordingly, market analysts and economists who have tried to study the behavior of U.S. financial markets wholly from the point of view of domestic economics and politics have failed to appreciate that both the bull market of the 1990s and the subsequent bear market were affected in no small measure by political developments in Third World countries.

If, therefore, neoliberalism rather than globalization is the culprit, this helps explain why the popular responses to the crises of the new global economy have been inadequate to the task of resolving the crises. Critics of the new global economy have unwittingly bought the neoliberal line that conflates globalization with neoliberalism, and therefore have all too often been tempted to resist the beast by retreating into a defensive parochialism. While it is true that neoliberal policies have driven the current wave of globalization and given it its peculiar character, recent technological developments ensured that some form of cultural globalization and economic integration would almost certainly have occurred. Yet there has been a popular tendency to see neoliberalism and globalization as one and the same thing. Perhaps the strongest current of this tendency has been found in the street protests that have dogged international financial gatherings ever since the Asian crisis. Yet as I will argue, the antiglobalizers have so far, with all good intentions, helped to consolidate the global hold of neoliberalism. Indeed, the so-called challenges to globalization, and the forces it has manifested, offer no solution to the regime crisis and often perpetuate what they seek to eliminate. What is needed is a new form of thinking that recognizes the unique opportunities presented by the technologies and changes behind globalization, while looking for an alternative to the neoliberal paradigm. To further complicate matters, a nuanced critique of neoliberalism is also required, for as we shall see, not everything about neoliberal globalization has been bad. Among other things,

the weakening of states has in some places permitted democratic movements to flower and has enabled small and medium-sized businesses to
challenge vested big interests.

The Rise and Fall of the Neoliberal Regime

Political elites succeed in consolidating their position when they establish distributional networks that solidify their support bases, and when
they construct accumulation regimes. Political elites may be coterminous with dominant classes, but they need not be so, and in modern
capitalist societies the two groups are typically distinct. Nonetheless,
they are closely related in bonds of mutual dependence. But while the
economic power of dominant classes or class fractions affords them a
high degree of political leverage, they exclude the masses from political
consideration at their own peril. Only in rare instances can elites construct stable and enduring political systems on a basis of mass exclu-
sion. When a regime does begin to malfunction in this way, it creates a
window of opportunity for rival elites to build up mass support bases in
order to overthrow the governors. This may take many forms depending
on the situation, including peaceful overthrow, revolution, anticolonial
struggle, and foreign invasion. All the same, regime change may not
lead to profound institutional change, but may occur within the context
of a stable institutional framework.

However, political regimes entail more than material accumulation
and distribution. They always entail a cultural or spiritual dimension.
Like material regimes, cultural paradigms are evolved by elites, largely
to serve the interests of dominant classes or class fractions, but nonetheless depend on mass consent for their secure existence. And generally,
the cultural content of a paradigm that is accepted by a society will be
that which corresponds to and serves their material interests. In this
way, material and cultural reality will tend to mirror one another.
Hence, stable regimes will be accompanied by a fair degree of cultural
hegemony and stability. Equally, sudden change in the material conditions of a people's existence will render prevailing ideas obsolete, initiating a period of cultural experimentation. Politics is thus a conversa-
tion between governors and governed. The former may set the agenda,
determining who talks and controlling the scheduling, so to speak, but
they will usually find it hard to silence the other participants altogether.

It is now widely accepted that the state was the institutional framework that emerged alongside capitalism, while the nation was the identity that grew beside it. Hence the nation-state is seen as the political

expression of modern capitalism. Even societies that sought to chart an alternative path to capitalist development, namely state socialism, accepted the nation-state as the foundation of political life, such that by the twentieth century the nation-state had become all but hegemonic in global politics. Nevertheless, the nation-state was not a regime but the framework within which regimes rose and fell (though national identity and the sovereign state would be integral elements of all the regimes that followed from its advent, widely seen as the French Revolution). In the post–World War II period, I will argue, two distinct if related regimes came to dominate much of the globe: in the First World, what came to be known as the Keynesian welfare state, and in the Third World, what can be called the developmentalist state (not to be confused with the developmental state, a term peculiar to the political economy of development). In addition to these, a third type of regime, communism, took hold in a smaller number of countries that nonetheless accounted for a good share of the planet's population. However, late in the twentieth century these regimes entered into crisis and permitted the rise of new elites who implemented neoliberal policy changes. These policy changes, in turn, restored the health of the accumulation regimes but created distributional crises, which ultimately provoked broader regime crises across the world.

In the developed countries, the crisis of neoliberalism has manifested itself in a turn against democracy, a retreat from politics (most pronounced among young people), and a growth in far-right and antisystemic political movements. These developments have been fed in part by a marginalization and loss of voice among the more vulnerable citizens in society, owing to the decline of the traditional left. Democracy is at greatest risk in the so-called new democracies, countries that have implemented or restored democratic systems in recent years. As liberal economic regimes have left many of the citizenries in these countries relatively (if not always absolutely) deprived in recent years, and as their spokespeople in the old left have gone over to the new right, they have turned their backs on their leaders, or in some cases turned against them, feeding a new grassroots left. The great wave of democratization that allegedly washed through much of the Third World in the last two decades or so of the twentieth century appeared to be poised for a reverse as the century came to a close.

Early neoliberal theorizing on the erosion of the state proposed the growth of "region-states" and increasingly autonomous regions as an alternative to the centralized apparatus of the nation-state. In fact, the nation-state has proved to be remarkably tenacious. Even in those places of the globe where its roots seem shallowest, as in some parts of

Africa, its imminent demise does not appear at all likely. Nevertheless, both de facto and de jure decentralization have whittled away the power of central governments in much of the world as governments, under pressure from globalization, have had to hive off responsibilities or reduce their fiscal base. In the most extreme cases, in the former socialist bloc, states have broken up altogether, leading to the creation of new states. In the less extreme cases, like Canada or Belgium, national states are under constant stress. And in several ethnically diverse countries, whether Trinidad and Tobago or Fiji, a resurgence of ethnic politics has fragmented the tenuous bonds of national identity. Where resource scarcities have become most pronounced, the violence has been greatest. Seen in this way, the 1994 Rwandan genocide appears not as a unique case of tribal barbarism, but simply as the far end of a spectrum of fragmentation and localization. Mirroring fissiparous trends identified and legitimized in recent philosophy, this process can be aptly termed postmodern politics.

Its logical corollary, not to mention its polar opposite, is what can be called fundamentalist politics. Although the doctrine of fundamentalism emerged from U.S. evangelical Christianity in the early twentieth century, the term has more recently been applied to describe certain socioreligious movements that have arisen in the Third World. The most significant of these has been Islamic fundamentalism, but there have also been fundamentalist movements in Judaism, Buddhism, and Hinduism. Fundamentalism is understood to mean a resistance to the intellectual and cultural pluralism that has arisen with modernity and even more so with postmodernity. Instead, stress is put on a return to the fundamentals, the basics, of a given faith. The irony is that fundamentalism, which in practice fiercely opposes postmodernism, owes more to it than it would like to admit. In particular, its vision of a past golden age is less a historical fact than an ahistorical artifact, invented more out of loyalty to present needs than to past truths.

Where postmodern and fundamentalist movements have established themselves, they have done so less because of their cultural critique than because of the ways they have exploited emergent regime crises. In particular, by plugging the distributional gaps left by retreating states, emergent elites have built up support networks that they have used to undermine the authority of governing elites, in a few cases actually overthrowing them. Yet despite their appearance of potency, I will argue that both postmodern and fundamentalist politics fail at what they often set out to do. Seen as being responses and even challenges to globalization, both exist in a curious symbiosis with it, and actually advance more than threaten it. The same will be said of the antisystemic tendencies that have arisen in liberal democracies. They may be lauded as instances of "resistance" and may certainly appear to threaten the hegemony of a decadent establishment, but in fact they have proved ineffective as a response. If anything, they have solidified the dominant role of the globalizing elites whose neoliberal policies have been responsible for the creation of these antisystemic tendencies.

Yet if no coherent alternative to the neoliberal regime has yet been produced, that does not mean the crisis does not exist. It merely means it festers quietly, and sometimes not so quietly. The practitioners of revolution, like Lenin and Gramsci, knew that a revolutionary situation could persist indefinitely. Systems do not merely collapse. They are pushed over the edge. Thus, revolutionary situations and revolutions are not one and the same. We are living through a revolutionary age, if by revolution we use the understanding given to us from the philosophy of science, specifically Thomas Kuhn's concept of the paradigm.[20] In other words, this book is not anticipating a new sweep of radical social revolutions, even though revolution is one possible response to a crisis; rather, it is anticipating paradigmatic shifts, although an interim period of crisis management can last for years, even decades. When a paradigm falls, Kuhn argued, a period of intense intellectual ferment follows, until a new paradigm manages to consolidate its hold over the community of scholars. Equally, when a regime falls, a period of intense political ferment follows, until a new one manages to win the assent of the political community in which it operates. We have arguably descended into the stage of collapse, but there is no reason to expect the situation to resolve itself of its own accord. Instead, moments of crisis will multiply and grow more intense, but each will be susceptible to management and temporary resolution. Arguably, most of the world's governments, and certainly the major economic powers of the Western world, have been managing crises without resolving them ever since the Asian crisis first broke in 1997. This is tantamount to saying that medical technology can stave off death in a critically ill patient for an almost indefinite amount of time; all the same, the resultant quality of the patient's life will bring such techniques of crisis management into question.

Arguably, the crisis that has been most acutely felt in the First World, though in this case it originated in the Third World, was the sharp end to the boom of the 1990s in the United States and the resultant plunge in global stock markets that began in 2000. Most analysts and economists have studied this development within the context of changes largely confined to the U.S. economy. However, as we shall see, the crisis had its origin far away, in the barrios and ghettos of the global political economy. Once again, this crisis proved resistant to the traditional policy interventions by national monetary authorities. Many pointed to the brevity and mildness of the U.S. recession of 2001 to make the point that the economy never really got off track, but the subsequent slowdown and resumed slide in equity markets worldwide showed just how complex the challenges had in fact become. The rules of the game have changed, and the solution—at least a solution that is to prove anything more than temporary—will have to take this new global reality into account.

Where this solution will come from and what shape it will take remain unclear. Marx, himself a dedicated theorist of crisis, maintained that the way we view the world is so bound up with our material conditions of existence that it is impossible to predict how the future will look, since all we can see is the present reality. Only in the midst of a revolution, when the force of events lifts the scales from our eyes, can we begin to see the unfolding shape of the new order. But if we are in such a moment of rapid change, it is time to begin trying to transcend the limitations of the present and see what a future regime might look like.

Outline of the Book

Chapter 2 operationalizes the concept of the regime, focusing on the aspects of material accumulation and distribution. It also looks at the dominant regimes of the post–World War II period—the Keynesian welfare state, the developmentalist state, and communism. Chapter 3 broadens the discussion by bringing in the important role of culture. I argue that each regime has produced its own distinct culture, while regime stability corresponds to cultural stability. In Chapter 4, I argue that the regimes of the postwar period have all been eclipsed over the past generation by a new type of regime, neoliberalism. The "neoliberal age," I will suggest, began on 11 September 1973, when a military coup overthrew Salvador Allende, the Chilean president. Over the next twenty years, the neoliberal wave spread across the world, carrying its own peculiar culture to far corners of the globe and washing up finally on the shores of communist states after the Berlin Wall fell in 1989. In the process, the world experienced one of the biggest economic booms in history; the flip side of this boom, though, was a widening pattern of income distribution, both within and across societies.

Chapter 5 takes up the practical manifestations of this widening gap between rich and poor, focusing on the trends discussed above—the

retreat from democracy, postmodern politics, and fundamentalist politics. None of these outcomes, however, herald any kind of resolution to
the regime crisis of neoliberalism. This crisis, in the meantime, has
heightened and spread, and in Chapter 6 I will show that it reached a
head with the crash of the New York stock market that began in 2000
and ushered in the beginning of a long global economic downturn.
Chapter 7 points the way forward. I argue that just as the theoretical
interpretation of these events requires a more globalized approach—a
transcending of analytical categories and approaches that evolved largely during the era of the nation-state—so too will the practical and policy
responses to the crisis of neoliberalism have to be global rather than
national.

Notes

1. *Analects,* quoted in Kung-chuan Hsiao, *A History of Chinese Political
Thought,* vol. 1 (Princeton: Princeton University Press, 1979).

2. See James C. Davies, "Towards a Theory of Revolution," *American
Sociological Review* 27 (1962): 5–18; Samuel Huntington, *Political Order in
Changing Societies* (New Haven: Yale University Press, 1968). More recently,
Huntington returned to this theme of cognitive dissonance in his work on
democratization, *The Third Wave* (Norman: University of Oklahoma Press,
1991), pp. 69–72.

3. Ted Robert Gurr, *Why Men Rebel* (Princeton: Princeton University
Press, 1970).

4. W. G. Runciman, *Relative Deprivation and Social Justice* (Berkeley:
University of California Press, 1966).

5. Alexis de Tocqueville, *The Ancien Regime and the French Revolution*
(New York: Garden City, 1955), p. 167.

6. Gurr, *Why Men Rebel,* p. 13.

7. See, for example, James C. Scott, *The Moral Economy of the Peasant*
(New Haven: Yale University Press, 1976); and Goran Hyden, *Beyond Ujamaa
in Tanzania* (London: Heinemann, 1980).

8. See, for example, Samuel Popkin, *The Rational Peasant* (Berkeley:
University of California Press, 1979).

9. Edward N. Muller and Mitchell A. Seligson, "Inequality and
Insurgency," *American Political Science Review* 81, no. 2 (1987): 425–450.

10. John Walton and David Seddon, *Free Markets and Food Riots: The
Politics of Global Adjustment* (Oxford: Blackwell, 1994).

11. Anthony Harriott, *Police and Crime Control in Jamaica* (Kingston:
University of the West Indies Press, 2000), p. 4.

12. See, for example, Cyril I. Obi, *Structural Adjustment, Oil, and
Popular Struggles: The Deepening Crisis of State Legitimacy in Nigeria,*
Monograph Series no. 1/97 (Dakar: Codesria, 1997); Alison Brysk and Carol
Wise, "Liberalization and Ethnic Conflict in Latin America," *Studies in*

Comparative International Development 32, no. 2 (1997): 76–104; Mitchell A. Seligson and John T. Passé-Smith, eds., *Development and Underdevelopment: The Political Economy of Global Inequality,* 2nd ed. (Boulder: Lynne Rienner, 1998), pt. 2; and Neil Harvey, *The Chiapas Rebellion: The Struggle for Land and Democracy* (Durham, N.C.: Duke University Press, 1998).

13. See John Rapley, *Understanding Development* (Boulder: Lynne Rienner, 1996), pp. 119–121.

14. See, for example, Friedrich Hayek, *The Constitution of Liberty* (London: Routledge, 1960).

15. President Bill Clinton's last treasury secretary once wrote an influential paper arguing that most of U.S. investment was accounted for by intergenerational transfers among the super-rich, suggesting that redistributive policies might eat into the savings rate. See Laurence J. Kotlikoff and Lawrence H. Summers, "The Role of Intergenerational Transfers in Aggregate Capital Formation," *Journal of Political Economy* 89 (1981): 706–732. President Clinton's own tax policies tended to continue the trend of favoring the wealthy, while his fiscal policies cut spending on the poor, as in welfare reform. Jeff Madrick in the *New York Times,* 7 June 2001, p. C2.

16. See, in particular, Torsten Persson and Guido Tabellini, "Is Inequality Harmful for Growth?" *American Economic Review* 84 (1994): 600–621. Compare Jeffery M. Paige, *Agrarian Revolution* (New York: Free Press, 1975).

17. See Richard Easterlin, *Growth Triumphant: The Twenty-First Century in Historical Perspective* (Ann Arbor: University of Michigan Press, 1996), chap. 10.

18. This is the case, for example, with Walton and Seddon, *Free Markets and Food Riots.*

19. This theory therefore bears a close resemblance to that put forward by James O'Connor in *The Fiscal Crisis of the State* (New York: St. Martin's Press, 1973), but differs in two important details. First, O'Connor's theory operates strictly within the confines of nation-states, whereas my theory put forth here applies to all political systems and is also displaced to the global level. Second, O'Connor's theory presumes an inevitable crisis caused by the clash between the competing objectives of accumulation and legitimation; my theory put forth here makes no such presumption. Equally, my theory put forth here also shows resemblance to that of the French regulationist school of political economy. However, regulation theory deals only with welfare states. Moreover, regulation theory describes the operations of a particular type of accumulation regime—Fordism—and analyzes the role consumption plays in that regime, rather than treating distribution for its political as well as economic functions.

20. Thomas S. Kuhn, *The Structure of Scientific Revolutions* (Chicago: University of Chicago Press, 1970).

2

The Material
Formation of Regimes

In contrast to the historians who once focused on the study of the great men of history, in the twentieth century there emerged what came to be known as social history, whereby historians looked beyond kings and parliaments and studied what was taking place on the ground. This came to be known as "history from below." Ordinary people, those whose names historians never recorded, were seen to make history to a much greater extent than had once been believed. In the first place, ordinary people had histories separate from those of their overseers. So, for example, the uniform image of medieval Europe, in which Catholicism was hegemonic, gave way to a more complex view of societies in which local pre-Christian beliefs and practices meshed with those of the new Church, preserving things like festivals for centuries. In the second place, kings and popes seldom if ever could act independently of the people. Rather than the image of omnipotent kings, lords, and popes that still lingers in popular imagery, at most times ordinary people enjoyed a measure of autonomy in their communities, and a ruler rode roughshod over them at his own risk. By concentrating their repressive resources in specific places, and for a set duration of time, medieval European kings could in fact bring rebellious peoples to heel and impose their uncontested authority. However, for the most part village communities carried on with a high degree of autonomy from lord and king, and resisted efforts by the former to overstep their powers beyond the limits set by tradition.[1] When crises made it impossible for the regime to fulfill its tasks, local networks developed to provide individuals with the material needs and security they required, even though formally the state continued to exist.[2] Nor was this a feature peculiar to medieval Europe. Recent research has suggested that the decay of the Roman Empire, which St. Augustine's contemporaries blamed on the rise of Christianity, did not so much result from as feed the rise of Christianity. When the imperial political structures failed to deliver resources the people needed, particularly during outbreaks of plague, the Christian churches filled the gap with such effectiveness as to undermine the social basis of the Roman state.[3]

Thus, even despotic leaders were in fact hemmed in by obligations to their underlings. In his historical novel *Doguicimi,* Paul Hazoumé has the Dahomean king—who appeared to foreign observers and his subjects as almighty—say of himself: "Imprisoned in tradition, obsessed with customs from which I must not stray by a single step, and petitioned by those in my entourage, I am, most of the time, no more than an instrument in a multitude of hands that are invisible to the people. The king is perhaps the person with the least freedom in his entire kingdom."[4] It is not merely his nobility whom he must serve, though, for the king has to perform a number of obligations he does not necessarily like because to refuse would anger his people. The restrictions of a nineteenth-century African king remind one of Machiavelli's advice to the prince, that the ruler of a religious people should himself appear to be religious, even if he has not a shred of piety in him, in order to retain the support of his followers.[5] This does not mean the ruler becomes a tool. But it does mean he must have sensitive political antennae. As S. E. Finer comments in his *History of Government,* "Where the claim of the ruler to authority is out of kilter with the prevalent belief-systems of the society, he must either 'change his plea,' that is, make himself acceptable in terms of that belief-system, or else delegitimize himself and fall."[6]

Over time many civilizations developed philosophical and even legal recognitions of the obligations of rulers to ruled. St. Thomas Aquinas's right of rebellion against a tyrant found its parallel in the Chinese emperor's having to retain the Mandate of Heaven, or the African emperor's having to enjoy the consent of his chiefs by not breaking with the ways of the ancestors. In the same vein, the Arab philosopher Ibn Khaldun wrote that "a ruler can only obtain power with the help of his own people" and that once the ruler began to claim all the glory for himself, the people would turn against him.[7]

If we start with these insights, we can develop a theory of politics that might explain contemporary events. Let us start with a definition. In most first-year university courses on politics, students begin with David Easton's famous definition that politics is the authoritative allocation of values. By values, Easton meant simply the things that human beings value. Value in this sense could be likened to the economic conception of utility. This left the definition sufficiently open to take account of those political struggles, such as the abortion debate, that did not entail control over or access to material resources. This book will divide the values or goods of politics into two broad categories, material and spiritual.

However, while access to spiritual goods plays an important role in politics, conflict over material goods makes up most of its content, for the following reasons. First is the sheer importance of material resources to human existence. One cannot engage in struggles over abortion or individual liberty unless one is first fed, clothed, and housed, and for the mass of humanity that has lived so far in this planet's history, satisfying basic needs has consumed much of life. Besides, the pursuit of nonmaterial values is facilitated, in most instances, by access to resources. The desire for learning is made easier by access to books or libraries. The desire for spiritual fulfillment is made easier by temples, churches, religious texts, and learned instructors who have themselves benefited from the fruits of educational establishments. The yearning for freedom is greatly enhanced by a political regime that commits its own legal and judiciary resources to the defense of those rights. And so to return to the analogy of the abortion struggle, the victors in this conflict will ultimately depend on the resources of a state (or similar body) to enforce the decisions they favor.

One might infer from this that in advanced industrial societies, the satisfaction of needs well beyond the basic has liberated people to turn politics over to higher pursuits. At times this has been so—the relative abundance of the industrial age has given rise to all forms of political experimentation—but in the main, prosperity has if anything intensified the struggle over resources. This results from what can be called the paradox of prosperity. As income grows, rather than sating demands, it creates new ones, and the faster income rises, the faster these new demands crop up.[8] As a result, expectations continually outrun the economy's ability to meet them, a phenomenon that is the subject of considerable debate. Some theologians and radical critics blame it on a society devoid of spirituality, which thus finds gratification in material stimulation alone, while some economists suggest the very nature of gratification means that wants have a tendency to accelerate exponentially.[9] The important point for this discussion is that while resource scarcity, whether real or contrived, intensifies conflict, the paradox of prosperity means that such struggles are not confined to poor societies with evident resource shortages. Demand for resources does not diminish with growth but actually increases.[10] Thus the rapid rises in prosperity experienced by a fifth of humanity over the past two centuries have unleashed a political struggle that is intensifying, not diminishing over time.

We must then ask how this competition for resources is played out. This takes us back to the point we began with, the relationship between elites and masses. In any human society beyond the most rudimentary level, economic elites emerge. Paul Samuelson once wrote that "if we were to make an income pyramid out of a child's toy building blocks, with each layer portraying $1,000 of income, the peak would be far higher than the Eiffel Tower, but almost all of us would be within a yard of the ground."[11] Wealth is typically even more unevenly distributed, reflecting the accumulation over time of differences in income. In capitalist societies, a relatively tiny share will control most of a country's corporate stock. But the rule is not peculiar to capitalism, it appears universally: societies committed to egalitarianism, as were the Soviet bloc states, may mitigate but never eliminate these inequalities. Moreover, if they eliminate concentrated ownership, they do little to change the concentration of control, and the distinction between the two may be a nicety: privatization in former socialist societies did not replace bureaucratic elites with capitalist ones, but merely legalized the effective ownership the former already enjoyed.[12] In Russia, for instance, it has been estimated that following the privatization of formerly state-owned enterprises, all but one-fifth of Russia's large enterprises remained in the hands of Soviet-era managers.[13]

Those at the top of the pyramid enjoy not only a disproportionate degree of control over society's economic output. So too will they tend to enjoy a disproportionate degree of political power. Few people, even in the most liberal of societies, will ever rise out of the social class into which they were born.[14] And just as the economy is dominated by relatively small groups, so too is the political process dominated by a surprisingly small number of people. Moreover, the politically powerful bear close connections to the economically privileged, so much so that in some societies there is no apparent distinction between the two groups.[15] Liberal democracies, supposedly rooted in the principle of perfect political equality, do not escape this rule, this "iron law of oligarchy" as the sociologist Robert Michels once called it. Even associations committed to democratic principles find it necessary to submit to the "iron law of oligarchy" if they are to be at all effective.[16]

What is the connection between these two groups? There was once a debate in political science between two competing schools of thought, the elite theorists and the class theorists. Elite theorists argued that in any organization, a small group, the elite, rose to dominance. Not only was this inevitable, but it was usually also seen as desirable, since the elite were believed to be more enlightened and better able to govern than the mass. Class theorists, however, dismissed the notion of a gifted elite and pointed out that membership in the ruling elite depended less on ability and intelligence and more on wealth. Political power, they argued, reflected economic power, and therefore what was important to study was not the behavior of political elites but the interests of the dominant class in society.

Yet while these two approaches have usually set themselves up against one another, they can be made complementary. It is a truism that in any organization, including any economic organization, a small group of individuals rises to the top. The attributes that propel them there are only sometimes economic. For while there are economic elites, so too are there elite athletes, scholars, and artists. Their gifts may be inherited or environmental, but very often they amount to what José Ortega y Gasset once called the willingness to "make great demands on themselves, piling up difficulties and duties."[17] Elites have the drive, vision, energy, and skills that enable them to take the lead in their respective fields. Let us say that these attributes, only occasionally physical, reflect what one might call a spiritual endowment. Yet membership in the elite is not determined solely by an individual's attributes. As C. Wright Mills argued in his classic study of the U.S. political elite, elites create selection mechanisms that enable them to filter new entrants to their ranks.[18] That way, an elite can actually freeze out some of the best and brightest.

This book will look principally at those elites who dominate the political process, namely political elites. These elites are composed of the individuals who hold high political or administrative offices or play leading roles in the political organizations and institutions—parties and interest groups—that direct society. Since politics concerns itself with the allocation of resources, it follows that control over resources affords one political power. Put simply, the greater one's wealth, the greater one's power. This is the golden rule of politics, that he—and historically, it has usually been a he—who has the gold makes the rules. Yet those with the gold do not always care to make the rules. Nor does wealth in itself afford one entry to the political elite: Ross Perot wanted desperately to turn his personal wealth into political capital, but U.S. political and cultural elites frustrated the transaction. If political power is determined by economic power, but membership in the political elite is not, it follows that economic power is a necessary but not sufficient condition for entry to the political elite. This, however, is not so simple a matter as saying that the political elite is drawn from the economic elite, for often the economic elite will be of little political consequence. Otherwise, we would never witness the spectacle of prominent businesspeople berating the government on the evening news. Rather, the power exercised by political elites will be shaped and limited by the material interests of the dominant economic group, which can be called a class or, in more complex societies where classes have many components, a class fraction.

The dominant class fraction may not be an elite, though. For it may lack the political organization or skilled leadership necessary for it to actually penetrate the political elite.[19] Nonetheless, if a class fraction's sway over the economy is great—if, for instance, it accounts for a particularly large share of economic output and is thus an important component of the political elite's resource base—it will not be regarded lightly by the political elite. This is because the political elite, to secure its position, must generate the resources demanded by its mass support base, and so must not antagonize those elements in society needed to carry out that task. The political elite may enjoy a high degree of autonomy relative to the dominant class or class fraction, but it can never separate itself from its environment.

This environment will shape or at least structure the political elite's behavior. To appreciate this environment, one must identify the dominant class or class fractions, their level of political organization—this is particularly important where a class fraction is, in the context of the overall economy, economically weak—and the class background of the political elite. Status, which is understood to be an indicator of whether an individual belongs to the elite or the mass, may be a spiritual identity, and class—owner versus producer—may be a material one. But the behavior of an elite will, regardless of its spiritual identity and orientation, be largely influenced by its material interests. Anybody can enter the political elite from outside society's dominant class, but will be unlikely to advance far or for very long if his or her political orientation differs profoundly from those of an economically powerful and/or well-organized dominant class or class fraction.

The main point is this: in all societies, as a rule, there will be a direct relationship between economic power and political power. Most of history's regimes acknowledged this openly, cementing clearly the link between control over economic resources and political power. However, liberal democratic regimes broke with tradition by creating the separation between private and public power. In point of fact, the link between economic and political power remains as strong as ever in modern liberal democracies, where the high costs of election campaigns have increased the dependence on money. And while anybody can contribute to an election campaign and participate in politics, it follows that candidates under pressure to enlarge their resources will inevitably have to turn to that small share of the population that controls most of the economy's income.

Explaining why minorities dominate the politics and economics of any society is probably an even more contentious topic than showing that they have done so. Some elite theorists accept the ancient view that some are born to rule and others to follow. Modern philosophers have generally eschewed the principle of hereditary rule in favor of the idea put forth by Nietzsche, that the *ubermensch,* or supermen, are those who invite suffering in order to strengthen themselves; the rest of humanity exists for their glory. This recalls the view of Ortega y Gasset, who, while less hostile to democracy than Nietzsche, shared his view of the elite as inviting challenges whereas the masses "demand nothing special of themselves . . . to live is to be every moment what they already are, without imposing on themselves any effort towards perfection; mere buoys that float on the waves."[20] At the other extreme from the elite theorists are radicals of various stripes, heirs to an equally ancient view that locates virtue in common folk (a view that Nietzsche for one spared no effort to ridicule). Marxists, for example, have always accepted the reality of minority dominance but have pointed out that it arose not from spiritual superiority, but from a control over wealth that at its inception often began with theft: those prominent business families who, generation after generation, passed their riches down to children who were often mediocre but whose position was unassailable, and whose wealth might have come from an ancestor who was a thief, slaver, or bootlegger. Radical feminists employ a similar framework but decry patriarchy rather than class rule, pointing to the historic preponderance of men in most ruling elites; Afrocentrists speak of white supremacy; and so forth.

As to interpretation, radicals see minority dominance as bad, elite theorists see it as inevitable if not good. Predictably, given their tendency to grab the middle ground, liberal theorists see it as inevitable but sufficiently open to reform to make it, if not perfect, at least the better of a bunch of bad choices. And so they consider liberal democracy the optimum trade-off between the apparently irreconcilable goals of freedom and equality: not true government by the people, which leads to the tyranny Ortega y Gasset so feared, but at least a regime in which the masses enjoy maximum power to rein in elites.[21]

This book will try neither to explain nor to interpret minority dominance. These are well-trodden terrains upon which improvements can scarcely be made. Instead, minority dominance will be taken for granted, and what appears to be a lesson of history will be accepted: that stable societies in which most citizens are apparently, on balance, happy with their lives have emerged from some types of minority dominance. By identifying the conditions of a stable regime, one can better understand why and when they break down. The question of whether fully egalitarian societies can be created will not be addressed in these pages. Not, however, because it is deemed irrelevant. Rather because the pressing questions for social scientists at the turn of this millennium are arguably of a different order.

The Role of the Masses

Although elite dominance is a fact of life, only in the most rudimentary societies can one speak of there being one elite, and even in those cases there is usually competition within the elite between strong personalities. In more complex societies, one will find elites at all levels of society, starting from the most basic of organizations, like the family, and at any given level there will usually be competing elites. Given the multiplicity of elites in most any society, elites are constantly vying with one another for influence if not dominance. Even in totalitarian societies in which the elite presents a facade of seamless unity, elite competition goes on beyond the public view, as studies of Soviet Russia revealed.[22] The competition may become a violent battle for supremacy, or it may remain a more amicable contest among friendly elites who nonetheless want to hedge their bets and retain secure positions of influence. But in the course of competition, elites will try to improve their position vis-à-vis their rivals by increasing their control over resources. The most potent resource in politics is people. Thus, political elites always seek to build up networks of supporters.

In simpler, relatively primitive societies, the division between elite and mass is fairly clear. In more complex societies, such as those of modern liberal democracies, the picture becomes more confusing. An individual may be linked into several elites, and at the same time be in the mass base of some others. Elites atop some networks may patronize not only their clients but also other elites, as happens when interest group leaders fund political candidates. Politics thus becomes a stew of competing elites, popular pressure, shifting alliances, and network building and atrophy. This complexity has led some to reject the argument that elites dominate the political process, at least in liberal democracies. However, just as an impressionist painting looks like a mess of color up close but takes on a powerful clarity at a distance, so too do the colors and hues of a society's politics come together into a clearer image once one backs away from the micropicture and takes a macroperspective. The fact is that in any society, a relatively small number of people enjoy an inordinate amount of income and power. Relative balances of power and ratios of income distribution will vary from society to society, but the basic rule has remained.

So why do the masses put up with rule by the few? In the past, a rather crude answer was sometimes offered that invoked ideology or brute force. Either the poor believed, falsely or otherwise—evidence on class mobility suggested it was usually the former—that through hard work they too could be rich one day, or they believed that their station in life was ordained by a power greater than them, or they were just plain ignorant that they were working as hard as someone else but earning a lot less for it. If the latter, once they became "conscious" and decided to rebel against their subjection, they faced elites whose control over resources included repressive power. The historical record indicated with depressing clarity that uprisings against the rich were never anything more than short-term successes. Reaction always followed, and the longer it was delayed, the harsher it was.

Glancing rapidly through history, this explanation seemed plausible. Where it ran aground—indeed, where orthodox Marxist theory ran into difficulties—was in recent history, in particular the history of Western liberal democracies. Given the Marxist definition of exploitation, of surpluses being appropriated by dominant classes from producing classes, the Western world's working classes were among history's most exploited people. They did most of the work but won comparatively few of the fruits of their labors. Given their relatively high level of consciousness—they were organized into unions and political parties that could operate freely, and Marxist professors lectured their children at university—they should have taken the logical next step into seizing control of the means of production. They did not.

Why was the working class, that exploited mass that was to be the standard-bearer of revolution, such a disappointment? Some Marxists blamed it on their having sold out to capitalism. Lenin himself decried unions for tying the working class more intimately into the operations of the capitalist economy. However, workers were not foolish. They knew what they wanted, they saw their options when they glanced further afield at supposedly communist societies, and they came to see that their interests were indeed bound up with contemporary capitalism. Their institutions, in particular their unions and the parties, which had successfully agitated for such things as wage and safety legislation, pensions, and unemployment insurance, had helped create a structure that secured them a share of society's output that they considered reasonable, and that certainly made it possible for them to enhance their living standards, particularly in the post–World War II period. That is why, in election after election, they consented to their "oppression" by supporting parties committed to the existing system. There were but few exceptions to this rule. Although French workers supported an unreconstructed Stalinist communist party for longer than most, in the main communist parties weaned themselves away from revolutionary doctrine and toward such ideas as Eurocommunism, which sought no fundamental changes to the political economy but merely a greater degree of redistribution. Moreover, where old-fashioned communist parties retained strong support, they did so by effectively performing many of the same functions the state was trying to perform in winning over the working class—namely, creating distributional networks to mobilize mass support.

The masses, though largely excluded from political decisionmaking—even in liberal democracies their political activity is for the most part confined to approving the decisions taken by elites—are not without their potency. People excluded from the political process, even when their control over resources is marginal or nonexistent, still seek access to resources, whether they take the form of physical security, spiritual comfort, or material benefits. Throughout most of history their means of securing resources and their expectations may have been considerably less than those of Europe's and North America's working classes since World War II, but they were seldom nonexistent. And when the mass believes that elites are depriving it of what it considers to be its just share of society's resources, it can undermine and even destroy ruling elites.

The key words in the sentence above are "believes" and "just share." Beliefs, as we all know, can be mistaken. They can also be manipulated by elites to serve their own interests. However, there is little evidence validating the description of ordinary folk as sponges who soak up the ideas fed to them by their leaders. The failed efforts of fallen totalitarian governments to "brainwash" their citizens by feeding them an endless diet of carefully monitored regimentation belies this assumption. When a belief system has consolidated its hegemony through repression—when disagreeing with it means going to jail—people will submit passively and retreat into apathy and resignation; it is this decay that is said to have hastened the downfall of Eastern Europe's former communist governments. Still, people do not just give up and accept the belief, and once liberated from it—when the Berlin Wall has fallen—most will quickly shed even the pretense of belief. As a rule, people will accept and hold to a belief not because they are required to, or because it is true or false. The veracity of a truth and its popularity may at times coincide, but most people—including most highly educated people—do not engage in the sort of philosophical reasoning involved in testing the validity of a hypothesis. Instead, people will accept or hold to a belief because they find it functional to their material interests (in fact, some philosophers hold that true truths are so disturbing, and thus so dysfunctional to human happiness and well-being, that it is better not to publicize them but to keep them the secret preserve of philosophers; thus Nietzsche suggested that poetic lies were needed to make life bearable, and a popular adage today says that while the truth will set you free, it will first make you miserable). And so, merely celebrating the cult of the individual and the doctrines of personal liberty, as liberal philosophers did, had little impact on nineteenth-century European working classes who were suffering from the bourgeoisie's newfound freedoms. Liberalism only became a widely accepted doctrine in Western societies when its promoters were able to successfully persuade the mass public that its ideas could benefit *them*. In general, this task has been done more by popularizers and sloganeers than by philosophers. The ideas may be evolved by the likes of Adam Smith and Robert Nozick, but it is the Horatio Algers and Madonnas who effectively communicate them to a mass public. And the latter do it not for philosophical reasons (generally), or because they are puppets of the bourgeoisie, but simply because the doctrine offers them high rates of return.

Ideas, like any other product, are released onto markets made up of human consumers. As neoclassical research has revealed, state regulation cannot entirely eliminate undesired economic activities, but drives some of it underground, all while placing a scarcity premium on the prices of the goods or services involved and thereby restricting their availability. So it goes with ideas. A mistake of some past theoretical work on media and propaganda has been the same mistake of the old political histories that assumed the masses behaved as the political elites said they should or said they did. Social history exposed both that error and the error that people also *believed* what the elites wanted them to. They might have observed certain practices because they deemed it in their best interest to do so, but we now know that, for example, long after the Roman Catholic Church had supposedly consolidated its hegemony over Europe, pagan beliefs and practices continued, often worming themselves into the practices of the Church itself. Where Christian beliefs, and not simply nominal Christian membership, were widely accepted, it now appears to have been the result of the fact that these beliefs were seen by people to serve their interests more effectively than other beliefs.[23]

Just as gifted minds all through history have produced visions of new inventions but have only been able to sell these ideas when a market to absorb them justified somebody else's investment, so it goes with ideas. When it comes to the ancestry of ideas, there is a ring of truth in Alfred North Whitehead's declaration that the European philosophical tradition consists of a series of footnotes to Plato. Many of the ideas we think of as recent have been around for a very long time. The Greek Cynic philosopher Diogenes celebrated the cult of the liberated individual long before John Stuart Mill's ancestors even came to England, and the list of other "modern" ideas that actually emerged somewhere else much earlier is a long one. However, when Martin Luther took direct aim at the Roman Catholic doctrine of salvation by stressing that salvation arose from individual faith alone, and not membership in the body of Christ as mediated by Holy Communion, he faced an environment different from that of earlier radical theologians. Now there were North European princes whose increasing economic autonomy had led them to seek a growing measure of autonomy from the papacy, and Luther's doctrine provided this.[24] Equally, Luther's mass appeal was exploited by all sorts of leaders anxious to emancipate the peasantry from their increasingly oppressive feudal bonds.

Capitalism had created a market for the doctrine of individualism and all the ideas bound up with it. In particular, the emerging bourgeoisie sought to emancipate itself from the feudal bonds that limited its boundaries for operation. However, Europe's emerging working classes, whose interests were still wrapped up in the collective nature of the industrial production process, found liberalism alien and retained their attachment to collectivist ideologies, initially of the traditional variety,[25] later of the new socialist strains (in contrast, in the United States, where there existed a large class of independent farmers, liberal ideas had an early resonance and became part and parcel of the national identity). Indeed, right through the nineteenth century the liberal regimes of the European bourgeoisie remained under threat, and in a few instances—most notably in 1848—came near to being toppled. Ideological hegemony did not save European capitalism. What did was incorporation of Europe's working classes into the regimes that had taken shape in modern states, politically through the extension of the franchise, which the working class had been demanding,[26] economically through the institution of basic welfare regimes and legislation to improve the conditions of workers.[27] Ideology may have helped motivate the demands of workers for these changes, but ideology did not account for the state's relenting: the first welfare state was created in Bismarck's Prussia, and was motivated not by liberal anguish over the lot of the poor but rather by a Machiavellian recognition of the truth in Abraham Lincoln's adage: the best way to eliminate your enemies is to make them your friends.

And with Europe's working classes coming to derive what they apparently considered their just share of capitalism's output, the destructive potency gradually waned, even if it would be some time before the threat disappeared altogether. This leads us into the consideration of "just share." Some students of modern Third World peasant economies have uncovered something that they have called the moral economy.[28] The idea is that in any society, people have not only economic expectations of the political economy in which they operate, but also moral ones. They can put up with a lot of poverty and hardship if they believe that elites are observing certain moral principles in the way they manage society's resources. People can tolerate a good deal of deprivation, suffering, and even death if they believe it is inevitable, or if they are persuaded that the future health of the system in which they exist depends on it. Critically, they will willingly put up with this suffering if they feel it is indeed "their" system, one that will resume the satisfaction of their or their loved ones' wants when it regains its capability to do so. Thus, people's resource expectations vary with the circumstances. Extreme poverty does not necessarily lead them to rebel; indeed, as we have seen, revolutions frequently occur during or immediately after periods of rising prosperity. Instead, what leads people to rebel is either the conviction that the moral codes of the political economy in which they operate have been violated, or the possibility of allying themselves to new elites who promise a superior moral code.[29] Historians of the French Revolution note that during the bread riots that preceded the revolution, when bakeries were looted the rioters usually left behind some payment, albeit less than the market price. They were not stealing bread so much as paying what they considered the just price.

There appears to be no conception of just share preprogrammed into us from birth. What is considered just share varies with context, and is equally a product of belief. As a society's prosperity rises, the expectations of its members increase. This helps explain why rapid economic growth gives rise to revolutions, either because the rising expectations it fosters run into the inevitable cyclical downturn that will strike any booming economy, or simply because the mass public believes that the elite is securing for itself an even larger share of the growing prosperity than it deserves. It was all very well to remind

European workers in the mid–nineteenth century that they were better fed and clothed than their ancestors, but it convinced few skeptics who saw that the relative improvement in working-class conditions had fallen behind the relative improvement in the conditions of the capitalist class. As for belief, people will formulate a different conception of just share based on the information at their disposal. Guest workers from the contemporary Caribbean sometimes return home from Europe or North America with expectations their countries find difficult to satisfy. In a similar vein, modern socialist states found it difficult to maintain their hegemony, and in many cases failed to maintain their existence, when the expectations of their citizenries changed thanks to the increased flow of information from Western societies.[30] To the extent that elites can control information, they can thus influence the beliefs regarding just share held by the mass, but they can seldom dictate them.

When an elite has created a strategy to generate and distribute resources to its support base, a regime—the prevailing way of doing things—has emerged. A viable regime depends upon two components, an accumulation strategy or regime and a distribution strategy or regime. If either breaks down, the regime enters a period of crisis and risks collapsing altogether. Indicators or symptoms of a crisis include rising political instability, antisocial behavior such as crime, violence, or anomie, antipolitical behavior or a retreat from involvement in politics, and a decline in civic engagement. It is important to note that measures of both inequality and instability are dynamic, not static. That is to say, there is no ideal level of income distribution that ensures stability, or a universal level of instability that can be characterized as critical. It will vary from society to society, since "normal" levels of income distribution and stability will vary greatly. For example, some societies can clearly tolerate higher levels of violence and aggression than others, while some find higher degrees of inequality acceptable. Yet within a given context, it is hypothesized, sudden changes in distribution will correlate over time with similar changes in stability.

Thus it cannot be overemphasized that the key variable in political stability is not absolute but relative prosperity. This is where sociologists and political scientists part company with economists. The latter generally see humans as rational utility-maximizers. In theory, therefore, as they obtain more of the things they value, their contentment should rise. So, all other things being equal, prosperity and contentment will rise together. This thesis is based on an atomistic conception of human society, in which individuals are essentially autonomous and therefore use themselves as reference points.[31] Thus, as they observe their own status in life improving, they will feel more contentment. Yet many and possibly most social scientists make a different assumption, namely that humans are social animals. As such, they use other humans as their reference points. As a result, there may well be times when an individual's absolute prosperity rises while his or her relative prosperity declines. That is to say, relative to past status, there may be an improvement, but relative to his or her reference point, there may be a deterioration. Another way of putting it is that the variable we have to pay close attention to is not immiseration but marginalization. Immiseration refers to an absolute in one's conditions of life, and is therefore individual. Marginalization is, by definition, a social phenomenon. It refers to the experience of being pushed to the margins of a given group. The key, then, is not what is happening to individuals as such, but what is happening to individuals in relation to the group to which they belong. This is a very important distinction. One of the key features of the global economy in the 1990s was that immiseration declined while marginalization rose, and it is the latter that ends up playing the determining role in political stability.

Distribution, then, appears to be key. Regimes can sometimes survive prolonged accumulation crises if they maintain a distribution regime that is widely perceived as fair. In contrast, even within periods of booming prosperity, the failure of a distribution regime can bring the whole regime down. To use Marxist terminology, regimes can more readily survive an accumulation crisis than they can a legitimation crisis. Fundamentally, a viable regime depends not on its accumulation strategy but on an effective distribution strategy, but to the extent that an accumulation crisis gradually provokes a distribution crisis, it will weaken a regime, perhaps fatally. Regimes may simply mediate and regulate the accumulation and distribution processes, as in minimalist states, or they may take full control of them, the most extreme examples being totalitarian states. Note that regimes are not coterminous with states or governments. Regimes exist within these, and several regimes can rise and fall within the same state, though outside of revolutionary periods only one regime will prevail. In normal times, networks that oppose the dominant elite can exist and operate, but typically they will become salient only when the regime ceases to function effectively.

The Changing Regimes of the Nation-State

Having put forth the rudiments that will be used to build a theory, it is now time to draw them together into some kind of coherent whole. First, in any given society an elite will emerge to gain control over a disproportionate share of the society's economic output. To secure its position of dominance, an elite will build up a political power base by establishing networks of support. In order to retain the commitment of its mass support base, an elite will grant access to a share of the economic output it has appropriated in the form of either goods or services, both material and spiritual. The share needed to satisfy the demands of the mass is contextual, and is governed by the mass's awareness of the society's level of output as well as the presence or absence of rival elites. Regarding output, rich societies produce higher wants and dynamic economies produce rising wants, to the extent that the masses are informed of the society's productive capacity. Such information can be manipulated but not wholly controlled by elites, since most of it is gleaned by observation, whether of prices in markets or mansions nearby. Regarding the presence of rival elite networks, the greater the range of choice, the higher the bargaining power of the mass. Where rival elites are absent, the dominant one enjoys almost untrammeled power. Where they abound and threaten, the dominant elite must remain sensitive to the demands of its mass base. In some respects, the mass can be considered like the market in a capitalist society: one speaks of the will of the market, which is never articulated through formal channels or given concrete expression, but whose signals are apparent to any good entrepreneur. If elites are seen as political entrepreneurs—they create regimes to suit their own interests—they must nonetheless remain cognizant of the demands and needs of their mass support base in all but the most exceptional cases.

There are, therefore, two things that can provoke a regime crisis: a sudden change in the distribution of resources, or a sudden change of context that brings rival elites onto the scene or at least creates opportunities for them to emerge. Regime crises do not resolve themselves, however, but are resolved either when the existing dominant elite reconstitutes a viable regime, or when a rival elite with an alternative distribution network is able to overthrow the ruling one and then build up a sufficient support network to be able to consolidate its position. One can use a medical analogy to illustrate the point: the symptoms of an illness do not themselves destroy the host, but they can render it sufficiently weak to make it prone to opportunistic infections.

So regimes are implied social contracts between elites and masses. For practical purposes, this makes them contracts between rich and poor. Both groups are parties to such contracts, though their relative power will vary with economic and political conditions, such that some contracts are effectively imposed by the rich. Either party can break the contract. When the rich do so, it is usually to liberate themselves from obligations to the poor; when the masses do so, it is usually because an opportunity has emerged to make a new contract with a rival elite. Either way, a broken social contract corresponds to a period of grave instability.

Political history is therefore not merely one of class conflict between rich and poor, as Marx supposed, but one between rich and rich—rival elites—in which the poor (who may be poor only in relative terms, as in the case of the industrial working class in the contemporary First World) play the role of arbiter. It is a history of the rise and fall of regimes. When an elite can consolidate its hegemony over rival elites, a regime comes into being. When its hegemony declines and rival networks threaten its sovereignty—its supreme authority—then a revolutionary moment emerges in which the shape of the regime to come is in question. This revolutionary period can last a very long time, until a new elite is able to reestablish its supremacy. During these periods of redefinition, geographical changes may well take place. If, for instance, no one elite can emerge to reoccupy the space once held by a fallen regime, the result may be the development of smaller political units under the control of different elites, or the colonization and incorporation by an outside elite.

Political regimes, therefore, depend on the assent of the mass support bases over which they preside. Corresponding to them are ideological and cultural verities, the superstructure of the age as Marx called it. To be durable, regimes must be made self-sustaining. That is, they must be able to generate resources to satisfy the demands of the mass. If elites are outstripped by rival elites in this task, they will find their position threatened, their authority undermined. If their mass support base erodes, society will enter a revolutionary phase; a social revolution need not follow, but a new regime will need to be developed before the crisis can be resolved. During this period, the intellectual verities upon which the old regime rested will also collapse, having failed to address the concerns of the mass market, having ceased to be functional to the interests of these consumers. This period may be short-lived, or it can go on for generations. These periods are times of instability, and also of tremendous intellectual and artistic creativity. What causes the rise and fall of regimes are economic and demographic changes. To the extent these changes make it impossible for an elite to continue generating, appropriating, or distributing resources to its supporters, its support base will crumble.

For the past two centuries, the dominant regimes on the planet have existed within the nation-state, the shell within which regimes rose and fell. The nation-state, the fusion of nationalism and the modern state, emerged as a result of the development of capitalism. Benedict Anderson has noted how print capitalism gave rise to the new identity of nationalism,[32] which took the place of parochial identities already eroded by urbanization and the decline of the feudal system. At the same time, the development of trade and urban industry both strengthened central states—thanks to their revenue-collection and improved communications technologies—and drew them into new areas of activity.[33] In order to manage capitalist growth and trade, states became involved in the provision of security—with royal and subsequently standing armies taking the place of the feudal military command structures, and police forces coming into being—the development of infrastructure, and the protection of public health. Meanwhile, the rising bourgeoisie penetrated the state and, where it was sufficiently powerful, pushed for liberal government,[34] in some countries using its wealth to buy offices. In this way were the feudal regimes of western Europe overthrown. Increasingly, it was central governments and not local authorities that managed accumulation.

In the early years of the nation-state, however, distribution was left largely to the market, with its attendant difficulties. In the early decades of industrialization, rural-urban migration caused a fall in the well-being of the growing working class, but in time urban incomes began to catch up. At the same time, the gap between rich and poor widened, giving rise to the swell of radical sentiment and activity that, by the mid–nineteenth century, was causing alarm to western Europe's new ruling classes (radical politics came a bit later to the United States). Partly in response to the threat, west European states in the latter half of the nineteenth century began implementing welfare measures designed to tackle some of the most glaring injustices of the industrial age. The fact is not lost on social historians that the first modern welfare state was initiated by Germany's conservative leader Otto von Bismarck, whose practice of realpolitik led him to understand that it would be easier to placate than to repress the growing working class. A distribution regime that provided more of the fruits of economic growth to the working class, coupled with the gradual extension of the franchise to the entire adult population, helped to win the working classes of the West over to the virtues of capitalism.

Come the twentieth century, the nation-state would find itself drawn further and further into the management of economy and society, through regulation, investment, protection of property, promotion of trade, provision of welfare services, and so forth. Part of this was a response to the increasingly complex needs of a capitalist economy.[35] At the same time, part was a response to the popular demands emanat-

ing from a capitalist society, in particular the demands for welfare services and some form of state protection coming from the industrial working class.[36] In this way, the working class, which when excluded from
the fruits of progress flirted with socialism, was brought into the new
regime. And while the intrusion of the state into the capitalist economy
was sometimes described by contemporary neoconservatives as a quiet
and slow surrender to socialism, in fact growing state intervention
aimed to enhance the operations of capitalism. The welfare state is con-
ventionally seen as having been born in 1883, when Germany introduced compulsory health insurance. After that, start dates varied, with,
for instance, the British welfare state originating around 1910 and the
U.S. one in the 1930s. Equally, coverage varied over time and place: if
the United Kingdom led in the extent of coverage in the 1940s, it was
soon overtaken by the Scandinavian countries.[37] In any event, the high-
water point in the development of the welfare state came after World
War II, at which time it was given intellectual sanction by the theory of
John Maynard Keynes, which maintained that the provision of a guar-
anteed level of demand would ensure that recessions did not become
aggravated in the future. To the extent that capitalism expanded rapidly
throughout much of the twentieth century, the effectiveness of such
intervention was made evident. Thus the welfare state, which began as a
series of pragmatic responses to social and economic conditions on the
ground, was developed into a programmatic imperative, and came to be
widely known as the Keynesian welfare state.

Hence from its inception, the nation-state housed the regimes of
emerging bourgeoisies in Europe and North America (though in the
United States, state development and centralization came later than in
Europe, and the welfare state never reached a comparable stage of
development). From there, it spread throughout the world, essentially as
a result of imperialism. It is not just that colonialism imposed structures
that replicated the modern state, with its fixed boundaries, centralized
authority, and bureaucratic apparatus. Not everywhere did colonialism
do so, at least not at first (semifeudal regimes in Latin America and
slave colonies in the West Indies and the American deep south come
rapidly to mind). However, non-European elites would find the nation-
state, and its cultural paradigm, suitable mechanisms with which to
withstand or roll back colonialism.

Yet as the era of independence approached in the Third World,
nationalist elites, who were typically trained in European schools and
thus wedded to the ideals of modernity, were not the only ones vying to
reclaim control of their governments. There were traditional ethnic,
religious, and regional elites as well, who frequently did not regard the

West as something to emulate. Thus, in some countries, bloody conflicts emerged as the new national governments sought to impose their rule. In Turkey, Egypt, and Persia, the state repressed religious elites; in Nigeria, a civil war broke out along regional lines; the Indian subcontinent would be split, violently, along religious lines, with Pakistan being further divided along linguistic ones. But in addition to the stick, control of the state also afforded the new governing elites a carrot. By taking over more and more resource-allocating functions, they could draw support away from rival elites by building up sometimes vast patronage networks.

The means for doing this, the state, now lay in their hands. The political exigency to consolidate the hold of the nation-state over peoples who, in their own minds, frequently did not yet constitute nations, combined with other elements to draw the state more deeply into the economy. In the twentieth century, the rise of business classes in Latin America had already caused states there to shift their orientation and press for a greater government role in the economy. When the African and Asian colonies gained their independence, though, the challenges were of a different order, namely to find a way to develop economies that lacked substantial business classes (this was especially so in Africa). Political elites in these new countries sought rapid development in order to lessen their dependence on their former colonial masters. By and large, they adopted versions of the Keynesian model that underpinned the welfare state, then blended them with new economic thinking that was emerging partly from the Third World in the postwar period—a school of thought called structuralism—to produce something that can be called the developmentalist state. Like Keynesianism, structuralism called for an active state role in the direction of a private economy, but not for quite the same reasons. If Keynesianism sought above all to manage demand, structuralism sought also to create supply. Faced with the challenges of "latecomer" status, it was held that a Third World society needed to shelter its industrial producers from import competition until they caught up with First World states; equally, they had to siphon resources from the primary sector to the secondary one if there was to be any hope of breaking out of the dependence on primary exports that, it was held, limited possibilities for long-term economic growth.

Like the Keynesian welfare state in the First World, the developmentalist state sought to manage capitalism in such a way as to produce rapid growth and modernization. Equally, it sought to consolidate the loyalty of new citizenries by assuming resource-allocating functions that had hitherto been performed by other agents. In Africa, for example, the decline of the village economy and society helped feed the rise of a new urban consciousness—ethnicity, sometimes called (probably inappropriately) tribalism—as new petty bourgeois elites built up support networks. By the twentieth century, therefore, the institutions and cultural paradigm of Western capitalism—nationalism and the nation-state—had become, with pockets of exception, virtually hegemonic across the globe.

In the late twentieth century, neoliberal globalization prompted a political and intellectual revolution and the collapse of a regime; this point shall be taken up in greater detail in Chapter 4. Early predictions foresaw the imminent death of the nation-state, but these proved to be premature. Its outer shell is likely to persist, but the regimes operating within it—the Keynesian welfare state and the developmentalist state—are either failing or at en end. In response, in many parts of the world, especially the Third World, the nation-state is being radically reconfigured, and in a few cases has all but collapsed.

It should now be apparent that the concept of the regime being used herein draws from the international relations tradition of political science, rather than the comparative politics tradition. The latter, the classic typology of liberal democracy, totalitarian state, and authoritarian state, refers to types of government, with particular attention to state-society relations. The former refers to norms that govern the operation of a given political system. Yet even though such a use of the term "regime" is not today commonplace in comparative politics, the term does have a lineage in the discipline. In *The History of Government,* for example, S. E. Finer draws upon some of the "classics" of comparative politics, in particular David Easton's book *Political System,* to define a regime as the "regularized method for ordering political relationships," thereby including norms, procedures, and both the formal and the informal structure of authority.[38] The key question, then, is: In any given political system, what is the policy framework and administrative, political, and institutional structure that mediates bonds between elites and masses, governors and governed, dominant and subordinate classes? Needless to say, there are few, if any, pure systems. Nevertheless, individual societies will gravitate toward one or another type at any given time.

Conclusion

This book posits that from the end of World War II until around the 1980s, there were three dominant types of political regime on the planet: the Keynesian welfare state, the developmentalist state, and the state socialist or communist regime. Loosely, these types correspond to the old typology of First World, Second World, and Third World, now largely disused but arguably still relevant. The Keynesian welfare state was to be found in the liberal democratic, capitalist countries of Western Europe and North America—a region often referred to as the West. The developmentalist state was to be found in the vast majority of the world's countries, the (mostly) former colonies that remained poor and lay in Latin America, most of Asia, all of Africa, and even a few countries in Europe—a region often referred to as the South. The communist regime was less widespread in application, though no less important for that. Located in the former Russian empire, or what came to be known as the Union of Soviet Socialist Republics (USSR), it spread to six neighboring states—Hungary, Poland, Czechoslovakia, Romania, Bulgaria, and the eastern portion of Germany—with the Soviet occupation at the end of World War II. Additionally, domestic insurgencies also brought communist regimes into being in Albania and Yugoslavia at around the same time. While communist governments also tried to impose the regime in some Third World countries—notably China, North Korea, Vietnam, Laos, Cuba, and briefly, Ethiopia, Mozambique, Angola, and Cambodia—the limited administrative capacity of Third World states meant that in some cases, especially in Africa, the resultant regimes would bear a closer resemblance to the developmentalist type than the communist one.

In very broad terms, the distinction among them was as follows. Named after its intellectual inspiration, Cambridge economist John Maynard Keynes, the Keynesian welfare state's accumulation regime involved extensive state guidance of a predominantly private economy. Its distribution regime involved the taxation of accumulated wealth—with an accent on progressive rates of taxation and a focus on taxing income rather than spending—and its subsequent redistribution via the welfare state, which provided extensive services and financial assistance in the form of income maintenance, pension benefits, education, healthcare, and housing (while the extent of welfare provision varied, from virtually universal coverage in the Scandinavian countries to a more limited provision in the United States, none of these areas of life were left untouched by any Western government). Although the economy was primarily a privately owned market one, state firms typically played an important role in the economy, and in some subsectors—steel, mining, air and rail transportation, public utilities, telephone service—were the dominant and even monopolistic players. Although in a few cases, notably Sweden, governments were even committed in principle to the eventual socialization or nationalization of the entire econo-my, the actual nationalizations that took place in Western countries were generally guided by pragmatic considerations having to do with the preservation of firms seen as either politically or economically strategic. Currency and financial markets were regulated to protect national interests. In principle, the government committed to managing economic growth through the use of fiscal policy ("demand manage-ment," as coined by Keynes). To this end, full employment became an overriding policy goal.

The developmentalist regime resembled the Keynesian one in most respects, though it varied in details and also drew its inspiration from a school of economics that had emerged from Third World acade-mies, structuralism. Essentially committed to the same principles as Keynesianism—state management of a private economy, with an impor-tant role by state firms and redistribution via a welfare state—the limit-ed bureaucratic and economic resources of most Third World states ensured that the welfare-state component remained much less devel-oped. Instead, a key patronage tool of Third World elites was state employment. This locked Third World states into a tendency toward bureaucratic expansion that surpassed even that of the West.[39] Given the undeveloped state of the economies in which they operated, these regimes generally set the accumulation of capital—and in particular, physical capital—as a key policy goal; to this end, they typically taxed the primary sector in order to generate funds to develop urban industry. Equally, their trade policies tended toward mercantilism, as they sought to protect domestic markets from import competition while they built their industrial bases. A few countries, notably in East Asia (and espe-cially South Korea and Taiwan), devoted their resources to building their export industries, but the norm was to use policies of import sub-stitution. Currency and financial markets were regulated to steer capital to urban industry. One of the practical consequences of this regime was that, as a rule, it fostered close linkages between political and economic elites, with bureaucrats patronizing firm managers in return for political support (a model that would be later derided as "crony capitalism").

The communist regime was built upon a simple premise, namely the complete fusion (in theory) of accumulation and distribution func-tions. In principle, there was no private economy, although even in the Soviet Union vestiges of one were tolerated, particularly in agriculture. Limited in its application to only a few countries, the model nonetheless held immense appeal to socialists around the world. While it proved effective at rapid capital formation in the early years of the Soviet industrial buildup, the rigidities of the accumulation regime caused the economic engine to sputter beginning in the 1970s. Meanwhile, the highly developed welfare state—of a First World magnitude in countries whose levels of development were still closer to those of the Third World—eventually placed an unbearable drain on the resources of the state.

More recently, a new type has emerged (or in some cases reemerged), and has been applied in varying degrees in most of the world. This is the neoliberal regime. In the neoliberal regime, the locus of accumulation shifts more unambiguously to the private sector. Via policies of privatization, the state renounces its direct role in accumulation,[40] and shifts its function from ownership to regulation.[41] At the same time, some regulations are streamlined, with the intention being to free the market to operate increasingly by its own logic. But it is not simply accumulation that shifts toward the private sector; so too does distribution. The welfare state is pared back and streamlined: some functions are left to the private sector altogether (private charities have taken up much of the work of poor relief in some countries, particularly in the Third World), some are funded by the state but contracted out to private or semiprivate bodies, and even those retained by the state are managed in a new way, through the adoption of public-sector reforms designed to inject market principles into the management of public services. The overriding policy goal of the neoliberal welfare state is to improve efficiency; the Keynesian principle that welfare programs serve to maintain demand levels necessary to economic growth is dismissed for its inflationary impact. The principle underlying economic management shifts from fiscal policy to monetary policy. To this end, central banks are granted more autonomy from elected officials, and the key role of public policy is no longer to maintain demand—full employment is thus abandoned as a policy goal—but rather macroeconomic stability, manifested particularly in low rates of inflation. Thus the government both reduces taxes and shifts the burden of taxation from income to consumption, with an eye to putting more money in the hands of those most likely to invest it. The government also attempts to arrest the growth of its spending as a share of gross output,[42] with the eventual goal being to eliminate deficits, thereby freeing up capital for private investors. The principle of the Keynesian welfare state that deficits are not a problem provided they do not grow faster than gross output, and indeed can be useful in helping to augment that output—a principle that was inspired by Keynesian economics but that took on a life of its own, of a sort Keynes might not have approved, since he saw deficit financing as a short-term measure—is discarded outright. The bureaucracy is reduced and, where possible, its functions are contracted out to private-sector agents.

As a rule, one can say that the Keynesian welfare state and the developmentalist state were national regimes, meaning that the state was used to effect development within national boundaries. Despite its internationalist rhetorical content, much the same was true of the communist regime. Neoliberalism, on the other hand, is more committed to the global economy, even if nation-states remain the principal agents driving globalization. Integration into the global economy is seen as the best way to raise output and efficiency. This reflects the impact of neoclassical trade theory, which runs directly counter in its arguments to the structuralist theory that underpinned the developmentalist state, and which rejected full integration if done too early in a country's development process. Coupled with the fact that in the Third World, neoliberal reforms were often implemented under external pressure—in particular from Western governments and the international financial organizations they dominated—the neoliberal model can be seen as more global than national. The polemical vision sometimes put across, that neoliberal policies were foisted on unwilling Third World governments that had no power to refuse them, seldom held true. In fact, local interests who were eager to integrate their countries more deeply into the global economy often forged alliances with powerful patrons in the international financial community. What is important to note, however, is that all the key players shared a global, and neoliberal, vision, which often emerged from their membership in what have been called international "epistemic communities."[43]

Indeed, neoliberal globalization has sounded the death knell of the old regimes. It is not that welfare states have disappeared, or that the old regimes will never return.[44] Rather, the reconfiguration of the state as a result of the imposition of neoliberal globalization has altered the relations among citizens, and between them and governing elites.

Geographers define globalization as time-space compression, economists as deepening integration, sociologists as cultural convergence. All, however, are describing what is essentially the same phenomenon. The process whereby one can speak of the emergence of "one world" is hardly novel, and so some critics dismiss talk of globalization as a fad. Indeed, European imperialism was arguably the first stage of globalization, and in terms of trade ties, it is true that the high-water mark came in the late nineteenth century. However, as we shall see in Chapter 4, if the quantity—to put it inelegantly—of globalization has not changed, its quality has. New communications technologies have made possible new forms of corporate organization, making the so-called global firm a reality in a few subsectors. This, in turn, has put both governments and the working class on the defensive. The result has been a shift in the balance of class power and a concentration of wealth on a global scale.

The important point for this book, though, is to note the distinction between globalization as a phenomenon, and the neoliberal variety with which it is currently associated. Neoliberal political and intellectual elites have conflated neoliberal policies with globalization and argued that the two go together. Yet there seems to be no reason why this should be so. As we shall see later in the book, there seem to be more fruitful possibilities in globalizing to resist neoliberalism, than in resisting neoliberalism by rejecting globalization, as is the current vogue.

A Note on Theory

Before we proceed into the heart of the book, a brief comment on theory is in order. Comparative politics has in recent years become polarized between two approaches, which can be called the rationalist approach and the culturalist approach.[45] Emerging from neoclassical economics, the rationalist approach presumes that all humans are fundamentally alike in being rational utility-maximizers. The immense variety one can observe in and among human societies does not reflect fundamental differences, but merely the different behaviors that people produce when faced with different incentive structures: for example, if honesty pays, people will be honest; if it does not, they will not. Guided by such a belief, rationalist approaches seek to uncover and explicate the universal rules that govern human behavior. The culturalist approach, on the other hand, is influenced by postmodern thought, and more specifically by poststructuralist thought, and believes that human society is so bewilderingly diverse that meaningful generalization is impossible. The best that scholars can try to do is apprehend the small fragment of existence they have chosen to master. Lying between these two extremes, in terrain that is occupied by most comparativists, lies what Peter Evans calls the "eclectic messy centre." This sees "particular cases as the building blocks for general theories and theories as lenses to identify what is interesting and significant about particular cases."[46]

This debate is a case in which art—to the extent that philosophical reflection involves an element of artifice—mirrors reality. This polarity reflects the new polarities of the global political economy, the tensions between homogenization and hyperdifferentiation, between globalization and localization. Moreover, the polarity is more apparent than real.

Both poles, which exist in a curious symbiosis, reflect the interests of the emerging elites and class fractions of the global economy. Each of these points will be taken up in turn as the book progresses, but the main point to be made here is that this book is placed squarely in the messy center of which Evans speaks. Let us liken theories to recipes. Different recipes emerge from different environments since they are tailored to suit local tastes, ingredients, nutritional needs, and so forth. The best of them emerge after a long process of trial and error. Some do not travel, others find universal appeal. But we persist in creating them and passing them on because without them, we could not assemble the mass of ingredients before us into a digestible whole. Once written down, they provide us with a reasonably accurate predictor of what will happen when certain variables are combined in certain ways. But they are never foolproof: the stomach of many a loving father has been fattened by the valiant efforts of children who tried their hand at cooking something that looked much better in the photograph. Followed slavishly, recipes are rendered useless by the absence of any single ingredient. But if used to inspire or stimulate imagination, to get one started, they become immensely useful.

And so, humbled by the knowledge that it is very difficult to find a perfect theory, that no matter how hard we try some case will emerge to render it useless, we persist in the endeavor of theorizing. Theories, like recipes, enrich our approach to the reality we confront. To say, as do the culturalists, that all reality is constructed, does not establish that the endeavor to theorize is futile. It can simply be taken to mean that we need to exercise our creativity with a strong aesthetic sense—an appreciation that reality can be made meaningful. It can also mean that we need to exercise our creativity with a sense of responsibility to the societies in which we live.

Throughout this book, a subtext will weave together the seemingly diverse dramas unfolding on its pages. It is that, possibly for the first time in human history, it is possible to speak of there being one world system. United by economic integration, this system has provoked political changes that, if differing immensely in character, are nonetheless united by the same essential causes. Whether the nation-state survives into the next century is not really the concern of this book. What is, is the fact that the global character of the crisis of our time has rendered the nation-state, on its own, incapable of rising to the challenges that have emerged. Even if nation-states continue to play the leading roles in the global political economy, global problems will nonetheless call for global solutions. It also seems evident that the solutions will be neither easy nor painless. The new global elite, overrepresented by but not confined to the First World, will have to reexamine its expectations of boundless prosperity accompanied by an apparently limitless freedom from obligations to others. Equally, we will have to transcend radical discourses that were happy to castigate the rich but somehow always managed to locate the source of oppression in the other, with the self only cast as the victim. Change must start closer to home.

Notes

1. Edward Britton, *The Community of the Vill* (London: Macmillan, 1977), pt. 5.

2. For an example, see Emmanuel Le Roy Ladurie, *The Peasants of Languedoc,* translated by John Day (Urbana: University of Illinois Press, 1974), p. 35.

3. Rodney Stark, *The Rise of Christianity* (San Francisco: HarperCollins, 1997).

4. Paul Hazoumé, *Doguicimi,* trans. Richard Bjornson (Boulder: Lynne Rienner, Three Continents, 1990), p. xxxv.

5. *The Prince,* chap. 18.

6. S. E. Finer, *The History of Government* (Oxford: Oxford University Press, 1997), vol. 1, p. 29.

7. Quoted in Albert Hourani, *A History of the Arab Peoples* (London: Faber and Faber, 1991), p. 210.

8. Richard Easterlin, "Income and Happiness: Towards a Unified Theory," *Economic Journal* 111 (July 2001): 465–484; Juliet B. Schor, *The Overspent American: Upscaling, Downshifting, and the New Consumer* (New York: Basic Books, 1998), chap. 1.

9. See Tibor Scitovsky, *The Joyless Economy* (New York: Oxford University Press, 1976). Scitovsky argues that pleasure comes from stimulus, and displeasure from a break in habit. New consumption thus brings pleasure, which, however, quickly becomes habitual and thus loses its stimulus value. Hence new consumption is sought, yet the old consumption habits cannot be replaced but must remain in place, as losing them amounts to a break in habit.

10. See, for instance, Richard Easterlin, *Growth Triumphant: The Twenty-First Century in Historical Perspective* (Ann Arbor: University of Michigan Press, 1996), chap. 10.

11. Quoted in Edward S. Greenberg, *The American Political System: A Radical Approach,* 5th ed. (Boston: Scott, Foresman, 1989), p. 97.

12. Egor Gaidar, "How the Nomenklatura 'Privatized' Its Own Power," *Russian Social Science Review* 37, no. 3 (1996): 23–34; Ol'ga V. Kryshtanovskaia, "Transformation of the Old Nomenklatura into a New Russian Elite," *Russian Social Science Review* 37, no. 4 (1996): 18–40.

13. So claims Grigory Yavlinsky. See *St. Petersburg Times,* 14 January 1997.

14. To illustrate, in Canada, one of the planet's richest countries, even

when policies of economic redistribution were at their height, studies of the upper class found that the great majority of its members came themselves from upper-class backgrounds. Given the numerically much larger lower classes, it followed that a very small proportion of the lower classes were rising out of their ranks. See Dennis Forcese, "Elites and Classes: The Structure of Inequality," in *Politics Canada,* 6th ed., edited by Paul W. Fox and Graham White (Toronto: McGraw-Hill Ryerson, 1987).

15. For case studies, see Ralph Miliband, *The State in Capitalist Society* (London: Weidenfeld and Nicolson, 1973); Edward S. Greenberg, *The American Political System* (Boston: Little, Brown, 1983); C. Wright Mills, *The Power Elite* (New York: Oxford University Press, 1957); and Wallace Clement, *The Canadian Corporate Elite* (Ottawa: Carleton University Press, 1986).

16. Robert Michels, in his landmark study of political parties, uncovered this apparently unavoidable rule of political life. See Robert Michels, *Political Parties* (New York: Free Press, 1962).

17. José Ortega y Gasset, *The Revolt of the Masses,* authorized translation (London: George Allen and Unwin, 1951), p. 10.

18. Mills, *Power Elite.*

19. Goran Therborn, "Classes and States: Welfare State Developments, 1881–1981," *Studies in Political Economy* 14 (1984): 7–42.

20. Ortega y Gasset, *Revolt of the Masses,* p. 10.

21. See, in particular, Robert A. Dahl, *Polyarchy* (New Haven: Yale University Press, 1971); and Robert A. Dahl, *Democracy and Its Critics* (New Haven: Yale University Press, 1989).

22. For a look at the practice of political machine-building in Soviet politics, see George W. Breslauer, "The Nature of Soviet Politics and the Gorbachev Leadership," in *The Gorbachev Era,* edited by Alexander Dallin and Condoleezza Rice (Stanford, Calif.: Stanford Alumni Association, 1986).

23. Stark, *Rise of Christianity.*

24. Bertrand Russell, *A History of Western Philosophy* (London: Unwin, 1984), p. 19.

25. Chantal Mouffe, "Working-Class Hegemony and the Struggle for Socialism," in *Studies in Political Economy* 12 (Fall 1983).

26. See, for instance, Dietrich Rueschmeyer, Evelyn Huber Stephens, and John D. Stephens, *Capitalist Development and Democracy* (Chicago: University of Chicago Press, 1992), which stresses the central role played by the working class in democratization.

27. On the role played by working-class demands in the construction of welfare states, see Peter Flora and Jens Alber, "Modernization, Democratization, and the Development of Welfare States in Western Europe," in *The Development of Welfare States in Europe and America,* edited by P. Flora and A. J. Heidenheimer (New Brunswick, N.J.: Transaction, 1984); and Ian Gough, *The Political Economy of the Welfare State* (London: Macmillan, 1979).

28. See, for example, James C. Scott, *The Moral Economy of the Peasant* (New Haven: Yale University Press, 1976); and Goran Hyden, *Beyond Ujamaa in Tanzania* (Berkeley: University of California Press, 1980).

29. Peasant rebellions have proved a popular object of study in exploring

what it is that makes people rebel. The moral economists, such as Scott (*Moral Economy*), stress the restoration of norms as an impetus to rebellion. In his influential survey of modern peasant wars, Eric R. Wolf agrees that peasant rebellions seek to restore lost traditional rights, and transform into revolutions when restoration becomes impossible, at which time peasants ally themselves with new elites. See Eric R. Wolf, *Peasant Wars of the Twentieth Century* (New York: Harper and Row, 1969). While Samuel Popkin stresses not the desire to preserve traditional norms but the opportunity for peasants to secure new ones as the motive behind rebellion, his theory still makes the governed active players in regime formation. See Samuel Popkin, *The Rational Peasant* (Berkeley: University of California Press, 1979). Equally, in her study of working-class movements, Chantal Mouffe suggests that industrial radicalism originated in movements that sought to preserve traditional rights. See Mouffe, "Working-Class Hegemony."

30. For example, John King Fairbank, in *China: A New History* (Cambridge: Harvard Belknap, 1992), argues that the recent democracy movement in China, which has posed a threat to the regime, emerged in part from the fact that Chinese intellectuals, once homegrown and parochial in their outlook, had, by virtue of the demands of modern technology, become much more international and cosmopolitan. In the course of their education, the students who massed in Tiananmen Square in 1989 picked up many new ideas that challenged the position of the Communist Party. Equally, Jerry F. Hough comments that "the exchange programs of the West were far more crucial in destroying communism than the military buildup of the early 1980s." See Jerry F. Hough, *Democratization and Revolution in the USSR, 1985–1991* (Washington, D.C.: Brookings Institution, 1997).

31. For a critique of atomism, see Charles Taylor, "Atomism," in Charles Taylor, *Philosophy and the Human Sciences* (Cambridge: Cambridge University Press, 1985).

32. Benedict Anderson, *Imagined Communities* (London: Verso, 1983).

33. Perry Anderson, *Lineages of the Absolutist State* (London: Routledge, 1974); Henry Jacoby, *The Bureaucratization of the World,* translated by Eveline L. Kanes (Berkeley: University of California Press, 1973); W. McNeill, *The Pursuit of Power* (Chicago: University of Chicago Press, 1982).

34. Barrington Moore, *Social Origins of Dictatorship and Democracy* (London: Penguin, 1966).

35. On this point, see Claus Offe, *Contradictions of the Welfare State,* edited by John Keane (Cambridge: MIT Press, 1984); Gough, *Political Economy of the Welfare State;* Anthony Giddens, *The Class Structure of the Advanced Societies* (London: Hutchinson University Library, 1973); and Karl Polanyi, *The Great Transformation* (New York: Rinehart, 1944).

36. See Flora and Alber, "Modernization, Democratization, and the Development of Welfare States"; Gough, *Political Economy of the Welfare State;* and Goran Therborn, "Classes and States."

37. Arnold J. Heidenheimer, Hugh Heclo, and Carolyn Teich Adams, *Comparative Public Policy* (New York: St. Martin's Press, 1983).

38. Finer, *History of Government,* vol. 1, p. 14.

39. By 1970, for example, 60 percent of Africa's wage earners were government employees, and during each year of the previous decade the civil service in Africa grew at an average annual rate of 7 percent. Naomi Chazan et al., *Politics and Society in Contemporary Africa,* 2nd ed. (Boulder: Lynne Rienner, 1992), p. 55.

40. In fact, as states privatized large firms, they often created a layer of small ones, such that the withdrawal from direct involvement in the economy was often tentative. In general, though, these new firms were created by the state to shift functions from the public to the private sector, such that their creation represented the increased application of market logic to the state. Accordingly, the idea that public-sector management should follow a different set of norms from private-sector management was largely abandoned. See Christopher Hood, *Explaining Economic Policy Reversals* (Philadelphia: Open University Press, 1994).

41. As Giandomenico Majone notes, the shift from deregulation was, like privatization, seldom unambiguous. As governments abandoned certain forms of regulation, they often took on new ones. For instance, in the United Kingdom the privatization of natural monopolies was followed by price regulation. The important thing to note, as with privatization, is that the changes in the regulatory regime were designed to make both the public sector and the private sector conform more to market rules. See Giandomenico Majone, ed., *Deregulation or Re-regulation?* (London: Pinter, 1990).

42. Contrary to dogmatic descriptions, the size of the Western state in its proportion to gross economic output did not shrink (though it often did in Third World and formerly communist countries). Nevertheless, given that the tendency in the early 1980s appeared to be toward continued growth, the slowdown and, in some places, the arrest of this process were significant.

43. Eric Helleiner, *States and the Re-emergence of Global Finance* (New York: Cornell University Press, 1994).

44. As Christopher Hood maintains, it is rare that discarded policy frameworks ever disappear forever. Hood, *Explaining Economic Policy Reversals.*

45. Peter J. Katzenstein in Atul Kohli et al., "The Role of Theory in Comparative Politics: A Symposium," *World Politics* 48, no. 1 (1996): 1–49.

46. Peter Evans in ibid.

3

Regime and Culture

Whether or not human beings can live on bread alone, the fact remains that aside from an intrepid few, they do not. In addition to their material needs and wants, humans also have what can be called spiritual needs and wants. The term "spiritual" here is used not as a synonym for "religious," however, but as a reference to those aspects of human existence that are immaterial. This introduces the common material-spiritual dichotomy that, to metaphysicians, is fraught with peril. Some philosophers see no distinction between spirit and matter; others see matter as an illusion and spirit the only essential reality; still others see spirit as nothing more than an epiphenomenon to matter. Regarding the last perspective, some scholars maintain that every mental state or emotion can be explained by complex chemical and electrical interactions within the brain, such that everything can be reduced to material phenomena. However, for the purposes of this book we do not need definitions of matter and spirit that pin down their objective reality, but simply definitions that ascertain their subjective reality to the political actors of the drama in question—namely human beings. Therefore, a definition of spirit and matter that is determined by the perception of the individual will be employed. Those needs and gratifications that are experienced as material will be such, those needs and gratifications that are experienced as spiritual will be such. In lay terms, if one can identify the body part that seeks gratification, one has a material need; if one cannot but experience the desire for gratification as a vague yearning, then regardless of the myriad material interactions that a biologist could explain if one had the time and patience, one nonetheless has a spiritual need. If an urge is nourished or satisfied with a material object or stimulus, then one has material gratification; if with an immaterial object or stimulus, then one has a spiritual gratification.

Emerging from this is a conception of balance whose importance will become apparent as the book progresses: when one type of gratification is used to satisfy the other type of need—if, say, emotional dissatisfaction (a spiritual longing) is nourished with impulse shopping (a material gratification) or if material suffering is nourished with religious escapism—an imbalance can emerge that can eventually hinder the health of the organism, both the human individual and, if such problems become widespread, the political regime in which he or she lives. Of course, the boundaries between the material and the spiritual are not always so clear, as we shall see. For example, many material objects— icons or status symbols, for instance—have spiritual significance to their users. Therefore, a full operationalization is probably impossible. The important point, though, is that as individuals come together into groups, the interaction of their personal spiritual realms gives rise to a shared realm that can be called a culture.

Yet while culture is often discussed in rather nebulous terms, as something that is "up there" or "in the air," it can also be seen itself as a form of economy comprising a multitude of transactions among consumers and producers of cultural goods. The cultural goods being produced and consumed include knowledge, law, symbols, morals, values, religion, philosophy, ideologies, music, literature, art, and popular entertainment. Such a good, when produced and consumed by only one person, is not considered cultural. Culture is social, it is shared. So a cultural good only becomes fully so when it is accepted by a group of people. One can approach the study of any given society by looking at the transactions among producers and consumers of cultural goods. The overall culture that emerges from an aggregation of these transactions, and which is spoken of in collective terms—the people's culture, the national culture, and so forth—will reflect the dominant demands within the economy for cultural goods (in fact, most societies will harbor a multitude of subcultures, but a given range of goods that is widely consumed will still produce what can be called a dominant culture). Culture is not set in stone, nor does it mold humans the way a child shapes putty. Culture is in flux to the extent that the demand for cultural goods is affected by the degree of choice—the more choice there is, the more cultural flux there will be—as well as the imperatives unleashed by economic changes—economic changes alter the market for cultural goods. In isolated communities dominated by a hegemonic elite, the lack of alternatives, coupled with a monopoly in supply, will produce a culture that seems rigid and into which individuals are socialized passively. But even this culture is fragile: if intruded upon by an outsider who can alter the economy of the society—colonialism being an instance—the culture can very rapidly collapse as the market for cultural goods is suddenly altered.[1]

However, while culture does not shape people like putty, all people are socialized into a culture. Typically, these cultural values will be internalized so deeply that violation of dominant mores may cause violent physical reaction, disgust, or self-loathing (psychological research reveals that the pain associated with the loss of a habit usually exceeds the pleasure or diminished pain associated with its initial formation).[2] One must not form the impression that people pick and choose their cultural goods the way they select among breakfast cereals in a supermarket. Except for relatively brief periods, usually periods of revolutionary transition, the market for cultural goods is seldom very free. Yet at the same time, there is a problem in seeing socialization as an autonomous process in which people are passive participants. This common view of socialization can be illustrated by a simple bivariate relationship, $x \rightarrow y$, in which x is the independent variable and y is the dependent variable. Acting autonomously, x determines the shape of y. Usually, this approach is wrapped up in a radical critique that decries the x group for inducting the y group into a false consciousness that serves the interests of the x group while hurting the y group. However, the critique permits that a few will rise from the oppressed y group to enter the ranks of the x group, from where they can build a counterculture to help overthrow the domination of the oppressor class.

This view is popular, especially among social science students, but it has an obvious flaw. If the x group is the oppressor group and the y group the oppressed, how is it that all the oppressors are creative enough to shape culture, while all but a few of the oppressed are passive and receive culture? The question is usually ignored. Equally, this thesis does not explain how those doing the cultural formation and socialization manage to stand above the process. The implicit though never stated assumption is that the two culture-creating groups—one on the side of darkness that forges the dominant culture, the other on the side of light that crafts the counterculture—are somehow superior to the rest of the population, a sort of Gnostic elect who can see the light where others see Walt Disney cartoons. All through history, the idea that a few are born to rule, know God, or see truth has been popular. Unfortunately, it has seldom been demonstrated in such a way as to provide an operational definition that makes it possible to differentiate the elect from the rest. Usually, those who are held to be above brainwashing or socialization are so held simply because they have declared themselves to be above it. To such theoretical lacunae one can add the empirical findings of cultural historians: there has always existed a cleavage between elite and mass cultures, even in societies with hegemonic ideologies, and elites have often bemoaned yet seldom been able to eliminate mass cultures they have seen as vulgar. The medieval minstrel finds his parallel in the modern professional wrestler.

Socialization is a transaction. However, it is a transaction in a market where the seller enjoys a degree of power over the buyer. And while some exercise more creative power than others, all members of a society participate in some way in the creation of culture. When there is no range of choice, it is functional to most individuals' interests to adopt the dominant cultural goods. Only born antinomians who value their freedom so highly as to accept ostracism—exceptional philosophers and poets—will accept the very high cost in social rejection entailed in a willful disregard of a society's norms. The higher the cost of breaking ranks, the higher the degree of conformity will be, and vice versa in a self-reinforcing circle. In the market for goods, economies of scale make it possible to lower the price of a mass-produced good, so that the greater the homogeneity in demand, the lower the cost of the item. Equally, those who demand specialized products will have to pay a premium for them.[3] In any society where a value is widely shared—this will always be the case in a society where a simple mode of production makes the economic interests of the mass broadly similar—the costs of breaking social ranks greatly outweigh the benefits for most people.

In any event, individuals do not sit down and run a cost-benefit analysis of adopting a given cultural good, but in effect that is what their intuition does for them. As in the relationship of the mass to the elites in political regimes, so too in culture: people will consume those cultural goods that they believe are functional to their personal material interests.[4] Importantly, *believing* that a given cultural good is functional to one's interests does not necessarily mean that it *is* functional. Poor information very often causes people to cleave to beliefs that ill-serve them. Furthermore, a given cultural good may not be shared by a whole population, but if a majority enjoy sufficient strength to impose it on the minority, it will be accepted by default, although instances of resistance are likely to arise (a fertile field of inquiry in this regard has been opened by feminist historians). People's personal interests will be shaped in large part by their material conditions, both economic and environmental. Geography, for instance, does not make culture, but it does incline its human occupants to prefer cultural goods that respond to the conditions produced by that geography over other possible choices. Some research suggests that even food recipes will reflect the environmental needs people face, with, for example, the antimicrobial properties of peppers explaining their widespread use in the tropics.[5] Other needs will inhere in the human species. Among these is the need all people have for social approbation. So, just as the costs of breaking with a dominant culture are high, the benefits forgone are many. An individual who has organized his or her life around a given set of values—marital fidelity, filial piety, traditional religious practice—will be loath to renounce those values after so much has been invested in them. That is why when new cultural goods begin gaining a mass market, it is mainly young people who do the consuming since they have not yet invested much in the old values.

In discussing the formation of culture, many students like to stress the role of history. Some scholars have tried to examine the peculiar cultural features of the founding fathers of new nations—the Puritan heritage of New England, the conservative statism of Anglican English Canada, the Calvinism that imbued South Africa's Boers.[6] Others have focused on the traumatic events that shaped a people's identity,[7] molding what some psychologists like to call shared memory or the collective unconscious. For example, the War of Independence gave Americans a passionate thirst for liberty while slavery so traumatized Africans in the diaspora that they could only overcome their emotional sense of inferiority by reclaiming their memory from the days before the slave trade.

History matters, but probably not as much as people often suppose. Memory is notoriously unreliable. People will often say that a given belief or value goes back deep into their history, but they seldom have ever researched the matter to verify the claim. More often what they are saying is that as far back as they can remember, the value has been with them. Often, that may not be far back. The way one recalls the past is shaped largely by contemporary events, only in part by authentic and unvarnished recollections. Take, for example, the widespread belief that values were immutable until the current generation came along and recklessly disregarded the time-honored ways. In fact, this perception of decay recurs in every generation, and may be one of the few cultural constants. Read the literature of Chinua Achebe from a half century ago, of Edith Wharton a century ago, and so forth back to biblical denunciations of the growing selfishness of the new generation. Youth always rebels, and culture is always in flux, constantly being redefined and reshaped to suit the changing needs of a people faced with changing material conditions. And while stories or myths can give a people a shared identity, these are not so much memories as tales, often largely fictitious, which continue to find an audience because of the contemporary needs they address.

Nonetheless, because the river is always flowing does not mean it has no constancy. One finds continuity in culture. History matters not because it forms people's memories; most people's memories are shaped by their own experiences, not those of their ancestors. But to the extent that a historical experience narrows the range of cultural options available to a people, and to the extent that one generation passes those on to the next, history structures the market for cultural goods. Medieval European laws barring Jews from landowning and public service steered Jews toward trade and the liberal professions. Subsequently, the specialized knowledge connected to those economic activities was passed from generation to generation. Other peoples lack that particular reservoir of practical knowledge, because historical circumstances did not compel or allow their ancestors to accumulate it. Should a historical experience exclude a given cultural good from consumption by society, the need for social approbation will incline most people to continue excluding it. Nevertheless, if their material circumstances change dramatically, people will discard some values and widen their search, even if only incrementally. History may incline a people in a given direction, but it does not enslave them. The cultural goods shaped by a given historical experience will be retained only to the extent that they continue to address the present material concerns of their holders.

The formation of culture resembles the polity and economy in one important respect: the rich dominate. The dominant culture of any given society will usually reflect, or at least seldom challenge, the economic and political interests of the dominant class or class fractions. However, just as in most political regimes the mass is not passive, so too it plays a determining role in the formation of culture. Ordinary people are not stupid, passive sponges for elite ideologies. On the other hand they are variously preoccupied with other matters, disinterested in philosophical debates, or little concerned with assessing the veracity or aesthetic value of a given cultural good. Moreover, the sheer volume of information available in the modern world is beyond the capacity of any one individual to gather together (this goes for members of the elite as well as for members of the mass). Nonetheless, humans feel the need to develop a broader picture of reality than that which they have formed on the basis of their own, narrow experiences. Only a handful of men have been to the moon. Most of the rest of humanity contents itself with accepting the truth of their claims regarding its existence, and we do not feel we can ignore the moon's existence just because it does not live in our neighborhood. Rather, our understanding of the moon as a piece of rock rather than, say, a god, affects our view of our place in the universe and of our potential as individuals. As Walter Lippmann put it eloquently in his 1922 classic *Public Opinion,* man "can just about span a sufficient portion of reality to manage his survival, and snatch what on the scale of time are but a few moments of insight and happiness. Yet this same creature has invented ways of seeing what no naked eye can see, or hearing what no ear could hear. . . . Gradually he makes for himself a trustworthy picture inside his head of the world beyond his reach."[8] He does this, according to Lippmann, through the use of symbols.

Because individuals cannot possibly grasp more than fragments of the total stock of information involved in public affairs, they distill reality into stored-up images, which they then use to filter and sort through the "trickle of information" that comes to them via the media. These symbols embody meanings that reflect the material concerns of their holders. In the United States, for example, the word *freedom* is a symbol that can encompass a wide variety of even contradictory substances. To a libertarian, it may imply the freedom from social controls, to a conservative the freedom of an unregulated economy, to a socialist the freedom from class oppression. But the word resonates among all Americans because the economy in which they operate has given a sufficient number of Americans a sense of personal liberty and economic independence to make "freedom" an important and functional symbol. It is a button that elites can press to open the door to the masses. Equally, elites who ridicule or debase the symbols that are dear to the majority will find their access to the masses limited or even closed.

Thus, although the mass may be an unequal participant in the process of cultural generation, it is not passive. Elites mislead or evade the masses not by telling them whatever it wants them to hear, but by employing the vague language of symbols to generate consensus. And cultural entrepreneurs must respond to existing demand within the market and produce goods that fit the basic outline of the symbols that hold meaning to the masses. Otherwise, the cultural goods they produce will fail to find a wide market. What matters to the masses, as with the purchase of any commodity, is the good's utility to them.

To say that the rich dominate the process of culture formation does not imply that political elites and the dominant class fractions of society sit down together and actually design a dominant culture and ideology, as some crude forms of radical thought have suggested. Anybody can produce a cultural good—a book, an idea, a religious doctrine, and so forth—but elite and/or corporate dominance of communications media ensures that while they may not produce culture, their interests filter the culture that is conveyed to a mass audience. In early societies, given the more primitive forms of technology, elites often enjoyed a stranglehold on the communications media. Subcultures beyond elite control always existed, but tended to be parochial, given the limited reach of the communications technology at the disposal of their purveyors. In medieval Europe, for instance, people lived in two worlds, the culture of Christendom on one level, and the culture of their village or region on the other. But the limited geographic reach of parochial subcultures meant that they seldom posed a threat to elite dominance. In modern societies, the greatly reduced cost of technology has made it impossible for elites to dictate cultural diffusion. Totalitarian regimes foundered on their efforts to do so. Nonetheless, while information is freely accessible, few people go to any significant lengths to find it, accepting instead what is readily accessible through the mass media. As a rule, the mass media in modern capitalist societies are dominated by fractions of capital. Nonetheless, control of culture is not always so simple a matter as an owner telling his writers and producers what to say (though it can be so). However, the perpetuation of cultural goods that serve the interests of the rich is often more subtle, an outcome less of conscious design than of the coalescence of economic decisions that favor those who do most of the consuming.

Let me illustrate this point with a simple analogy. In Jamaica, bank queues can stretch such a distance that a customer depositing his $500 can wait an hour for service. As one waits patiently, every once in a while one sees a customer, usually in a suit and typically carrying a briefcase, enter and go straight to the back of the bank, where the manager will usher him to a seat with a broad smile. This, of course, is the customer coming to make a $50,000 deposit. It annoys all the ordinary folk in the line, but most of them aspire to make it to the back someday and so keep quiet. As for the bank manager, he is simply doing what he is paid to do. He can ill-afford to alienate the few depositors who hold most of his bank's deposits, but can take his chances on angering a few of the customers in the queue. The point about markets is this: free market dogmatists celebrate them as the most democratic of institutions, since no government can dictate what they produce, and since they have proven to be the most efficient way of identifying and satisfying consumer demand. In short, they give the people what they want. What could be more democratic? In principle, this is true. But as with the case of our wealthy bank customer, while markets aggregate expressions of consumer desires, they do so not on the principle of one person, one vote, but rather one dollar, one vote. They will therefore tend to reflect the wishes of the small number of consumers with the greatest purchasing power.

So it is in the market for cultural goods, even in the freest of markets. There is no backroom dealing in this process, no conspiratorial effort to warp people's minds. The process is simpler than that, and at the same time so complex that its participants are usually unaware of their participation in the process of cultural diffusion. Thus a middle-class businessman will shrug uncomprehendingly when his daughter comes home from university during spring break and informs him that the bourgeoisie to which he belongs has warped the minds of the nation with its dominant ideology. He will be at pains to recall any of the secret meetings at which he and his peers ostensibly got together to define this ideology.

Yet they have defined it. They have done it via their purchasing decisions about where to advertise their products. It is not that they choose only to advertise in media that reflect their ideology; few are so sophisticated (or unsophisticated, depending on one's perspective). Rather, they advertise in those publications that can sell their wares. This does not necessarily mean those publications that reach a large audience, but rather those that can create a demand among consumers for the goods and services producers are trying to sell. Walter Lippmann pointed out that while the media are seen as a key element in democracy, as providers of the information that the public requires in order to make informed decisions regarding public policy, in fact newspapers, magazines, and radio and television stations are businesses like any other. Unless owned or subsidized by the state, they will normally be required to show a profit if they are to remain in business. And "a newspaper which angers those whom it pays best to reach through advertisements is a bad medium for any advertiser."[9] The mass media themselves produce a commodity that they then sell. Although most people think of the buyer as the mass market, this is at best half true. Most media today depend mainly on advertising for their revenue. The commodity produced and sold—to businesses—by the mass media is markets.[10]

As capitalism developed, the shift from sales to advertising as a source of revenue for the mass media strengthened the latter's role in the dissemination of cultural goods that reproduced the interests of capital.[11] It is not that corporate advertisers pressure the media in which they advertise to carry certain stories and not others. This does happen, but only occasionally, and usually reflects narrow concerns of direct interest to the advertiser. An automobile firm will pull its ads from a magazine that slams its product, and more conservative companies, anxious not to be associated with a risqué article or news story, will often demand prior warning of its publication or ask that their advertisement appear in another part of the publication.[12] However, an advertiser will happily associate with any cultural entrepreneur that can sell its products. So, for example, a magazine that rails against the evils of conspicuous consumption will neither attract nor help develop a market for, say, jewelry producers. Thus, while some advertisers eschew controversy, others seek it out. As one industry analyst put it, "the 'vice' peddlers (booze and cigarettes), along with some apparel and consumer electronics products, actually like being surrounded by edgy editorial copy—unless their own product is zapped."[13]

Thus this process of market aggregation of demand for cultural goods will privilege some producers of cultural goods over others. But in transmitting these cultural goods to a wide audience, communications media and cultural entrepreneurs cannot simply disregard the mass market, since these are the ultimate consumers of the finished product. In one sense, capitalist development has strengthened the role of the masses by enhancing their market power, and thus their role in the determination of cultural content. The purchasing power of most individuals may be limited, but taken together the mass is an important consumer, especially in advanced capitalist societies. While it seldom shapes the formation of culture, the mass determines culture by plebiscite, preferring some goods over others through its patterns of consumption. Thus, purveyors of cultural goods must remain sensitive to the demands of the mass market, and frame their products in the terms that suit the market's demands. So, while cultural goods are transmitted from elite to mass, the flow is not quite unidirectional. There is a feedback mechanism, with producers conducting market research and creating focus groups to identify what the public wants so as to create a link between producer and consumer. The producer must identify the symbols that resonate in the mass public, and cloak his product in these.

A case drawn from the contemporary United States can illustrate. Feminist theorists who developed the original case for abortion rights usually grounded their argument in a critique of patriarchy, and saw abortion as an act of liberation. Such an argument would have failed to persuade many Americans, most of whom had their doubts about feminism, would have found the theory impenetrable, and in any event remained wedded to Christian moral principles. However, these Americans were also mostly well-to-do property owners who were among the first people in history to enjoy a measure of what we may call financial freedom. To them, especially in their guise of consumers, the principle of choice enjoyed deep resonance. The very word "choice" evokes strong positive feelings in most poll respondents, in a way it does not in societies where poverty still makes choice an alien concept to most people. By marketing abortion rights as a victory for choice, the abortion-rights lobby very effectively tailored a cultural product to suit the mass market, gaining wider support for its proposals than it might have in an audience who remained troubled by the act of abortion itself.[14]

In a rapidly changing society, like that of modern capitalism, culture is in rapid flux. Speaking of earlier civilizations, scholars can talk of the culture or beliefs of a people as remaining fundamentally unchanged over centuries. In contrast, anyone comparing, say, sexual morality in the present-day United States to that of just a few generations ago will notice striking change. This is because contrary to what popular radicalism suggests, there is not and probably never has been a monolithic culture and ideology of capitalism. The bourgeoisie is composed of several fractions with highly divergent interests, both material and cultural. A U.S. textiles producer who depends for his well-being on sales to the domestic market will oppose free trade, lest his firm be swamped by cheap Third World imports. In contrast, a candy producer who would like to import cheap sugar rather than buy from protected U.S. farmers will favor free trade. Thus, contemporary Marxists have gone beyond the study of class alone to focus on the study of class fractions, to help account for why two governments that are both judged to be procapitalist will nonetheless produce strikingly different policies.

So it goes with culture. Though often derided as conservative, bourgeois cultures vary. Some fractions of capital are deeply conservative, others can be boldly liberal. Victorian England may have produced a rigid moral code, but this reflected in large measure the economic interests of the then-dominant class fractions. Early-nineteenth-century British capitalism was founded on the production of capital goods and infrastructural development. A mass market had not yet emerged, there being only a limited class of relatively rich buyers for consumer goods. Demand, therefore, was chiefly for industrial products, so the need to create mass markets was not pressing. What was pressing was the need to speed up the rate of capital formation in an economy with a lot of unused capacity, to lower costs by keeping wages down and stabilizing a labor force that was threatened with social dissolution, not to mention outbreaks of epidemics due to urban crowding. The "Victorian" values of thrift, self-denial, moral probity, and sexual restraint were all consonant with these needs. It was not only the bourgeoisie who favored them. The popularity of Methodism among the working classes revealed that there was felt to be a need among Britain's poor to advance themselves through strict morality. To the extent that this culture raised family incomes, it met this need.

Fast-forward a century or so, and the situation has changed greatly. It behooves many people to account for the wholesale abandonment of moral codes that seemed perfectly useful just a few decades ago, but the change is not that difficult to understand. For the economy changed a great deal in the intervening period. The limits of expansion on the basis of capital goods production had been reached toward the end of the nineteenth century. With the British mainland crisscrossed with railways and canals, profit rates began to decline. Lenin suggested in *Imperialism, the Highest Stage of Capitalism* that this is why capitalists began to look overseas for investment opportunities, and ended up colonizing most of the globe. Lenin, though, overlooked what in hindsight would be an obvious untapped market: production not of capital but of consumer goods. Beginning in the late nineteenth century and continuing into the twentieth, partly in response to the demands of working classes, partly in response to the needs of capital, political elites began restructuring economies in such a way as to steer more of their revenue into the hands of the mass public, through such means as labor and welfare legislation. The rest, as we know, is history. But the long-term impact on the culture of capitalism would be profound. The values of thrift and restraint did not sell goods. Rather, the values of having fun and letting go began to creep in. And by the late twentieth century, the growth of a "pink" market—homosexuals with high disposable incomes but no families—made the libertarian principles underlying gay rights good business. It was not just a matter of advertising in gay publications to reach the market; it was a matter of advertising in publications, gay or otherwise, which created a market. Popular media that not only celebrated hedonistic lifestyles, but sometimes also ridiculed traditional ones or dismissed them as impossible or pleasureless ideals, were those that attracted the advertising dollars of the mushrooming consumer goods industries. Magazines that decried capitalism or praised the virtues of social responsibility might still have found large markets in the Third World, and today Louis Farrakhan's call for traditional morality resonates among some African Americans who have been largely excluded from the benefits of the growth in consumer power and still feel the need to reap the benefits of stable family life. But in most of the First World, traditional morality is being rolled back for the simple reason that it is an obstacle to the growth of the emerging dominant fractions of capital.

An irony that emerges from this is that cultural entrepreneurs who market themselves as antinomians, rebels, or iconoclasts are usually anything but. Rather, they help sweep aside the obstacles to further capital accumulation as surely as gentleman parliamentarians in nineteenth-century Britain did when they changed the trade laws. The Spice Girls may have trumpeted an allegedly subversive feminist message, but they were the brainchild of middle-aged male marketing geniuses who built their success on extensive research to match their products to the demands of the market.[15] Similarly, Benjamin Barber has commented that "gangsta rappers think they are using rock to take on the official culture. But of course the official culture owns them rock, stock, and barrel and it is they who are being used. . . . The rockers and rappers may end up in jail, but the record companies and cable stations keep raking in the dough."[16] Similarly, some left-wing commentators maintain that the counterculture of the 1960s was anything but: it did not challenge the staid culture of a hegemonic bourgeoisie, as its exponents often claimed, but was in the vanguard of capitalist development, sweeping aside the underbrush that inhibited consumption and thereby opening up new markets and raising profits for capital.

Neoliberal defenders of contemporary capitalism will say that producers of mass consumption goods are merely giving the people what they want. Indeed, they will add, far from capital reigning supreme, the consumer is sovereign. That is true, to an extent, but the process goes deeper. Contrary to the assumption underlying conventional economic theory, wants are not a given. People do not simply have desires that they then set about meeting. Many of the products people desire today they may well not have desired a generation or so ago, because the products did not then exist. Advertising is not just a means of making the public aware that you offer a product. Were it so, the advertising industry would be leaner than it is today—over $50 billion a year and rising in the United States alone, larger than most of the world's national economies—and could depend on a relatively small number of well-placed ads drawing public attention to one's good or service. It would certainly not rely on multimillion-dollar endorsements from celebrities or expensive productions designed to create an image surrounding a product. Suffice it to say here that advertising must create demand, and to keep the economy growing, it must constantly create *new* demand and not simply address *existing* demand. If capitalism were a matter of satisfying given wants, the economy would grow only slightly more rapidly than the population. By creating new wants it has managed to achieve high rates of dynamism long after the limits of capital goods development have been reached.

In fact, it seems reasonable to argue that without such cultural diffusion, many of the wants we now take for granted would have never come into existence. The commonsense view that rising prosperity has not brought an equivalent rise in happiness is borne out by research showing that the boom in consumption in recent decades has done little to make people happier, and if anything has corresponded with an increase in unhappiness.[17] This is not a celebration of poverty, or a denial that there may be an optimum level of consumption that brings real joy. Yet without a doubt, those who benefit the most from stimulating consumption are the sellers of the wares, not the buyers. Gianni Versace became fabulously wealthy off promotion of the fashion industry. Most of his customers ran up credit card debts.

The stress on journalistic objectivity or artistic freedom leads many involved in the mass media to noble achievements, yet individual ideals cannot alter the fact that the mass media do not and cannot convey unvarnished truths to the mass public. It is not just that the mass media are not democratic. In fact, they do give the people what they want, but from a narrow range of options. The cultural milieu in which people swim is largely determined by the dominant elite. Enthusiasts of the Internet will often wax eloquent about the democratizing nature of the communications revolution, but while the technology makes information easily accessible, for as long as purchasing power is concentrated, the culture that emerges from the Internet will reflect the interests of this privileged group. The voices of the poor and oppressed, though they may find the occasional website on the Internet, are unlikely to be heard in any meaningful way.

Those who dominate the process of cultural formation cannot get people to consume just any product. But what of a situation where an elite has an interest in getting the mass to believe something that is foolish or simply false? Can it be done? The answer is yes, but cultural entrepreneurs must in this case be clever artificers. Georges Sorel argued that some of the most potent myths were false, but that what mattered was not that they were true, but that people *believed* they were true.[18] A poetic lie will often vanquish a mundane truth, especially if the latter is unpalatable. Most of us are capable of believing quite silly things if we judge that it serves our material and spiritual interests. People especially believe what they want to believe. The belief may not serve their actual interests, but their own ignorance or fallibility may cause them to believe nonetheless in its value. So, many intellectuals criticize some forms of religion for keeping people in doubt and ignorance and thereby inhibiting their progress, but the short-term spiritual benefits provided by those religious beliefs obviously outweigh the short-term costs of renouncing them.

Implicit in the foregoing discussion is the suggestion that reality and the perception thereof differ. This is hardly a radical idea, but in recent years some philosophers have made much of it, arguing that reality is wholly contextual, subjective, and reflective of the interests of the dominant group in society, and thus worthy of "deconstruction." This is really just a fancy way of saying "strip it bare and expose it for what it is." The poststructuralists are probably correct to assert that culture and discourse are largely products of a process that privileges the interests of dominant groups in society. The truths with which we are familiar are therefore worthy of close scrutiny. However, it appears to be a non sequitur to proceed from that conclusion to the further one that there is no such thing as absolute truth or objective reality.[19] Rather, all we can say is what has been known for centuries, that humans can be poetic and persuasive liars. Objective truth may well be difficult to apprehend, but that fact in itself does not allow us to conclude that it does not exist, or even that it is impossible to find. In short, while this discussion of culture owes an obvious debt to poststructuralist theory, this is no paean to postmodernism. The latter, as will be argued later, is the discourse of the emerging dominant class fractions in the global political economy, and may well be helping to worsen the lot of the poor.

The Culture(s) of Neoliberalism

In light of the foregoing, what can we say about the cultures of, respectively, the Keynesian welfare state, the developmentalist state, communism, and neoliberalism? How did regime changes correspond to cultural revolutions? Given that the first regimes bound citizens in relationships of vertical loyalty to the state, which looked after many and often most of their material needs, loyalty and a sense of collective identity were bound to be strong. Collectivism was seen as virtue, the cardinal one in communist countries; greed was seen as a vice, and self-sacrifice a virtue. Faith in modernity remained strong, nationalism took primacy over other forms of identity, and the state was seen as enlightened (whereas markets, if sometimes seen as useful tools, were also seen as feeding humans' baser instincts).

As the state withdrew from its resource-provision role, therefore, it was to be expected that individuals would become more focused on their own needs, and less willing to make sacrifices for others, from whom there was no longer a guarantee of reciprocation.[20] Individualism and thus competitiveness would rise, and collectivism would diminish; accordingly, greed would come to be celebrated as a virtue, and self-sacrifice as a folly. Identities would become narrower as people gravitated toward parochial groups that they saw as serving their needs, particularly when (as we shall see in subsequent chapters) new elites had built networks of support by exploiting the opportunities of the new global economy. Nationalism, in particular, no longer seen as a unifying force but as a strategy by a dominant group to repress minorities, would suffer; identity politics would thus emerge. A duality, of globalism and localism, would become dominant, especially among the dynamic young entrepreneurs who would come to lead the new global economy. Modernism as the guiding faith would give way to postmodernism in its various incarnations. Equally, amid the anarchy of postmodernity, fundamentalisms would reemerge in a quest to reimpose order on a disordered society.

Many studies have tracked the growth of individualism, civic disengagement, and materialism. One of the facts that appears to recur is that these trends seem most manifest among young people (which is to be expected since, as argued above, new cultural traits are most likely to show up in young people). An annual survey among entrants to U.S. universities called *The American Freshman,* which was initiated in 1966, has tracked such changes.[21] In the first year of the study, 57 percent of college freshmen felt that keeping up with political affairs was very important and 29.9 percent discussed politics frequently; by 1997 those figures had decreased by half, to 26.7 percent and 13.7 percent respectively. In 1968 only 40.8 percent of freshmen said that an essential purpose of education was to become financially well-off, whereas more than twice that number said that developing a philosophy was a key goal; by 1997, 74.9 percent said that financial security was an essential purpose of higher education, and the importance of developing a philosophy remained important to only 40.8 percent of college freshmen. Youth voting, which normally trails the overall vote to begin with, reached low points in the United States by the end of the 1990s.[22] Such tendencies are mirrored in Europe, where a 2001 survey found that one in two young Europeans did not belong to any organization or association.[23]

Such selfishness, to the point that social ramifications of acts are now dismissed, has become increasingly common. Even in law-loving Canada, young people are now twice as likely as the average Canadian to cheat on taxes or buy smuggled goods.[24] In the First World, such anomie came to be reflected in the 1990s in a youth culture that was remarkably similar across societies and characterized by cynicism, resignation, and a sometimes crass materialism. The lyrics of what was once called the anthem of America's Generation X, Nirvana's "Smells

Like Teen Spirit," probably captured the political attitude of the generation: "I feel stupid, and contagious, Here we are now, entertain us."

The conventional explanations for the concentration of asocial and antisocial tendencies among young people tend to relate it to formative events and factors that affected the generations born after the war in distinct and peculiar ways.[25] However, another way of interpreting the data is to connect the attitudes of young people to the very different policy environment into which they have emerged.[26] At least one commentator on the *American Freshmen* survey noted that the apparent increase in materialism was in part affected by the rising cost of college education to the students.[27] Equally, greater insecurity in the job market, coupled with a loss of faith in the institutions that might once have helped them to face such a challenge, has been said to have led the post-1960s generation of Americans to feel that the state can no longer help them through their trying times.[28] Put simply, in an age when social bonds and obligations were attenuated, even severed, self-sacrifice became dysfunctional; if self-sacrifice is to not become dysfunctional to the individual, it requires some sort of collective enforcement—sometimes legal obligation, but more often moral sanction—to prevent the free-rider effect from coming into play. Otherwise, individuals will have every interest in deriving the benefits of the whole while eschewing contributions to that whole. And given that such moral sanctions came to diminish with the celebration of individual freedom, while the benefits were not seen to be accruing by many members of society, self-sacrifice simply became dysfunctional to one's material well-being. In this context, only those with a strong principled commitment to self-sacrifice—in particular, certain types of religious people—continued to abide by its practices.

Culturally, the shift toward the celebration of greed and selfishness seems evident to most people. Even if the data remain essentially anecdotal, the wealth of it makes the cultural shift that has been taking place over the past generation evident to anyone old enough to have observed it. If, in Western societies, the 1960s were the decade of love and revolution, by the 1970s the shift toward what Christopher Lasch called "the culture of narcissism" was well under way.[29] And so the syrupy celebration of love and fidelity of the 1970s, "I Got You, Babe," by Sonny and Cher, metamorphosed into the 1990s remake by Cher, featuring Beavis and Butthead, in which the singer dropped hints of scorn for her former husband and used the song to celebrate her liberation. Similarly, a Champion clothing publicity campaign at around the same time deliberately ridiculed the social orientations of a previous generation with an advertisement that featured a game of beach volleyball and the caption

"They say you can serve the ball or your fellow man? I say, here it comes, man." *The Brady Bunch* ceded place to *Married with Children;* both were caricatures, but of very different realities.

Social commentators have noted similar cultural shifts in other societies, corresponding to similar periods in time. The old Chinese activists of the Cultural Revolution, whatever their excesses had been in the late 1960s, would nonetheless maintain that they acted in service of a greater goal. In the competitive climate of the 1990s, they would find themselves marginalized and ridiculed by a younger generation who would wonder what they had to show for their efforts.[30] Polls in India have also detected a clear shift toward materialism and civic disengagement, and away from idealism and political involvement. A 1996 survey among college students there found that 60 percent listed their top priority as getting a good job, while a mere 18 percent listed service to community as their top priority;[31] today, most young Indians have no interest in politics and nearly half of them do not vote.[32]

The contestation of nationalism by new identities, both local and global, is testified to by the rising visibility of identity politics, and regionalist and ethnic movements (to be discussed in more detail in Chapter 5). In many Third World societies, nationalism has suffered serious setbacks, as the nation-state has become increasingly remote from the lives of ordinary people. Particularly in Africa, where talk of failed states is most widespread, nationalism has in many countries failed to take deep roots. As the already fragile state has withdrawn, clan, ethnic, religious, and regional loyalties—never far from the surface—have reappeared. Ethnic and regional politics have become particularly vociferous as a result, as we shall see later in the book.

Technological changes merged with material ones to make possible this fragmentation of culture. Hyperdifferentiation—the explosion of choice to which sociologists refer—enabled many communities to emerge from beneath national cultures. In the days before satellite television and the Internet, it had been easier for governments to exercise a degree of control (virtually complete, in the case of the communist countries) over the cultural diet of their citizens. But as the bonds between citizens and national elites attenuated as a result of the material changes of the neoliberal age, the emergence of new communities could easily find cultural expression, especially as the Internet allowed them to transcend the limitations of space in communicating with one another. The Internet has been a tool that has been used to great effect by some of the antistate militants of the neoliberal age, from Islamists to those of the far right. Globalization and localization go hand in hand. Returning to the question of the peculiar role of young people in the

United States, when they are involved in politics, they are today more likely to be involved in grassroots volunteer work rather than overarching struggles, where they apparently feel they can make a difference.[33] As one member of the so-called Generation Seattle that resists neoliberal globalization put it, if the twentieth century was the century of the big projects, the twenty-first century is the century of small, local struggles.[34]

Much is often made of the materialistic tendencies of neoliberalism vis-à-vis its predecessors. One often hears older intellectuals bemoan the fact that while their generation was committed to goals that surpassed their personal interests—patriotism, nation building, revolution—the younger generation is concerned only with their personal indulgence. In other words, it is said that there was a stronger spiritual dimension to the regimes that predated the neoliberal era. Too much may be made of this distinction. By its very nature, the modernity that underpinned the Keynesian welfare state, the developmentalist state, and communism was as materialist as anything that followed. Social service was not glorified as it was by conservative ideologies, as a duty to a higher order, but as a contractual obligation to a society that was benefiting all its members. Rather, the principal distinction between neoliberalism and its predecessors is that the former sees the material gratifications as being wholly individual, rather than collective. Hence it is no accident that as modernism and nationalism went into decline in Christian societies, so too did the traditional churches that laid great stress on collective salvation. Within Christianity, the fastest-growing movement today is pentecostalism,[35] with its emphasis on personal salvation and—when coupled with the so-called faith gospel—the material gain that can come to an individual (not a community) through personal redemption. As with other cultural innovations, pentecostalism seems to have immense appeal to young people, and often speaks to their material concerns more effectively than do the traditional churches.[36] Evangelical Christianity is booming in Latin America, sub-Saharan Africa, the former Soviet Union and East Bloc states, and the Philippines—that is to say, in nominally Christian cultures in which the collectivist doctrines of traditional churches do not correspond to the material realities of a more atomized society. In the industrial democracies, meanwhile, one sees a similar trend in the growth of so-called New Age religions, as well as an adapted Buddhism, which are united in their quest for a personal development that frequently writes the community—and with it any obligations to its other members, in particular its less fortunate ones—out of the picture. Such religions, one could say, represent the religious face of neoliberalism: no more or less materialistic than the older religions, but far more individualistic.

Yet if the culture of neoliberalism was no more materialistic than its predecessors, it is perhaps true that it tended toward what might be called hyperconsumerism—a belief that pleasure comes from the consumption of material stimuli (including bodily stimuli, which would allow for a stress on the sexual aspect), and that greater happiness comes from constantly rising levels of consumption. This arguably reached its peak in the 1990s, a decade during which Westerners, and most especially Americans, went on one of history's biggest buying binges, the consumption of pornography exploded, and pharmaceutical companies pared back their production of tropical medicines for poor countries[37] and shifted their resources into developing treatments for baldness, impotence, and obesity for the markets of the rich world. What lay behind this was one of the temporary features of the neoliberal global economy. Liberalization of trade and capital markets led hundreds of billions of dollars—much of it emanating from Third World countries[38]—to flow into the U.S. economy over the course of the 1990s as foreign money subsidized the U.S. trade deficit. This vast influx of capital, running at several hundred billion dollars per year by the end of the decade, found its way into U.S. stock and bond markets. As a result, investment was abundant and cheap. This meant the government could tolerate a decline in the savings rate to historic lows, and thus a surge in consumption. So whereas the phenomenon of declining savings would have ordinarily raised capital costs to business, a peculiar feature of the boom economy was that U.S. firms were able to promote heavy consumption with no cost to their bottom lines, and thus reap huge profits. They promoted this consumption by sponsoring, through advertising, cultural products—television shows, music, and the like—that transmitted such cultural values. Thus the logic of capital rather than the achievements of sexual revolutionaries (though the latter may have in fact been serving the former)[39] lay behind the appearance of television programs like *Sex in the City* in the late 1990s. Emblematic of this peculiar economy was a U.S. president whose own lifestyle typified the hedonism of the "greed is good" generation.[40] Of course, the economy was built atop a fragile foundation, as the foreign capital would begin to leave in the new century. Equally deleterious was the fact that the globalization of cultural industries spread this culture to countries whose economic structure could ill-afford even a temporary shift to high consumption and low savings. In poor countries with high degrees of inequality, this conspired to depress savings rates during the 1990s, ensuring that any economic growth that occurred was shallow, unsustainable, and dependent entirely on exports to the swimming economies of the First World.[41]

Conclusion

The quarter century that followed World War II proved to be the "golden age" of the statist regimes (the Keynesian welfare state, the developmentalist state, and communism). Recovery from war prompted a burst of economic growth in Western Europe and North America, which in turn drove up demand for the exports of the newly independent states of the Third World. There thus followed a period of sustained growth, which touched most of the world. Even the communist countries—the Soviet Union, its six European buffer states and a small network of allies in the Third World, and China—were growing, although they were not keeping up with some of their capitalist rivals. Moreover, the growth was broadly distributed via increasingly generous welfare states. The state-led economy thus created a market for state-led ideals, including those of nationalism, solidarity, community, and self-sacrifice. By the early 1970s, though, the economic growth rate in most of the Western countries was slowing. Productivity gains failed to keep pace with income growth, and rising pressure from the dynamic East Asian economies (in particular Japan) forced Western corporations to find ways to reduce labor costs. Recession hit the First World, though the oil shock, by swelling the coffers of banks with Arab deposits, enabled Third World governments to borrow their way through the decade. But when recession returned with the second oil shock in 1979, Third World countries were hit by the debt crisis and were forced to turn to the lending agencies of the First World for assistance.

By then, First World governments had shifted rightward under the influence of a new middle-class politics. These governments were increasingly calling for an abandonment of the Keynesian compromise and a restoration of the free market. By and large, their assault on the welfare state failed to make much headway among programs popular with the middle class, but did cut deeply into those that targeted the more politically marginalized poor, not to mention poor countries. Meanwhile, Third World countries were running into problems of their own. In many countries, particularly in Africa, the expansion of the distribution regimes used to consolidate the power of new governing elites outstripped accumulation, and by the 1980s several governments were headed for fiscal crises. At the same time, Third World governments that had borrowed petrodollars when they were cheap during the oil boom of the mid-1970s ran into a double barrier. As the politics of the First World shifted rightward, monetarist policies of tackling inflation by raising interest rates came into vogue. By raising credit costs and the value of the currency—the U.S. dollar—in which most international debt was denoted, the costs to debtor governments surged. Second, the monetarist recipe, as it was meant to do, had the effect of sinking First World economies into recession. This led to sudden drops in demand for Third World exports, depriving governments there of the revenue they needed to pay those same debts and forcing them to turn to the international lending agencies at the very time that these agencies were coming further under the sway of neoliberal thought. The price of bailouts to Third World governments was an acceptance of the "structural adjustment" programs then being promoted by the lending agencies. The neoliberal age had begun.

Notes

1. In *Magic and the Millennium* (London: Heinemann, 1973), Bryan R. Wilson shows how many Third World millenarian movements, which often borrowed their eschatologies from the colonizers, originated in response to the economic and social disruptions caused by colonial penetration. The theme of the abandonment of traditional beliefs that are seen to have been compromised by their inability to insulate peoples against colonial penetration, who then adopted either the cultural beliefs of the colonists or anticolonial syncretic beliefs that nonetheless drew heavily from missionaries, is also found in African literature at around the time of independence.

2. Tibor Scitovsky infers from this that accumulated goods—one can add cultural goods—bring little additional pleasure once people have become accustomed to them, but that people are loath to renounce them. See Tibor Scitovsky, *The Joyless Economy: An Inquiry into Human Satisfaction and Consumer Dissatisfaction* (New York: Oxford University Press, 1976), chap. 6.

3. See Scitovsky, *Joyless Economy,* p. 10.

4. Research into television viewing shows that rather than being simply socialized by what they see, people tend to watch the shows that reflect their views and interests. Gerhardt D. Wiebe, "The Social Effects of Broadcasting," in *Mass Culture Revisited,* edited by Bernard Rosenberg and David Manning White (New York: Van Nostrand Reinhold, 1971).

5. See Paul W. Sherman and Jennifer Billing, "Antimicrobial Functions of Spices: Why Some Like It Hot," *Quarterly Review of Biology* 73, no. 1 (March 1998).

6. See Louis Hartz et al., *The Founding of New Societies* (New York: Harcourt and Brace, 1964).

7. See S. M. Lipset, *Revolution and Counter-Revolution* (New York: Anchor Books, 1970).

8. Walter Lippmann, *Public Opinion* (New York: Harcourt, Brace, 1922), p. 29.

9. Ibid., p. 324.

10. Robert A. Hackett, "For a Socialist Perspective on the News Media,"

Studies in Political Economy 19 (Spring 1986): 141–156. The theory that the mass media constitute a means of production was originally developed by Dallas Smythe.

11. Hackett, "For a Socialist Perspective."

12. For examples of this, see Russ Baker, "The Squeeze," *Columbia Journalism Review,* September–October 1997. The anxiety of corporate advertisers not to antagonize their customers further illustrates the claim that the elite cannot feed the masses any cultural product, but must take note of their wishes as well.

13. Ibid.

14. On the ambivalence of Americans toward abortion, see Barbara Hinkson Craig and David M. O'Brien, *Abortion and American Politics* (Chatham, N.J.: Chatham House, 1993), chap. 7.

15. Compare David Harvey, *The Condition of Postmodernity: An Enquiry into the Origins of Cultural Change* (Oxford: Blackwell, 1990); and Thomas Frank, *The Conquest of Cool: Business Culture, Counterculture, and the Rise of Hip Consumerism* (Chicago: University of Chicago Press, 1997).

16. Benjamin Barber, *Jihad vs. McWorld* (New York: Ballantine Books, 1996), pp. 110–111.

17. One U.S. study found that although wealth doubled in the four decades after 1957, those who declared themselves to be very happy declined substantially (*Outlook Magazine, The Sunday Gleaner,* Kingston, 12 October 1997). See also the United Nations Development Programme's 1998 *Human Development Report* (New York: United Nations, 1998); and Juliet B. Schor, *The Overspent American: Upscaling, Downshifting, and the New Consumer* (New York: Basic Books, 1998). Similarly, "The Canadian Mental Health Association survey reveals an unmistakable link between stress levels and income." Peter Shawn Taylor, "Melancholy Babies," *Saturday Night Magazine,* Toronto, May 1996. For a theoretical treatment of this apparent paradox, see Scitovsky, *Joyless Economy;* and Richard Easterlin, *Growth Triumphant: The Twenty-First Century in Historical Perspective* (Ann Arbor: University of Michigan Press, 1996), chap. 10.

18. Georges Sorel, *Réflexions sur la violence,* 11th ed. (Paris: Librairie Marcel Rivière et Cie., 1950).

19. Compare Margaret McCabe's observations in the *Times Literary Supplement* (London), 13 June 1997, p. 14. McCabe says, "The observation that there are attitudes which are peculiar to one culture delivers no conclusion about whether there are any values which transcend culture and locale."

20. If moral demands are universally enforced, their burden is not great. The problem is that when people are free to choose not to accept the burden, those who do so are left shouldering a greater burden. See Liam B. Murphy, *Moral Demands in Nonideal Theory* (New York: Oxford University Press, 2000).

21. Published by the Higher Education Research Institute of the Graduate School of Education and Information Studies, University of California–Los Angeles. For a recent commentary, see Sheilah Mann, "What the Survey of American College Freshmen Tells Us About Their Interest in Politics and

Political Science," *PS: Political Science and Politics* 32, no. 2 (June 1999): 263–268.

22. Mark Strama, "Overcoming Cynicism: Youth Participation and Electoral Politics," *National Civic Review* 87, no. 1 (Spring 1988): 71–77.

23. Eurobarometer: http://europa.eu.int/comm/public_opinion/archives/eb/ebs_151_summ_en.pdf.

24. *The Globe and Mail* (Toronto), 9 January 1996, p. A1.

25. Robert Putnam attributes it to the role of television, as does Juliet Schor, pointing out that it is only in the post-1960s period that television comes to occupy such an important place in people's lives. See Robert Putnam, "Tuning In, Tuning Out: The Strange Disappearance of Social Capital in America," *PS: Political Science and Politics* 28, no. 4 (December 1995): 664–683; and Schor, *The Overspent American,* chap. 1.

26. On this point, compare Shalom H. Schwartz, Anat Bardi, and Gabriel Bianchi, "Value Adaptation to the Imposition and Collapse of Communist Regimes in East-Central Europe," in *Political Psychology,* edited by Stanley A. Renshon and John Duckitt (New York: New York University Press, 2000). In a study of communist societies, Schwartz, Bardi, and Bianchi found that values were formed not so much by material conditions or indoctrination, but by the adaptations individuals made to the material conditions of their existence.

27. Daniel Cheever, president of Simmons College in Boston, quoted in the *New York Times,* 12 January 1998.

28. W. Lance Bennett, "The Uncivic Culture: Communitarianism, Identity, and the Rise of Lifestyle Politics," *PS: Political Science and Politics* 31, no. 4 (December 1998): 741–761.

29. Christopher Lasch, *The Culture of Narcissism* (New York: W. W. Norton, 1979).

30. See James Kynge, "China's Twenty-First-Century Cultural Revolution," *Financial Times* (London), 3 January 2001.

31. The survey was done by the Bombay firm Marketing and Research Group Ltd. *The Globe and Mail* (Toronto), 6 January 1996.

32. *Financial Times* (London), 17 February 1998.

33. Strama, "Overcoming Cynicism"; compare Bennett, "Uncivic Culture."

34. Christian Losson and Paul Quinio, *Génération Seattle* (Paris: Grasset, 2002), pp. 29–30.

35. Allan Figueroa Deck, review in *Theological Studies* 57, no. 1 (March 1996): 153.

36. See, for example, Paul Gifford, *African Christianity* (Bloomington: Indiana University Press, 1998).

37. BBC World Service, 30 October 2000.

38. From 1990 to 1999, U.S. accumulated financial surplus (foreign investments in the United States minus U.S. investments abroad) came to $1.14 trillion. Much of this found its way into the stock market. Indeed, by 1999 foreign investors were pouring nearly as much money ($299 billion) into the U.S. stock market as ordinary Americans (who placed $390 billion into stock and money-market mutual funds in that year). See U.S. Department of Commerce,

Bureau of Economic Analysis, for details. Figures on U.S. mutual funds taken from Investment Company Institute data (www.ici.org).

39. See Frank, *Conquest of Cool.*

40. As much as anyone, Bill Clinton bought into this rhetoric, which has its roots in neoclassical and libertarian thought (see, for example, Ayn Rand, *The Virtue of Selfishness* [New York: New American Library, 1964]; this doctrine of unintended consequences originated in Bernard Mandeville's seventeenth-century treatise *The Fable of the Bees,* was elaborated by Adam Smith in the *Wealth of Nations,* and arguably reached its apogee in Nietzsche's inversion of vice and virtue in *The Anti-Christ*). During his "poverty tour" of the United States near the end of his presidency, Clinton called on U.S. businesses to invest in depressed communities not because it was morally right, but because it would make them rich. In fact, markets seldom miss an opportunity to make a profit, and the reason these areas were neglected was because conditions within them made returns so low. Only an ethic of responsibility that led firms to absorb some losses in the pursuit of collective goods, or government investments to augment returns in these areas, would have drawn in investment.

41. The African continent was a case in point. See the 2000 report on development by the United Nations Economic Commission for Africa, *Transforming Africa's Economies* (Addis Ababa: United Nations, 2001).

4

Neoliberal Globalization
and the Crisis of the State

Neoliberalism can be taken to be a fusion of neoclassical economic theory with neoclassical liberal political thought. Neoclassical economics dates back to the late nineteenth century, when the "marginalist revolution" formalized the philosophy of Adam Smith. It receded to the margins of economic thought during the Keynesian age, but returned gradually, its principal tenets being kept alive by brilliant thinkers such as Friedrich Hayek and Milton Friedman. Although it has come to be seen as dogmatic, in no small part because of the nonacademic literature of Hayek and Friedman (with provocative titles like *The Fatal Conceit, The Road to Serfdom,* and *Free to Choose*), in fact most neoclassical economists are economic technicians, concerned with minutiae like incentive structures and rent seeking. Nonetheless, neoclassical economists converge around a faith in entrepreneurship and free markets and a suspicion of the state.

Among the tenets of neoclassical economic theory are beliefs that markets are efficient and clear; that individuals are rational utility-maximizers; that the price mechanism offers the best means of distilling all information available in an economy; that a stable macroeconomic environment—characterized by low inflation, secure property rights, and restrained government—will attract private investment and lead to growth, and that the best way to effect this macroeconomic stability is through monetary rather than fiscal policy; that an unfettered market will eventually disperse the fruits of growth to all its participants; that inequality raises investment; that public investment crowds out private investment (by competing for scarce capital and thereby imposing a premium on the cost of capital); that political considerations typically

75

interfere with economic logic, such that greater government involvement in the economy tends to lead to less growth; that greater trade leads to a greater realization of comparative advantage, resulting in efficiency and income gains; that greater competition accelerates innovation and restrains price inflation; and that rules are always preferable to discretion in government economic policy, since the former can easily be integrated into prices whereas the latter tend to distort them, while the rational expectations school of neoclassical economics goes even further and argues that all government policies are anticipated by economic agents in such a way as to neutralize their intended impact (thereby rendering government policy ineffective).[1] The practical upshot of this worldview is that the government should withdraw as much as possible from management of the economy and leave its operations to relatively unconstrained entrepreneurs, with market logic governing their activities. To this end, reduced government spending and employment, deregulation, greater autonomy for central banks, a shift in tax from income toward consumption and a reduction in top rates, and privatization all form part of the neoclassical prescription for economic growth. Neoclassical theorists are typically less dogmatic than their neoliberal popularizers: they do not consider all government policy bad, and foresee a continued (if pared-back) role for government in the economy. Nonetheless, the overall thrust is toward reducing government's involvement in the economy and freeing up the market.

In their faith in individual initiative and their consequent belief in the virtue of individual liberty, the neoclassical economists resemble neoclassical liberal philosophers, whose wellspring was the same as the thinking of Adam Smith. Classical liberal philosophy, associated with such names as Thomas Hobbes, John Locke, and John Stuart Mill, saw individuals as the building blocks of society and stressed the need for individual freedom from the depredations of the state. Yet in the course of the nineteenth century, liberal theory grew mindful of the private violations of individual liberty that could occur, and increasingly looked to the state to ensure people the realization of their rights. The emphasis came to be placed on positive freedom. By the end of the century, liberal thinkers like L. T. Hobhouse could expound philosophies that were close to socialism,[2] a fact that did not escape the notice of Friedrich Hayek.[3] In response to what was seen as a liberal thrust toward more and more state power, classical liberal philosophy began to revive in the postwar period in the work of such writers as Robert Nozick.[4] Equally significant were the attempts by neoclassical economists like Friedrich Hayek[5] and Mancur Olson,[6] among others, to extrapolate from their economic conclusions and make inferences that would apply in the political sphere. The principal thrust of this "economic approach to politics" was that in all areas of life, not just the market, individuals behaved self-interestedly, and that the most rational society was one that permitted them to do so with maximum freedom.[7]

The fusion of neoclassical economics and neoclassical liberal thought was effected in the 1970s by conservative politicians and the intellectuals who surrounded them. As this fusion took place, the more technical aspects of neoclassical economics were discarded and the resultant school of thought tended to be more dogmatic and uncompromising in its assertions about the role of the state and the individual. Neoliberalism saw society as nothing more than a collection of individuals—Margaret Thatcher famously declared there was indeed no such thing as society—and thus sought to restore freedom to individuals, particularly in the economy. In its early stages, neoliberalism was a bit muddle-headed as it combined economic freedom with the political and social restraint of conservative morality, but by the 1990s a new generation of neoliberal politicians, typified by Bill Clinton and Tony Blair, had resolved this tension by extending individual liberty to all spheres of life. In any event, neoliberalism aimed to roll back the power of the state and free up the market. In the Third World, neoliberalism emerged less for political reasons and more as a result of the needs to adjust to international requirements. Nonetheless, it would be wrong to suggest that neoliberal policies were foisted upon Third World governments by First World lenders, as is often suggested. In fact, the accumulation crises of Third World regimes had, by the 1970s, drawn the developmentalist state into question. Neoliberal policy elites were thus in the ascendant and arguing for a shift in policy orientation. Indeed, some of the earliest experiments in structural adjustment, in Chile, Turkey, Ghana, and Côte d'Ivoire, were drawn up mainly by local policymakers.[8]

Historians might one day trace the start of the neoliberal age to the overthrow of Salvador Allende in Chile in 1973. The new president, Augusto Pinochet, brought the "Chicago Boys"—Chilean economists trained at or influenced by the University of Chicago—to power, and they set about implementing a campaign of monetarist "shock therapy." By the end of the decade, neoliberal politicians were in office in the United States and Britain. France held out and went socialist, but then produced what would be Keynesianism's last stand, a program that failed and gave rise to an abrupt about-face in 1983. By this time, neoliberal policies were being adopted even by left-wing governments in the First World. In the Third World, the wave of structural adjustment rolled on, finally washing up against the last holdouts, in the Middle

East, after the Gulf War in the early 1990s. Around then, the fall of the Berlin Wall and the ascent of (sometimes nominally) liberal governments in the former Soviet bloc brought on a wave of shock therapy in several formerly communist societies. By the time the left started coming back to power in the industrial democracies, it had shed its Keynesian and statist clothing and been won over to the virtues of neoliberalism. All that was left to be done was to give it a kinder, gentler image than that imparted to it by its earlier, revolutionary generation.

What lay behind the decline of the old regimes—the Keynesian welfare state, the developmentalist state, and communism—appears to have been both the eventual failures of their accumulation regimes and, paradoxically, the successes of their distribution regimes. On the one hand, all three regimes were effective at engineering growth and physical capital accumulation; on the other hand, they tended to become bound with rigidities that rendered them less able to respond flexibly to the challenges of an increasingly global economy. By the 1970s, all three were in crisis. In the Western states, productivity was declining; given the continued generosity of the welfare state (including the legal protections it gave to unionized labor), this meant inflation would start rising, even in the midst of recession. Equally, as economies integrated, the effectiveness of Keynesian reflationary strategies was eroded by the possibilities of capital export (something that defeated France's effort at Keynesian reflation in the early 1980s, when the additional money pumped into the French economy simply found its way to foreign firms). In the Third World, the economic boom of the 1950s and 1960s gave way to the sluggish growth, rising debt, and declining commodity prices (with the obvious exception of oil) from the 1970s. Industries built up during the boom days reached the limits of national markets and found it difficult to move into export markets, which placed growing strains on current accounts. In the communist countries, the rapid physical capital formation of the early postwar period relied on the installation of additional plant. However, central planning was ill-adapted to the task of raising labor productivity or improving product quality, and the result was a slowdown in economic growth that had become endemic by the 1970s. Everywhere, the rise of the East Asian economies posed a threat. To Western countries, Asian imports forced firms and governments to look for new ways to cut costs and raise productivity in order to remain competitive. To China, the dynamism of Taiwan and Hong Kong threatened the legitimacy, not to mention the comparative viability, of the Maoist model.[9] Third World countries were equally penalized by the dynamism of both primary and secondary producers in East and Southeast Asia, who were capturing their market shares for traditional exports and penetrating their markets.

Meanwhile, the growth of the middle class, due in part to the education provided by the state, and also in part to the needs of the increasingly sophisticated postwar economy, figured as a significant development almost everywhere. In the 1970s, this new middle class provided the political support for a turn against the existing regimes. If the old regimes had been built upon a marriage of dominant economic elites with urban working classes, the equation had broken down by the 1970s. In the communist countries, the new middle class—more globalized than peasantries and working classes—was exposed to cultural influences from abroad. Its wants were thus shaped in ways that ruling elites found impossible to meet within the context of existing accumulation regimes.[10] In Europe and North America, whereas the working classes feared the specter of unemployment, the property-owning, comparatively prosperous middle classes feared the specter of inflation, which not only eroded their buying power but increased their mortgage payments. Keynesian reflationary strategies, which by the late 1970s were aggravating inflation, began to look less attractive than neoliberal calls for a war on inflation.

As the postwar regimes gave way to the neoliberal one, so too did the cultural paradigm shift. In the place of modernity came postmodernity and its rival twin, fundamentalism (which both rejected yet emerged from postmodernism).[11] The solidarity and cooperation of the modern age gave way to the individualism and celebration of competition of the neoliberal market. The state was no longer seen as the rational agent of progress; rather it was the corrupt brake on progress. The market was now the measure of civilization, the venue where individuals enjoyed maximum freedom to develop and exploit their talents. In the industrial countries, the growth of a large middle class, which saw itself as more independent and was less unionized than the working class, created a constituency whose relationship to the state was ambivalent. This effect was exaggerated in Third World countries, where both large industrialists and urban workers had benefited from state patronage; it was the small class of middle entrepreneurs who had been truly independent, and who bore much of the brunt of government retrenchment,[12] and who thus came to regard the state with some hostility. In the late twentieth century, the shift in industrial organization away from large units of production toward large networks of small units[13]—a shift made possible by globalization—created a growing class of independent, relatively prosperous entrepreneurs who, however, jealously guarded their independence from the state. This middle class provided the support base for political movements that challenged the authority of the state, whether the far right in Western Europe[14] or Islamist organizations in the Muslim world.[15] As they provided the constituency in favor of policies of economic liberalization, they helped further build the base against the state. For as governments cut into their spending and thereby threw more and more people outside the distributional networks of the state, citizens were forced to rely on their own wherewithal for their well-being. Small-scale trade and entrepreneurship developed as a coping mechanism,[16] and so the state indeed came to be seen not as friend but rather enemy, particularly in the Third World. In the First World, as governments cut their spending programs but kept taxing their citizenries in order to pay off the debts accumulated under the previous regime, the fruits of progress and the role of the state in such became less evident. As the national glue weakened in many societies, nationalism would increasingly give way to multiplying assertions of more localized identity, such as regionalism and tribalism, or to overarching ones, such as religious fundamentalism. Such new forms of identity would reflect the new realities of the global economy: greater integration eroded national boundaries, but smaller and more flexible production units eroded the economic role of the nation-state. It retained its sovereignty, but it was now a contested sovereignty.

Can all this be blamed on globalization? Yes, and no. No, in that what really lay behind the reconfiguration of societies, and that produced the conditions giving rise to the political and cultural changes, were neoliberal policies, not globalization. Yet to the extent that neoliberal policy changes made possible a variety of globalization, one that strengthened the hand of globalizing fractions of capital at the expense of those fractions of capital most dependent on the state, globalization is the proximate and ultimate cause of the regime crisis. However, for both better and worse, globalization is not always all it is cracked up to be. Yet it remains profoundly important.

Globalization and the Income Gap

Contrary to the depictions of some propagandists, globalization is not an autonomous juggernaut—a force of nature is how former U.S. president Bill Clinton once described it—rolling along its own merry way and crushing any opposition that comes across its path. Driven by the fractions that benefit the most from liberalization,[17] and managed by political elites responding to these challenges,[18] globalization has all along been a directed process. However, once globalization's ball got rolling it would prove very difficult to resist. Countries get into spirals whereby incremental integration into the global economy necessitates a subsequent further integration. As the market for imports to a Third World country widens a bit, consumers there develop a taste for a new product, which puts pressure on the country's foreign currency reserves. This then forces the government to reorient its production toward export markets, which may necessitate a trading agreement, which in turn may require further cuts to import restrictions, and so forth. Thus, political elites can resist globalization only at the expense of welfare costs to at least parts of their population. Given increasing labor mobility—particularly among highly skilled professionals—and increased access to information from abroad (thanks to the information revolution, which will be discussed below), it seems likely that people will rebel against attempts at nationalism and protectionism on the part of their governments. The problem, though, is that what people do to advance their interests as consumers can undermine their interests as producers, with debilitating effects for the political regime within which they live.

It is important to be clear about what "globalization" is, and what it is not, for it is a term that has come to be wrapped up in dogma. Although almost everyone has something to say about the topic, broadly speaking there are three branches—economic, political, and sociological—to the discussion of globalization. In each there is a lively debate pitting those who think of globalization as a major change to the global political economy against those who say its scope is exaggerated. The strong view of globalization posits a virtual change of era, from that of the nation-state to a new, as yet unspecified domain. Economically, globalization is drawing all the world's countries into a single global economy, with the flow of capital, goods, and services increasing in all directions. The value of world trade increased sixteenfold from 1950 to 1995, with the ratio of world exports to world gross domestic product (GDP) more than doubling over the period;[19] firms are farming out more of their production to overseas suppliers;[20] and the growth in overseas investment and international capital flows has shot ahead of economic growth rates.[21] The effects of such integration are apparent to all: when Thailand's currency crashed in 1997, stock exchanges from New York to Johannesburg plummeted. New forms of business enterprise arise: the multinational corporation, with branches in several countries, is replaced by the transnational corporation (TNC), which sources out different parts of the production process such that it operates as a single, global unit. Thus, borders are not so much crossed as transcended, making the world seem like a single place.[22] Political scientists who ponder the effects of these changes on politics argue that the nation-state is losing its sovereignty, and may even be facing extinction. Unable to control the flow of wealth across national boundaries, forced to pare back the state's reach in order to allow their economies to become more internationally competitive, national governments are becoming increasingly irrelevant. With capital so mobile, governments must cut tax rates in order to attract investment, which means they must scale back spending. The nation-state, rooted in territory, becomes increasingly impotent when faced with the so-called borderless world. Its economic geography is transformed: cities once connected to regional hinterlands are supplanted by global cities, the bases of the new TNCs. These firms' profits drive up property values and create demand for high-quality business districts, hotels, and restaurants. Older businesses are driven out of the city, and a widening gap between rich and poor emerges.[23] New territorial configurations then develop, reflecting the emerging flow of goods, services, and capital, giving rise to region-states that are gradually hollowing out the nation-state.[24] Sociologists stress this deterritorialization, arguing that the information flows made possible by the communications revolution are overwhelming parochial and national cultures, giving rise to an increasingly homogeneous global culture. In 1950, 25 million tourists traveled abroad; in 1995, 561 million did so,[25] mainly Westerners who exposed other peoples to their ways. Everywhere, satellite technology and videocassettes have helped bring U.S. cultural fare into people's homes.[26] Everywhere, the Internet is doing the same thing, delinking information and space and creating a single global community dominated by U.S. media. Everywhere, elites appear to be embracing the Enlightenment heritage and democratic ideals, signaling the apparent triumph of the West.

However, there are those who argue that most of this is overplayed. In terms of economics, globalization is neither new nor particularly striking. A global economy first began to emerge half a millennium ago when Europeans started to travel the globe in new ships able to cover long distances. Since then, globalization has evolved gradually. In terms of the relative volume of world trade, its high-water mark was not today but in the late nineteenth and early twentieth centuries, when European imperialism drew much of the planet into its economic orbit.[27] The recent move toward global integration is merely the rebound from the retreat that took place after the Great Depression. Despite talk of global markets, in most countries most output continues to be sold locally; while financial markets are highly globalized, most investment continues to be financed at home;[28] when it comes to labor markets, language and cultural barriers will keep them closed for the foreseeable future.

As for TNCs, there are actually very few truly globalized companies, and most firms remain less mobile than portrayals of free-flowing capital suggest.[29] Politically, reports of the nation-state's demise are considerably exaggerated. Nor are they particularly new, and in light of past reports about the obsolescence of the state, they deserve to be taken with a grain of salt. In fact, in terms of the share of GDP consumed by public spending in First World countries, the state is not retreating but has remained more or less stationary.[30] Sociologically, globalization is real and territory is becoming less salient in the definition of culture. But this does not necessarily mean we are seeing the emergence of a global and homogeneous culture. For globalization has created an explosion in choice, what some theorists call hyperdifferentiation.[31] And while it seems like the Internet could create a virtual global community, to date most Internet users have limited themselves to the more mundane tasks of checking the news and financial statements (such as the information for the following endnote).[32] As for homogenization, Samuel Huntington argues that the consumption of imported commodities in no way entails the consumption of the producer country's values. If anything, he suggests, increased proximity may drive people further apart culturally.[33] While the U.S. film industry has taken over much of the globe, pockets of resistance remain, notably France and India, while other cultural industries remain much more competitive.

Which of these competing takes on globalization has it right? For the purposes of this book, what matters is that globalization represents not a quantitative change but a qualitative one. It may not extinguish the nation-state, but it is altering the way it operates. While it is true that First World states have maintained their share of overall consumption, much of it is now consumed by debt servicing and entitlements like pensions, meaning that spending elsewhere has had to be trimmed. In the Third World, meanwhile, cuts in public spending have been far deeper. Even though only a few firms are truly globalized, increased capital mobility and possibilities to shift production, while not threatening states' existences, have reduced their margin for maneuver when it comes to such things as fiscal policy. Forced to cut taxes or to shift them away from highly mobile capital, governments have found it impossible to preserve the income distribution patterns of the post–World War II regimes. Moreover, the character of the economy has everywhere changed: large firms, often closely connected to political elites, have lost ground relative to the increase in small and medium-sized firms.[34] And while the only labor market likely to ever become globalized is that for high-skilled labor, this too has important effects on income distribution: with executive wages set in global cities but worker wages set in shanty towns, it is not difficult to see in which direction the global political economy is headed, namely increased inequality.[35] Moreover, while information technology may increase productivity, Third World countries, unable to make the initial investments in hardware and human capital, are likely to fall further behind the First World.[36] The political implications of this, as we shall begin to see, have been great. And both the globalization and the localization of culture are having profound effects on ideology and political discourse. The main impact of globalization has been to erode the regimes of postwar politics, especially through the way it has altered income distribution and weakened the state's patronage power.

So, yes, globalization has a centuries-long history. But we have arguably begun a new chapter in that history. We can see it as the confluence of three different streams. One was the postwar rise of East Asia and a few other newly industrialized countries, which put great pressure on the manufacturing sectors of the Western economies and provoked a shift in the weight of the latter's economies toward the service sectors.[37] The second was the opening up of Third World economies, in large measure prized open by the conditionalities of Third World structural adjustment programs. The third has been the end of the Cold War, which brought the last major holdout against globalization, the former Soviet bloc, into the fold. All these processes were aided by the communications revolution. Greater access to Western information delegitimized the ruling elite in the eyes of the Soviet public.[38] Meanwhile, reduced communications costs made it possible for Western firms to make themselves more competitive with their East Asian rivals. This forced Western governments to lower their production costs in order to keep capital at home and entailed streamlined regulations and lower taxes, implying reduced government spending and welfare benefits.

Therefore, pressure to liberalize, which had begun in the first monetarist wave, only intensified. It did not subside once economic growth resumed later in the 1980s. Intensifying this pressure was the fact that government discretion in budget cutting had become quite limited. Many spending commitments had been made in an age when expectations were high, but were coming due in an age when performance was lower. An obvious instance of this dissonance was in pension programs: First World governments had taken on obligations to support a babyboomer generation in its old age, but slowed economic and demographic growth promised to create an aging population who would consume more and more of state revenue. The economically obvious solution, of cutting into pension programs, has never been politically obvious: the large and politically active babyboomer constituency would prove to be a risky one for any government to antagonize, and as their ranks swell the growing political clout of the retired has made pension reform a minefield in many countries. Governments looked elsewhere to trim spending, namely to programs that benefited the most vulnerable but also least politically mobilized segments of society.

Capital had become mobile, so governments had to work harder to attract and keep it. New production technologies had emerged to make it possible for producers to take advantage of new opportunities for investment in regions with lower costs. In particular, the communications revolution had greatly reduced the cost of transport and information flows, making it possible to globalize the production and sale of many goods and services. Airfares, for instance, are one of the few items whose price has decreased not only in real but in nominal terms as well over the past few decades. Due to new technologies like containerization, shipping goods became cheaper.[39] New computing technology made it possible for managers in one country to keep a close eye on the operations of plants in far-off lands. Whereas every stage of automobile assembly used to occur in one place, it now became possible to break down the process and source out those tasks that could take advantage of cheap foreign labor. Typically, what happened was that management, engineering, and design took place in a First World country, along with the most skilled forms of construction, while most of the assembly and the more basic production tasks would take place in a Third World country. By the 1990s, one in three cars bearing a German trademark was in fact produced outside of Germany,[40] while the French car maker Renault spent more money in France selling its cars than it did producing them,[41] having moved most of its production facilities overseas. Benjamin Barber came to ask, "Whose national workforce do you fault on a defective integrated circuit labeled: 'Made in one or more of the following countries: Korea, Hong Kong, Malaysia, Singapore, Taiwan, Mauritius, Thailand, Indonesia, Mexico, Philippines. The exact country of origin is unknown.'"[42]

Globalization allowed many large companies to revitalize themselves and return to profitability once again. But it had a different impact on these companies' home economies. Whereas at one time the restoration of the corporate sector's health "trickled down" to the population at large in the form of job creation, this was no longer the case. "Downsizing" and "rationalization" began a cycle of massive layoffs that gained speed in the 1980s and 1990s, all while corporate profits boomed. One must bear in mind that such private-sector layoffs or austerity programs—the shift from full-time to part-time work and the increased use of short-term contracts[43]—took place at the same time that the public sector was retrenching. Even if public-sector spending as a share of GDP remained stable in most First World countries, debt servicing and entitlement programs (like pensions) consumed so much money that cuts had to be made elsewhere. The situation in Third World countries was even worse. Thus, globalization and state retrenchment produced a situation in which income polarized, with owners of capital making increased profits and highly trained and skilled labor doing well, but with low-skilled labor losing out. In Germany, while exports increased in the 1990s, employment declined, forcing the government to try to prevent further employment loss by further reducing employee benefits, lessening the incentive to firms to move offshore to low-wage zones. Yet move they continued to do: while domestic investment remained slack in Germany, investment by German firms overseas was booming.[44]

In Canada, soaring share prices and bank profits coexisted with rising unemployment,[45] while in the United States the pay of top executives rose nearly twenty times faster than that of the average U.S. worker, whose pay barely kept pace with inflation[46] (the net worth of the poorest Americans actually fell).[47] Such trends persisted even after growth resumed. In the United States, after years of outsourcing, the U.S. automobile industry began resuming hiring in the mid-1990s, but the workers taken on had to settle for lower wages and benefits than they would once have earned.[48] Overall, incomes for most working Americans remained flat throughout the decade, while they soared for the wealthy.[49] In Canada, from 1994 to 1996, corporate pretax profits grew by 50 percent, but job cuts continued;[50] after the economy resumed its growth, wage settlements continued to lag behind.[51]

Western economies did not become "postindustrial," as was sometimes supposed. Manufacturing remained almost everywhere the driving force, but it had become highly productive and so shed much of its labor force.[52] Overall employment in the First World economies eventually picked back up, but most new jobs were in the service sector, where wages and rates of unionization were much lower, and where women were more strongly represented than men. This narrowed the wage gap between men and women, but widened the gap between rich and poor.[53] Those hardest hit, in the traditional working class, would form a disorganized yet potent army of what came to be known as the "angry white males."

There was, admittedly, some debate over just how bad the income distribution figures had become. In the 1980s, research uncovered an alarming polarization between rich and poor in most societies.[54] There emerged a picture of a decade in which a small class of entrepreneurs and financial speculators had become fabulously wealthy at the expense of the bulk of the population, even in the most buoyant economies (in the boom days preceding the 1997 East Asian crisis, Hong Kong speculators made huge returns and spent them lavishly on cars, jewelry, and other luxury goods; however, inflation forced the wider public to buy fewer nonessential goods).[55] Later research added nuances to this picture, though. While income differentials widened in most Western societies—and it is worth noting that the effect was most pronounced in the United States, where the market is most free—they were largely offset by changes in other sources of income.[56] In some countries, notably the United States, tax cuts actually improved the situation of the middle classes, although lingering job insecurity made many people *feel* no more prosperous even if, on paper, they were. On the other hand, what the income story does not capture is the effect of the government spending that enabled such tax breaks. Many public services available free or at low cost were now withdrawn or had user fees attached, from welfare programs to bus services to university tuition. Middle and upper classes could offset these expenses with their enhanced posttax income, but the poorest found that their standard of living was eroded. In Russia, with the implosion of the once-extensive welfare state, the number of diphtheria cases rose from 2,000 in 1991 to 48,000 just three years later.[57] Even after average real incomes returned to their mid-1980s levels, increased inequalities left most Russians with a seriously diminished standard of living, not to mention a shorter life expectancy,[58] while United Nations Children's Fund (UNICEF) reported that the education of East European children dropped after the fall of communism.[59] By the end of the 1990s, Mexico's richest billionaire had an income greater than the combined incomes of the country's 17 million poorest citizens,[60] while the 200 richest people in the United States were together worth more than all of China, with its billion-plus souls.[61] This changing pattern of income distribution was worsened by the ways in which cuts in public expenditure fell on the population. Well-organized, more-privileged interests were able to close ranks and defend their programs more effectively than were the disorganized mass, who tended to be the poorer citizens of society. In consequence, well-intentioned but politically expendable programs, from welfare to foreign aid, tended to feel the brunt of budget cuts. In the United States, despite the boom, cuts to the food stamp program augmented the number of working poor,[62] while the number of hungry children—one in six—saw no reduction from the supposed prosperity.[63] Equally, tax reforms that shifted the burden of taxation away from income and toward consumption, and away from capital and toward labor (since the latter was less mobile and thus less able to move to tax havens),[64] introduced a regressive element in taxation: increasingly, the poorer segments of society were bearing, in proportionate terms, a greater share of the tax burden. As the twenty-first century dawned, the number of poor across the planet was on the upswing.[65] Yet so too was the number of billionaires.[66]

Added to this intracountry income distribution was the intercountry pattern. In per capita terms, the income gap between the First World and the Third World has been continuously widening;[67] the picture is worsened by the fact that in many Third World countries, a good portion of income is being used to pay off debts to First World creditors. Sadly, this picture shows no signs of becoming any less ugly. Greater efficiency in industrial production in First World countries has lessened demand for primary products, upon exports of which most Third World countries continue to depend. In effect, the prices on primary and secondary goods have become "uncoupled," such that First World economic growth will no longer lead to equivalent demand for Third World goods. Exacerbating this is the shift from labor-intensive to knowledge-intensive production, which will further hurt Third World countries that lack the resources needed to develop the infrastructure and human capital required to make them competitive.[68] As the First World gets richer, the Third World will fall further behind. By the end of the twentieth century, the average African household consumed 20 percent less than it had twenty-five years before.[69] The gap between the richest fifth of the planet's population and its poorest fifth doubled over a similar period.[70]

Nevertheless, and this is the important point, the principal polarity is not between rich and poor countries, but between rich and poor people across the globe. Many conscientious people decry the exploitation of poor countries by rich ones, but this obscures much of what is happening. By driving up the wages of highly skilled professionals, who thanks to the communications revolution can now forge close bonds with counterparts around the world, globalization has created what some call the new global middle class. Nodes of wealth can emerge in the poorest lands. India, for example, has produced some of the planet's most advanced computing centers. But these herald few benefits to the people cramped into the slums surrounding them. The rich have forsaken the poor. And because the cleavage between rich and poor transcends the nation-state, the struggle to rectify it must do so as well. This means that the age of national liberation as a progressive ideal has probably now passed.

The important thing to bear in mind at this point is not that poverty has worsened, for globally it has not. The 1990s saw a reduction in both the absolute number and the proportion of poor people on the planet[71] (although admittedly the results varied greatly by region and a reversal began in the wake of the Asian financial crisis). Rather, as poverty declined, the gap between rich and poor widened. Put differently, although absolute prosperity rose, relative prosperity declined for a growing part of the world's population. And as I have argued, this is the more important of the two facts. Immiseration has declined, but marginalization has increased, and it is in these circumstances that regime crisis is most likely to manifest itself.

The Crisis of the Neoliberal Regime

What has come of all these changes? The erosion in the state's ability to distribute resources to its support base has eroded the loyalty of those at the bottom. Excluded altogether from the regime, or increasingly marginal within it, people have begun to look elsewhere in their search for resources; they may be objectively better off, but feel subjectively marginalized. Where political entrepreneurs have filled the gap, offering access to the resources people seek, they have been able to create rival political networks to that of the state. Two responses to the change in the political regime have emerged. One is material, the other cultural and intellectual. As suggested earlier in the book, the two interact closely.

Let us start with the material response to the regime crisis. The search for a greater share of resources has led many people to look beyond the state to new elites as patrons. The greater the constraints on state distribution, the more advanced is this effect. So, Third World countries coping with the impact of severe budget cuts imposed by the need to adjust their economies to the new demands of the global economy have, in some places, virtually ceased to enjoy any meaningful measure of support from their citizenries. In the very worst cases, nation-states have, for all intents and purposes, disappeared. The small elites that still lay claim to them enjoy no connection to a mass support base. Their regime is extinct. In most countries, though, political elites have managed to retain a role in resource allocation, so the existence of the nation-state is not in question. Nevertheless, its composition is being fundamentally altered almost everywhere.

Cuts in public expenditure have weakened the power of central governments. They have thus found it less easy to confront the challenges of emergent rival elites. Equally, as people find themselves squeezed out of the regime, their cultural links to the elite weaken. A period of cultural revolution begins, as the search for a new paradigm starts. The hypothesis here is quite simple: people will not willingly obey the rules of a regime that does not serve them. They will not respect a set of morals that appear not to serve their interests, but rather to exist for the benefit of a privileged few. Radicals call this process in which ordinary people abandon traditional precepts hegemonic dissolution, suggesting that the hegemonic culture and discourse of a decaying dominant class is bringing down with it the moral principles that kept it in place. Conservatives prefer to call the process moral decay or decline. One way in which the process manifests itself is in a growing cynicism toward and nonparticipation in the political process, and an open questioning of traditional moral principles. In many countries, older citizens worry about the rise of a generation, called Generation X or Y or Z, steeped in cynicism and dismissive of the ideals of their elders. Related to this has been a worrying erosion of what has come to be called civil society. Robert Putnam considers the decline of bowling clubs in the United States an indicator of a worrying trend toward the fragmentation of society.[72] The fragmented Weimar Republic permitted the rise of the Nazi Party in Germany in the 1930s, and ever since then political scientists have used fragmentation as an omen of things to come.[73] We are unlikely to see a return to Nazism anywhere, but already in the industrial democracies there have been many disturbing developments. In particular, as we shall see, the turn away from politics, particularly among young people, has permitted the rise of extremist political movements with an antiglobalization agenda (insofar as they oppose immigration), heralding worsening conflicts as globalization advances.

The repudiation of past ideals has very often been connected to a wholesale repudiation of modernity and the ideal of progress. The chief political victim of this ideological shift has been what we might call the traditional left: modern liberals, socialists, and communists. The decline of the left in the era of neoliberalism fed one of the challenges facing the industrial democracies, the rise of right-wing extremists, from neofascist parties in France to militia movements in the United States and anti-immigrant movements just about everywhere. Cultural shifts underlay this desertion from left to far right, but there has been more to the rising popularity of these movements than that. From the outset, extremist movements made significant inroads into the ranks of the poor and working classes by making direct appeals to the material concerns that have arisen over the past generation. In contrast, parties of the left soon became mired in arcane ideological debates and pursued what could be called postmodern political agendas that won them some support among emerging elites, but lost them support among the poor.

The latter, I will suggest, came to prefer the "fundamentalist" appeals of the far right.

This trend in the First World is mirrored by a similar if distinct trend in the Third World toward a different kind of fundamentalism. These are religious fundamentalisms, whether Muslim fundamentalism in the Muslim world, Hindu fundamentalism in India, or evangelical Christianity in Latin America, the Caribbean, sub-Saharan Africa, and the former Soviet East Bloc states. With the possible exception of evangelical Christianity, the appeal of these movements once again owes something to the fact that they not only promise access to resources denied the poor by retreating states, but in many cases actually deliver them. Only a small percentage of the followings of these movements are attracted to them by their religious appeals (although those so attracted go on to provide the fervor that makes these movements so well organized). Most have developed their loyalty because these movements, in varying ways, have taken on many of the tasks—providing accommodation, housing, jobs, security, credit, and so forth—once performed by the state. In these cases, people kicked out of one distributional network are entering another. Where they retain a foot in each camp, the situation is tense, uncertain, and all too often violent. Where people have left the state in droves and moved into a new, rival network, the nation-state faces severe challenges to its sovereignty. In a few instances, it has already collapsed.

Throughout the world, we are seeing the return of tribal politics. With the universalist appeals of modernism set to one side, societies have fragmented and been reconstituted into smaller, exclusive groups led by emergent political elites. A peculiar feature of this process, found particularly in First World societies, has been the development of what has been called identity politics—a type of postmodern politics spearheaded by elites who make claims to radical agendas but usually succeed more in reinforcing the privileges of a lucky few. Elsewhere, such tribalization often feeds a resurgent ethnonationalism, as in Yugoslavia or Rwanda. Often the nationalism is less violent and strives to be more civil, as in French Canada or Belgium or Scotland. Often it feeds into regional autonomy movements, whether in northern Italy or Somaliland. However, whatever the peculiar characteristics of any one case, the underlying causes remain essentially the same: a fight over a diminished resource base.

One of the things that has weakened the ability of governments to effectively confront these challenges has been the reorganization of public sectors. To make economies more responsive to global trends, political elites have allowed not only firms but public administrations to be more flexible and sensitive to economic forces at the local level. Unwieldy central administrations have often been blamed for inhibiting business activity. Therefore, administrative decentralization, whether de jure or de facto, has taken many of the policy levers and resources from the central state apparatus and handed them to local administrations.[74] In some places, like France or Canada, this decentralization has provided a trade-off for the effects of retrenchment: with the government having to restrict its resource-allocating power, it loses disciplinary powers over local organs of administration, which demand increased autonomy in return. In some places, notably the United States, decentralization has been linked to ideological struggles between those who see the central state as an agent of transformation and those who see it as an unresponsive bully trampling on the rights of lower authorities. In other locales, notably Third World countries, decentralization has been proposed as a means to improve the quality of "governance" and reduce corruption. In some places, namely the so-called economies in transition (former communist economies), decentralization has been a pragmatic response to what has been a sudden relinquishing of power from the center. In all these cases, power still resides in the state, but it is a very different state. Nor has there been a simple transfer of authority from the center to the regions. In the process, there has been some hemorrhaging, as public power has been taken up by private agents. In some cases this has been drastic, as in Russia, where contracts have been enforced by gangs since the state currently lacks the machinery to do so effectively. Organized crime, one should observe, is not new to Russia. But whereas organized criminals once had to cooperate with Soviet authorities who monopolized resource distribution, the privatization of their assets—well over half of Russia's capital is now said to be in criminal hands—has given them a frightening degree of autonomy from the legal authorities.[75]

Just as income has polarized between the First World and the Third World, so too has it polarized within nation-states. The move toward regional trading blocs has removed much of the authority once vested in national governments. At the same time, decentralization of power within nation-states has shifted power downward. So, as some authority moves upward and other moves downward, the center weakens. In a few cases it has difficulty holding. For this reason, not surprisingly, regional nationalist movements—like Quebec separatists or Catalan and Scottish nationalists—often see themselves as the wave of the future and push for greater integration into a global market while they push for segregation from the existing political arrangements that limit their power. Even where separation is not an issue, regional authorities have been able to increase their powers at the expense of central states. So, China's reforms have restored the traditional power of regional elites, which had been largely repressed by the Maoist state. Similarly, the move away from a centrally planned economy toward an increasingly liberalized and open one in India has removed many of the levers from the federal government, enhancing the powers of the states. And in Russia, Moscow's once-authoritarian power has been hollowed out by regional barons eager to exploit the weaknesses of the center. In extreme cases, this leads to what can be called postmodern politics, with the collided atom firing its particles in different directions. Weaker states face collapse. Whereas stronger ones withstand and have adapted to the crisis, they have taken on a new form to do so. At the very least, there has come a return to the decentralized state, as in the United States, a process that has not taken place without some pain and political soul-searching.

Technological changes and alterations in the global political economy have created new opportunities for organizations that transcend international boundaries. Algerian Islamists may have a leadership in France, with connections to similar movements elsewhere in the Arab world and patrons in the Persian Gulf. The complexity of the challenge that has emerged was made clear by the 11 September 2001 attacks on U.S. soil, in which an international network was able to pull off what no government had succeeded in doing in two centuries, namely launch an assault on U.S. military headquarters. Such organization obviously makes it possible for these kinds of movements to find ways of evading state crackdowns. An equal threat to national sovereignty is posed by the rise of international drug cartels and crime syndicates that stretch around the world. In the autumn of 1998, a Japanese man was arrested at an Italian airport for trying to smuggle a Chinese girl he had bought in Thailand into the European child sex market. Such international challenges demand international responses, but the imperatives of national politics often frustrate the emergence of such coordinated responses. When the U.S. government proposed using its warships to patrol Caribbean waters to intercept drug shipments, the governments of Jamaica and Barbados, not surprisingly, took offense at the affront to their national sovereignty. But these governments were caught between a rock and a hard place: on one hand, a bullying superpower posed a clear challenge to their sovereignty; on the other, drug cartels operating within the Caribbean islands were already eating away at the sovereignty of these states. It is not just that drug cartels are well armed and well financed and have wormed their way into the political systems of some

Latin American and Caribbean states.[76] It is also that they have, in an era of reduced state largesse, been able to buy the loyalty of some of the world's poorest citizens. A senior officer in the Jamaican security establishment once commented to me that all the weaponry the United States cared to give him would not make it possible to win the war on drugs, because in large stretches of inner-city Kingston children were fed, clothed, and schooled by drug money. Only a concerted effort to wean people away from these distributional networks and back into the formal political sphere will make it possible to begin pulling the carpet out from under the cartels. And poor countries with large debt loads, under pressure to keep their industry competitive in a hostile international trading environment, simply cannot marshal the resources necessary to this task. And so for all but the youngest among us, the world into which we are emerging looks very different from the world in which we grew up.

The Reappearance of the Local

In mathematics and logic, identity is taken to be that relationship represented by the equal-sign ($=$). When it comes to human identity, though, the relationship is more likely to begin with the unequal-sign ($\neq$). The formation of identity very often begins not with an assertion—what I am—but with a negation—what I am not.[77] For as long as one can take the stability and acceptance of one's group for granted, identity remains a subconscious thing. It is when that group breaks up, or casts one out, or when one is lifted from it, that questions of identity become pressing.[78] The search for identity can be long and painful, but it usually emerges from those already suffering some form of alienation.

This was to be the general rule for that most potent of modern identities, nationalism. Nationalist leaders typically emerged not from the soil they would come to venerate as sacred, but within exile communities. When Europeans first began venturing overseas in the Age of Exploration, they developed national identities to help preserve their integrity when they came across alien cultures whose practices and beliefs challenged their convictions of universality. Consequently, increased migration, especially within empires, created communities of exiles all over the world. In exile, these people faced a rejection that made them search for an identity in which they too could take pride. Often, they also felt the insecurity of a minority group: even if they never intended to return to their "homeland," knowing that they had a "patch" to which they could retreat in an emergency gave them a sense of stability in a world of uncertainty. If there is but one general rule of nationalism, it is that it emerged in diasporas or exile communities.[79]

Similarly, in his history of the southern United States, Gavin Wright found that the "southern" mentality legendary in U.S. history emerged less from the poor residents of the south than from upwardly mobile southerners transplanted to the north, who sought to preserve something which in their old environment had never been threatened.[80] This is a staple by-product of emigration: the Scots who went to Cape Breton did a better job of preserving their Gallic language than the Scots back home, and immigrant communities everywhere preserve cultural practices like artifacts, often casting them in amber and maintaining them long after they have disappeared in the homeland. And like the displaced southern whites of whom Wright spoke, studies in the contemporary United States suggest that black consciousness, and with it the strong sense of grievance against whites, emerges not from among the underclass who suffer the most from America's racist history, but from the emerging black middle class who have benefited most in recent years from government programs designed to reverse past discrimination.[81] In part this may arise from the paradox unleashed by rising expectations, but it also reflects another fact: the black underclass are so isolated from white America that they take their condition for granted, and most of the enemies with whom they come into contact are other blacks, be they drug dealers or robbers. In contrast, more successful blacks are lifted from their environments and put into surroundings dominated by whites and in which they still, despite government programs, feel unwanted and frowned upon. The quest to discover who they are has been shaped by a declaration of who they are not having been thrust upon them.

Just as the black nationalism of displaced African Americans can become militant in its assertions of identity, so too have some of the more violent forms of nationalism that have resurfaced in recent years been nurtured in expatriate communities. Whereas Croats and Serbs had, by force of circumstances, learned to live together in Yugoslavia, expatriate communities preserved a hardened identity and nursed, and at times perhaps even invented, historic grudges, fueling much of the hard-line nationalist politics that drove the Yugoslav conflict.[82] Equally, in northeast Africa (notably Rwanda and Burundi), emigrant communities have driven the rise of ethnonationalism.[83] And while Islamist intellectuals may appear like hidebound traditionalists seeking to preserve a dying way of life, in point of fact they are typically highly educated, cosmopolitan, literate in several languages, and have lived and studied abroad for lengthy periods of time.[84] Indeed, Arab and Indian guest workers in Saudi Arabia have kept alive—even created—the dream of an independent Palestine, a Khalistan, or a more purely Hindu India, in part by the remittance of funds to the organizations promoting these goals, in part by the ideological constructions they have crafted in their efforts to find themselves a psychological homeland in their strange environment.[85] And one can add that so-called postcolonial critiques of Western literature, which seek to expose the underlying racism and imperialism of much Western writing on the Third World, are in fact products not of Third World academies but of Third World intellectuals working at First World universities.[86]

The point is that cultural resistance to globalization emerges not from traditional and parochial communities seeking to withstand the tide of cultural homogenization, but from those individuals who are already swimming in the new global environment and tasting its fruits. Following this line of reasoning, one can expect that in times of great social dislocation—when more people find themselves lifted from their old environment—the search for cultural identity will strengthen. As globalization advances, so too does localization. On the one hand diasporas seek their roots, while on the other their host communities, faced with this alien other, retreat behind walls of defensive parochialism.[87] To the extent that it increases the flow of information and people, globalization is causing a renewed rearguard attack to preserve identity. This, as we know, has already been manifest in the so-called culture wars of recent years. Hindu fundamentalists in India, Islamist intellectuals in Turkey, and the preachers of militia movements in the United States are all united in their conviction that their cultures and ways of life are threatened by the beast of internationalization, even if they differ greatly over the characterization of this beast. Moreover, the diasporas that have yielded the intellectual and financial resources driving much of localization will probably augment in importance, uniquely situated as they are to exploit the advantages of globalization. Tending to congregate in global cities, and being cosmopolitan and internationally connected, diasporas are particularly advantaged to penetrate the global economy.[88]

However, there is something of an irony in these wars to preserve culture. The militants in the struggle are often motivated by a sincere conviction that the cultural homogenization wrought by globalization will cause their people to lose their identities. If anything, though, globalization is producing the opposite result. Cuts in public services and growing income differentials are marginalizing less privileged citizens all over the world, driving them deeper into their home environments, both economic and cultural. Jamaican nationalists, recalling the island's insularity during the heyday of socialist experimentation in the 1970s, bemoan their people's "deculturation." The advent of cable television and videocassette recorders, coupled with the trend toward imported fashions and the sweep of U.S. fast food outlets across the island, makes it seem like Jamaicans are plunging headlong into the emerging universal culture of which U.S. intellectuals like Francis Fukuyama speak. However, worsening poverty and declining education standards, due in no small part to cuts in public expenditure, are deepening vernacular culture.[89] Jamaicans in the ghetto may watch U.S. soap operas, but the gap between the lives they lead and those they observe is widening. Given verbal expression, the lives are diverging: the dancehall culture of Jamaican music today no longer expresses itself in English, but in a Creole that is increasingly impenetrable to those outside the ghetto.

In fact, this probably reveals the real threat of globalization to elite intellectuals. Increasingly, one finds that older Jamaicans find it hard to understand the patois and culture of the ghetto. Vernacular culture is strengthening. To middle-class Jamaicans, it is becoming more vulgar, which literally means it is becoming more and more a product of the common people. While vernacular culture has strengthened, the widened ideological market caused by the downfall of old paradigms, coupled with the increased access to information caused by the information revolution, has weakened links between old elites and the masses.

New elites can step into the breach and challenge the old elites, but appeals to cultural integrity will on their own do little to build up a mass base for their political campaigns. Ideologies enjoy public acceptance to the extent that they address the material interests of that public. In her study of the spread of British national identity, Linda Colley shows how the growth of commerce, which depended upon and fed the rise of the nation-state, brought material benefits to a substantial constituency whose loyalty to its patron—the nation-state—was thereby solidified. She quotes Miroslav Hroch, who once said that "national ideology is effective where it reflects (even though in a merely illusory fashion) the interests of the groups to which it makes its appeal, or contains at least in part the kind of programme which is close to their interests."[90] The same can be said for any ideology. Political entrepreneurs seeking to build a counterhegemonic ideology will win popular acceptance for it only if they couple it with a resource-distribution strategy. Where new elites have successfully married ideology with practical action, they have been most effective at challenging decadent elites. Where their appeal has remained cultural, so has it remained limited.

This does not mean that the mobility of information and population

causes the poor no fear of cultural assimilation. In fact, support for
politicians espousing nativist policies—whether opposing immigration
or favoring preferential treatment in employment for locals—is
strongest where one finds high concentrations of recent immigrants. In
reaction, locals abandon traditional parties. The French National Front
has drawn most of its support from working-class communities with
high immigrant populations, as did the late German Republikaner
Party;[91] the militantly nativist Indian party Shiv Sena has its power base
in Mumbai, where Maharashtrians feel swamped by the immigrant
community of southern Indians, and not in the surrounding countryside
where immigrants are not a threat;[92] it has long been held that the support pillars of apartheid in South Africa were among the Boer working
and farming population who came into the greatest contact with blacks,
and who therefore had reason to fear being swamped if the gates were
brought down; and many argued that support for former neo-Nazi
David Duke in his campaign for the Louisiana governorship in 1990
came from among poor whites in communities with large black populations.[93] Nonetheless, if one probes the sources of discontent, one finds
that the concerns of the supporters of extremist politicians are not primarily cultural, but economic. The French National Front's appeals for
a return to traditional morality find little support among devout
Catholics, who support the traditional center-right parties; most
National Front supporters are in fact not religious.[94] Similarly, while
India's Hindu-nationalist Bharatiya Janata Party activists are likely to
be religious, the party's supporters are generally not so.[95] As we shall
see later, their concerns, along with those of supporters of Shiv Sena,
the Republikaner, and U.S. far-right groups, have been primarily material, not cultural. Similarly, it has been argued that support for apartheid
crumbled when it ceased to appear to be an economically viable strategy able to deliver the material benefits to its supporters as it once did.[96]
Thus, trying to build a rival network to that of a state on cultural
appeals alone will only ever capture a limited support base.

Having said that, culture is important in any political struggle. It is
not simply a concern of elites suffering from alienation and identity
crises. Just as elites cannot build effective counterhegemonic strategies
on cultural appeals alone, nor can they do it simply by buying support.
An elite can build up a support network on the basis of resource distribution, but if that alone is the basis for winning support, the support
will be very fickle indeed: it will disappear as soon as the supply of
resources dries up. A distribution strategy is reinforced by a culture that
is encompassing and complete. Political elites must fill stomachs, yes,
but they must also win hearts and minds.

It has been said that one of the failings of Islamist political strategies has been their inability to develop a countercultural project.[97] When it comes to cultural warfare, Islamic fundamentalism, much like its counterparts in Judaism and Christianity, opposes more than it proposes. The excessive preoccupation with a radical materialist critique at the expense of spiritual matters has also been used to explain the failure of liberation theology to take deep root in Latin America or to stem the tide of evangelical Protestantism.[98] Cultural concerns matter, though they probably still matter more to the elite than to the mass. It is not that the masses are any less cultured than elites, save in the sense that distinguishes "high" and "low" cultures; it is rather that the changes in the global economy have created differing demands for cultural products.

Conclusion

If one were to sum up the material and cultural responses to the crisis of the neoliberal regime in one word, it would be "fragmentation." As regimes have collapsed, or been blown open, or partially dismantled, a floating mass of atoms has been released. When galaxies explode and their matter is released, a similar type of fragmentation results, scattering debris in space. In time, though, the matter begins to coalesce into new bodies, and a new system comes into being. Much the same can be said in politics. Being social animals, humans do not wander alone for long. They seek new bodies to which to belong. As we shall see in the next chapter, this has created opportunities for emergent political elites. However, as we shall also see, the new configurations appear unlikely to resolve the crisis, since they fail to effectively address its underlying causes. As such, the new regimes can be only temporary phenomena, and so the crisis has persisted through their emergence and growth.

Notes

1. For some of the "classics" in the resurgence of neoclassical economics, refer to Milton Friedman, "The Role of Monetary Policy," *American Economic Review* 58 (1968): 1–17; Bela Balassa et al., *The Structure of Protection in Developing Countries* (Baltimore: Johns Hopkins University Press for the World Bank and Inter-American Development Bank, 1971); Jagdish Bhagwati, "Directly Unproductive, Profit-Seeking (DUP) Activities," *Journal of Political Economy* 90 (1982): 988–1002; Harry G. Johnson, *Money, Trade, and Economic Growth* (London: George Allen and Unwin, 1964); Anne O. Krueger, "The Political Economy of the Rent-Seeking Society," *American*

Economic Review 64 (June 1974): 291–303; Anne O. Krueger, "Trade Strategies and Employment in Developing Countries," *Finance and Development* 21, no. 4 (June 1984): 23–26; Hla Myint, "Economic Theory and the Underdeveloped Countries," *Journal of Political Economy* 73 (1965): 477–491; Friedrich Hayek, *The Fatal Conceit: The Errors of Socialism* (London: Routledge, 1988); Friedrich Hayek, *The Constitution of Liberty* (London: Routledge, 1960); P. T. Bauer, *The Rubber Industry: A Study in Competition and Monopoly* (Cambridge: Harvard University Press, 1948); P. T. Bauer, *West African Trade: A Study of Competition, Oligopoly, and Monopoly in a Changing Economy* (Cambridge: Cambridge University Press, 1954); Laurence J. Kotlikoff and Lawrence H. Summers, "The Role of Intergenerational Transfers in Aggregate Capital Accumulation," *Journal of Political Economy* 89 (1981): 706–732; and Douglas C. North and Robert Paul Thomas, *The Rise of the Western World* (Cambridge: Cambridge University Press, 1973).

2. L. T. Hobhouse, *Liberalism* (New York: Henry Holt, 1911).

3. See Hayek, *Fatal Conceit,* p. 110.

4. See Robert Nozick, *Anarchy, State, and Utopia* (Oxford: Blackwell, 1974). It is noteworthy that Nozick's famous book began as a critique of John Rawls's attempt in *A Theory of Justice* (Cambridge: Harvard Belknap, 1971) to justify the welfare state within the context of liberal thought.

5. Hayek, *Fatal Conceit;* and Hayek, *Constitution of Liberty.*

6. Mancur Olson Jr., *The Logic of Collective Action* (Cambridge: Cambridge University Press, 1965).

7. For a fuller discussion, see Kristen Renwick Monroe, ed., *The Economic Approach to Politics* (New York: HarperCollins, 1991).

8. John Rapley, *Understanding Development,* 2nd ed. (Boulder: Lynne Rienner, 2002), p. 64.

9. Gordon White, *Riding the Tiger: The Politics of Economic Reform in Post-Mao China* (Stanford, Calif.: Stanford University Press, 1993).

10. Robert V. Daniels, *The End of the Communist Revolution* (London: Routledge, 1993), p. 68. Compare John King Fairbank, *China: A New History* (Cambridge: Harvard Belknap, 1992), pp. 422, 431. As Jerry Hough put it, "The exchange programs of the West were far more crucial in destroying communism than the military buildup of the early 1980s." Jerry F. Hough, *Democratization and Revolution in the USSR, 1985–1991* (Washington, D.C.: Brookings Institution, 1997), p. 497.

11. Compare Michael Hardt and Antonio Negri, *Empire* (Cambridge: Harvard University Press, 2000).

12. John Lucas, "The Politics of Business Associations in the Developing World," *Journal of Developing Areas* 32, no. 1 (Fall 1997): 71–96.

13. While the number of large firms in the global economy has remained relatively constant in recent years, the number of small and medium-sized enterprises has exploded. See Peter F. Drucker, "The Changed World Economy," *Foreign Affairs* 64, no. 4 (Spring 1986): 768–791. In the United States, meanwhile, although large firms created no net new employment after the 1970s, employment grew rapidly, with the slack being taken up by small

firms and the self-employed. See Robert B. Reich, *The Work of Nations* (New York: Alfred A. Knopf, 1991), p. 95.

14. Roger Karapin, "Radical-Right and Neo-Fascist Political Parties in Western Europe," *Comparative Politics* 30 (1998): 213–234, esp. p. 223; Hans-Georg Betz, "The New Politics of Resentment: Radical Right-Wing Populist Parties in Western Europe," *Comparative Politics* 25 (1993): 413–427.

15. See Ilkay Sunar and Binnaz Toprak, "Islam in Politics: The Case of Turkey," *Government and Opposition* 18 (1983): 421–441; and Samuel Huntington, *The Clash of Civilizations and the Remaking of World Order* (New York: Simon and Schuster, 1996), p. 113.

16. In China, for instance, employees of state firms who lose their jobs to rationalization have generally gone on either to form their own businesses or to join the businesses already formed by those who preceded them in the rolls of the redundant. See Trish Saywell, "Little Pioneers," *Far Eastern Economic Review,* 6 August 1998. See also Henry Sender, "Prolonging the Pain," *Far Eastern Economic Review,* 20 May 1999.

17. On the transnational capitalist class that is driving globalization, see Leslie Sklair, *Sociology of the Global System* (Baltimore: Johns Hopkins University Press, 1991), pp. 133–137.

18. See Eric Helleiner, *States and the Re-emergence of Global Finance* (New York: Cornell University Press, 1994). Helleiner argues that nation-states use international financial liberalization to discipline domestic economies.

19. "Trade Winds," *The Economist* (London), 8 November 1997.

20. Robert C. Feenstra and Gordon H. Hansen, "Globalization, Outsourcing, and Wage Inequality," *American Economic Review* 86, no. 2 (1996): 234–239.

21. Blanca Heredia, "Prosper or Perish? Development in the Age of Global Capital," *Current History* 96, no. 613 (November 1997): 383–388; Wolfgang H. Reinicke, "Global Public Policy," *Foreign Affairs* 76, no. 6 (November–December 1997): 127–138.

22. Jan Aart Scholte, "Global Capitalism and the State," *International Affairs* 73, no. 3 (1997): 427–452.

23. Saskia Sassen, "Cities and Communities in the Global Economy," *American Behavioural Scientist* 39 (1996): 629–639.

24. Kenichi Ohmae, "The Rise of the Region State," *Foreign Affairs* 72, no. 2 (Spring 1993): 78–87. Compare Susan Strange, *The Retreat of the State: The Diffusion of Power in the World Economy* (Cambridge: Cambridge University Press, 1997).

25. *Financial Times* (London), 3 August 1996.

26. Benjamin Barber, *Jihad vs. McWorld* (New York: Ballantine Books, 1996).

27. Paul Hirst and Grahame Thompson, *Globalization in Question: The International Economy and the Possibilities of Governance* (Cambridge: Polity Press, 1996); Ankie Hoogvelt, *Globalisation and the Postcolonial World* (London: Macmillan, 1997); Paul Hirst, "The Global Economy: Myths and Realities," *International Affairs* 73, no. 3 (1997): 409–426.

28. "Capital Goes Global," *The Economist* (London), 25 October 1997.

29. Hirst and Thompson, *Globalization in Question;* "Worldbeater, Inc.," *The Economist* (London), 22 November 1997.

30. "Bearing the Weight of the Market," *The Economist* (London), 6 December 1997.

31. See Malcolm Waters, *Globalization* (London: Routledge, 1995).

32. *Los Angeles Times,* 14 October 1997.

33. Huntington, *Clash of Civilizations,* chap. 3.

34. Drucker, "Changed World Economy." Looking at the United States, Robert Reich points out that from 1975 to 1990, the 500 largest U.S. firms failed to create a single new job, but the number of small firms and self-employed people exploded. Reich, *Work of Nations,* p. 95.

35. See "Trade Winds," *The Economist* (London), 8 November 1997. See also Jeffrey D. Sachs and Howard J. Shatz, "U.S. Trade with Developing Countries and Wage Inequality," *American Economic Review* 86, no. 2 (1996): 234–239.

36. Michael Connors, *The Race to the Intelligent State* (Oxford: Capstone, 1997).

37. Benjamin Barber points out that the United States, for example, can only be seen as a declining economy if one is looking at its manufacturing sector. Barber, *Jihad vs. McWorld.*

38. Scott Shane, *Dismantling Utopia* (Chicago: Ivan R. Dee, 1995).

39. "Delivering the Goods," *The Economist* (London), 15 November 1997.

40. Commerzbank, *Sector Report: Forecast for German Industry 1996/97* (Frankfurt am Main: Commerzbank, February 1996), p. 9.

41. *Le Nouvel Observateur* (Paris), 26 January–1 February 1995, pp. 12–14.

42. Barber, *Jihad vs. McWorld,* p. 14.

43. While the shift to short-term contracts has not, except for low-income males, shortened the average length of job tenure in Europe, they probably have increased the contract holders' sense of insecurity. See Simon Burgess, "You're All Right, Jack," *Times Higher Education Supplement* (London), 26 December 1997, p. 11.

44. Commerzbank, *Sector Report.*

45. *Maclean's Magazine* (Toronto), 28 October 1996. UNICEF, *State of the World's Children* (New York: Oxford University Press, for UNICEF, December 1997), reports that the Chinese boom coexisted with widening income distribution and worsening malnutrition, while the Center for Budget Policy and Priorities reported in December 1998 that in the United States, the income gap between the top 20 percent (largely in the service sector) and the bottom 20 percent (largely in manufacturing) widened.

46. In the 1990s, CEO pay rose 535 percent, while average compensation for workers rose 32 percent. Inflation, meanwhile, went up 27.5 percent, swallowing nearly all the modest income gains made by workers, this according to a study by the Institute for Policy Studies reported on cnnfn.com, 30 August 2000. Similarly, the Center on Budget and Policy Priorities, in a report released 18 January 2000, said that from 1988 to 1998, earnings for the poorest fifth of U.S. families rose less than 1 percent, while those of the richest fifth jumped 15 percent.

47. U.S. Federal Reserve statistics, taken from cnnfn.com.

48. *Financial Times* (London), 23–24 March 1996.

49. Late in 1997, the U.S. Center on Budget and Policy Priorities reported that over the previous two decades, the income of the richest fifth of Americans had risen 30 percent, while that of the poorest fifth had fallen 21 percent. *The Economist* (London), 20 December 1997. In real terms, median family incomes actually fell until the short-lived 1997 surge in wage earnings finally took them above 1990 levels, according to the U.S. Census Bureau.

50. Canadian Press, 19 March 1996.

51. Canadian Press, 18 October 1995.

52. In the United States, for instance, the proportion of manufacturing jobs in the economy was nearly halved from 1950 to 1995, with most of the drop coming after 1970. See Allen Gerlach, "Economic Decline and the Crisis of American Liberalism," *Contemporary Review* 270, no. 1572 (January 1997): 1–7.

53. *Financial Times* (London), 13 May 1998.

54. For details on the U.S. case, see Michael Lind, *The Next American Nation* (New York: Free Press, 1996), pp. 154, 181, 191, 193, 195–196, 201; Paul Krugman, *The Age of Diminished Expectations,* rev. and updated ed. (Cambridge: MIT Press, 1994), chap. 2; Christopher Lasch, *The Revolt of the Elites and the Betrayal of Democracy* (New York: W. W. Norton, 1995), pp. 31–33; and Reich, *Work of Nations.*

55. *Times of India,* 28 October 1997. A United Nations report suggested that widening income gaps were a feature of the whole Southeast Asian boom. Radio Deutsch Welle, 16 April 1996. In China, despite its own economic surge, the World Bank estimated that 350 million people lived in poverty by the end of the 1990s. BBC World Service, 7 May 1997. And in Indonesia, although the income gap narrowed from 1970 to 1990, it began widening again in the boom years leading up to 1996, at which time the social tensions became enormous and riots broke out. *Far Eastern Economic Review,* 28 May 1998.

56. Peter Gottschalk and Timothy M. Smeeding, "Cross-National Comparisons of Earnings and Income Inequality," *Journal of Economic Literature* 35 (1997). 633–687.

57. *The Independent* (London), 29 June 1995.

58. Vladimir Popov, "Emerging Structure of Russian Capitalism," *Development* 40, no. 3 (1997): 37–45.

59. BBC World Service, 26 May 1998.

60. Judith Adler Hellman, lecture at the University of the West Indies, Mona, Jamaica, 19 February 1998.

61. As reported in *Forbes* magazine, 21 June 1999.

62. *Financial Times* (London), 11 February 2000.

63. This was reported by the Center on Hunger and Poverty at Tufts University. CNN, 20 June 2000.

64. "Bearing the Weight of the Market," *The Economist* (London), 6 December 1997.

65. In mid-1999, the World Bank reported that from 1993 to 1995, the number of people living on less than a dollar a day rose from 1.3 billion to 1.5 billion. *Financial Times* (London), 4 June 1999.

66. This according to *Forbes* magazine.

67. Hoogvelt, *Globalisation and the Postcolonial World,* p. 85.

68. Drucker, "Changed World Economy."

69. United Nations Development Programme's 1998 *Human Development Report* (New York: United Nations, 1998).

70. As reported by Oxfam in the *Financial Times* (London), 21 June 1995.

71. World Bank, *World Development Indicators 2002* (Baltimore: Johns Hopkins University Press, 2002).

72. Robert Putnam, "Bowling Alone: America's Declining Social Capital," *Journal of Democracy* 6, no. 1 (1995): 65–78.

73. See Sheri Berman, "Civil Society and the Collapse of the Weimar Republic," *World Politics* 49, no. 3 (1997): 401–429, which takes issue with conventional wisdom and suggests that what permitted the rise of Nazism in Germany was not a weak civil society, for it was quite vibrant, but rather a fragmented one, enabling the Nazis to penetrate and unify some of its diverse fractions.

74. The evidence as to whether or not decentralization has had the desired effect of making public administrations more responsive to local needs, thereby enhancing state effectiveness, has been mixed. See Tim Besley, "Decentralising Governance," *Risk and Regulation,* Spring 2002, p. 8; and Barbara Ingham and A. K. M. Kalam, "Decentralization and Development: Theory and Evidence from Bangladesh, *Public Administration and Development* 12 (1992): 373–385, and the survey of findings on pp. 1–122.

75. Tanya Frisby, "The Rise of Organised Crime in Russia: Its Roots and Social Significance," *Europe-Asia Studies* 50, no. 1 (1998): 27–49.

76. Trevor Munroe and Ivelaw L. Griffith suggest that in St. Kitts and Nevis, both government and opposition parties have now been penetrated by drug interests. See Trevor Munroe and Ivelaw L. Griffith, "Drugs and Democratic Governance in the Caribbean," in *Democracy and Human Rights in the Caribbean,* edited by Ivelaw L. Griffith and Betty N. Sedoc-Dahlberg (Boulder: Westview Press, 1997), p. 87.

77. Samuel Huntington, in *The Clash of Civilizations,* cites distinctiveness theory from social psychology to make this point: "People define their identity by what they are not" (p. 67). Discussing the formation of British national identity, Linda Colley writes that "men and women decide who they are by reference to who and what they are not. Once confronted with an obviously alien 'Them,' an otherwise diverse community can become a reassuring or merely desperate 'Us.'" What drew the English, Scots, and Welsh together was the fact that they were not Roman Catholics, as were the ever-threatening French. See Linda Colley, *Britons: Forging the Nation, 1701–1837* (New Haven: Yale University Press, 1992).

78. E. Roosens in *Creating Ethnicity* (London: Sage, 1989) adds: "In order to see and use one's own culture as a right, one must first have gained distance from that culture. . . . This creates a paradox, for the ethnic claims and slogans are mainly formulated by people who seem to have markedly moved away from their own culture of origin, which they want to 'keep'" (pp. 150–151).

79. Kathryn Manzo, *Creating Boundaries: The Politics of Race and Nation* (Boulder: Lynne Rienner, 1996); Robin Cohen, *Global Diasporas: An Introduction* (London: UCL Press, 1997). Case studies seem to bear this out. On nationalism in Latin America, see Benedict Anderson, *Imagined Communities* (London: Verso, 1983), p. 58 n; in Africa, see Reinhart Kössler and Henning Melber, "The Concept of Civil Society and the Process of Nation-Building in Africa," *Internationale Politik und Gesellschaft [International Politics and Society]* 1 (1996): 69–80; and compare Michael G. Schatzberg, "Ethnicity and Class at the Local Levels: Bars and Bureaucrats in Lisala, Zaire," *Comparative Politics* 13 (1981): 461–478, which shows a similar logic at work in the formation of ethnic consciousness.

80. Gavin Wright, *Old South, New South: Revolutions in the Southern Economy Since the Civil War* (New York: Basic Books, 1986), p. 8.

81. Jennifer L. Hochschild, *Facing Up to the American Dream: Race, Class, and the Soul of the Nation* (Princeton: Princeton University Press, 1996).

82. See, for example, Robert J. Donia and John V. A. Fine, *Bosnia and Hercegovina: A Tradition Betrayed* (New York: Columbia University Press, 1994).

83. David Turton, "War and Ethnicity: Global Connections and Local Violence in Northeast Africa and Former Yugoslavia," *Oxford Development Studies* 25, no. 1 (1997): 77–94.

84. See, for example, Metin Heper, "Islam and Democracy in Turkey: Toward a Reconciliation?" *Middle East Journal* 51, no. 1 (Winter 1997): 32–45. Compare Gilles Kepel, *The Revenge of God,* translated by Alan Braley (Cambridge: Polity Press, 1994). In looking at Islamic, Christian, and Jewish fundamentalisms, Kepel points to the commonality not only of the high education of their leaderships, but also of a tendency toward technical education.

85. Arjun Appadurai, *Modernity at Large: Cultural Dimensions of Globalization* (Minneapolis: University of Minnesota Press, 1996).

86. Hoogvelt, *Globalisation and the Postcolonial World,* p. 156.

87. Stuart Hall, "The Question of Cultural Identity," in *Modernity and Its Futures,* edited by Stuart Hall, David Held, and Tony McGrew (Cambridge: Polity Press in association with the Open University, 1992). Compare Huntington, *Clash of Civilizations,* p. 68.

88. Cohen, *Global Diasporas.*

89. While acknowledging that the status of vernacular has improved in the Caribbean, Hubert Devonish adds that the quality of English has declined because education reforms failed to draw a sharp distinction between the two languages by recognizing Creole as a language. See Hubert Devonish, "Walking Around the Language Barrier: A Caribbean View of the Ebonics Controversy," *Small Axe* 2 (September 1997): 63–76.

90. Colley, *Britons,* p. 12. Colley also quotes an obscure eighteenth-century Cambridge don who said, "National courage will be proportional to the share of property which each individual possesses, or hopes to possess" (p. 71).

91. Hans-Georg Betz, *Radical Right-Wing Populism in Western Europe* (London: Macmillan, 1994), chap. 5. See also *Le Nouvel Observateur* (Paris), 17 November 1996, pp. 60–61.

92. Dipankar Gupta, *Nativism in a Metropolis: The Shiv Sena in Bombay* (New Delhi: Manohar, 1982).

93. One must note, though, that this thesis of "racial threat" has been hotly debated. Compare, for example, Michael W. Giles and Melanie A. Buckner, "David Duke and Black Threat: An Old Hypothesis Revisited," *Journal of Politics* 55 (1993): 702–713, with D. Stephen Voss, "Beyond Racial Threat: Failure of an Old Hypothesis in the New South," *Journal of Politics* 58 (1996): 1156–1170.

94. Betz, *Radical Right-Wing Populism*. See also Nonna Mayer and Pascal Perrineau, *Le Front National à Découvert* (Paris: Presses de la Fondation Nationale des Sciences Politiques, 1996), chap. 5.

95. Pradeep Chhibber, "Who Voted for the Bharatiya Janata Party?" *British Journal of Political Science* 27, no. 4 (October 1987): 631–639.

96. Jonathan Hyslop, "Problems of Explanation in the Study of Afrikaner Nationalism: A Case Study of the West Rand," *Journal of Southern African Studies* 22 (1996): 373–385.

97. Olivier Roy, *The Failure of Political Islam* (Cambridge, Mass: Harvard University Press, 1994).

98. Carol Ann Drogus, "The Rise and Decline of Liberation Theology: Churches, Faith, and Political Change in Latin America," *Comparative Politics* 27 (1995): 465–477.

5

Manifestations of the Crisis

Manifestations of a regime crisis can be merely symptomatic, in which case they have no significance beyond themselves. In these cases, the symptoms point to a disorder in the regime and indicate its malfunctioning, and as such draw our attention to the need for reform. However, in and of themselves they need not bring about the collapse of the regime, because rival elites to the dominant one have not exploited them effectively. Recent concerns about the erosion of liberal democracy and the growth of what might be called postmodern politics are such symptoms. Antisystemic tendencies have emerged, but no counterelite as yet poses an effective challenge to the neoliberal regime whose malfunctioning has spawned them.

However, in some cases, the manifestations may also have a looping effect, in which case they feed back into the regime and threaten its existence. In these cases, counterhegemonic elites have emerged to pose an effective challenge to the dominant elite, and are manipulating the crisis to threaten the regime's existence. An example of this is fundamentalist politics. In itself, fundamentalism has failed as yet to provide a workable alternative to the neoliberal regime. This has led some scholars to dismiss it out of hand.[1] Nonetheless, as we shall see, it has produced sufficiently effective threats that it has led to a severe erosion in the neoliberal regime.

Democracy on the Defensive

In the early 1990s a wave of optimism about the future of liberal democracy piggybacked into the academic literature on the back of

107

communism's downfall.[2] Within a few short years, though, setbacks to the democratic "wave" caused the literature to become a good deal more gloomy.[3] Indeed, many scholars began to wonder if democracy was threatened in its very heartland, in Western Europe and North America. The cause of their growing pessimism has been a decline in political participation and partisanship, rising cynicism about democratic politics, the emergence of antisystemic movements or movements with an ambivalent attachment to liberal and democratic principles, and a general fragmentation of society, with the result being a weakening of the communities that are supposed to provide the foundation of a democratic system.

It would probably be mistaken to try to make a definitive conclusion as to the balance sheet of democratization. In the past few years, there have been significant improvements in the human rights records of many countries of the Third World. On the other hand, the setbacks of recent years, as well as the resurgence of populist politics, threaten to undermine some of these achievements.[4] But the point that is germane to this argument is not the current status of democracy globally. Rather, the hypothesis is that the rise of the far right and far left in the First World, and the return of populism in the Third World, threaten to roll back neoliberalism while fueling the movements that could destroy it (such as Islamic fundamentalism).

The decline in partisanship may not reflect a turn away from participatory politics so much as a change in its character. In most Western societies, party identification and loyalty has been in consistent decline throughout the postwar period. From the early postwar period, when, for example, most British workers supported the Labour Party unquestioningly,[5] voters reached the point in the 1990s that in some elections, most entered the polling booths still undecided as to their political allegiance.[6] This reflected the decline of working-class culture, brought on by rising prosperity, the move to the suburbs, the erosion of working-class cultural institutions and practices due to the privatization of leisure (the retreat into homes, where entertainment increasingly revolved around the television and later the computer), the numerical decline of the working class—in the German Land of North Rhine/Westphalia, for instance, the number of miners fell from 600,000 in the mid-1950s to 100,000 by the 1990s[7]—along with its cultural decomposition, and the weakening of the union movement in most Western countries in the 1980s and 1990s.[8] The result was that parties of the left had smaller support bases. For its part, the rising class of homeowners tended to support conservative political agendas, as

Margaret Thatcher calculated to her advantage in privatizing Britain's council houses.

So, to supplement their depleted ranks, leftist parties made appeals to new constituencies. Theorists observing the student ferment of the decade argued that such groups, which had not yet entered the "Establishment" and so had not been tainted by bourgeois ideology, offered the wave on which a socialist revolution could crest.[9] Yet the appeal to the new left—environmentalists, feminists, gay rights activists—carried risks. Most obviously, the demands of the new left often ran contrary to those of the old left, which while economically radical could be socially quite conservative.[10] The left was caught between a rock and a hard place. Those parties whose ideology remained true to their working-class roots, like the French Communist Party, experienced a slow but inexorable erosion. Yet those that tried the "rainbow coalition" approach often eroded as well, as working-class voters left to, in many cases, support new parties of the far right (as we shall see below).

However, as parties diminished in importance, they did not cede to vacuums but to new forms of political organization, namely interest and lobby groups. In the postwar period, the number of lobby groups mushroomed in all Western societies. From the point of view of voters who, in a prosperous age, increasingly defined themselves as consumers, lobby groups were attractive because they enabled citizens to channel their energies in ways that best addressed their needs.[11] On the other hand, they contributed to a further fragmentation of political society and, according to some scholars, reinforced the dominance of small, well-organized minorities.[12] The result was that when apparent political resource scarcities would emerge in the 1980s and 1990s, well-secured groups would be able to secure their interests at the expense of the less-mobilized portion of the electorate. This meant that cutbacks, when they came, would fall disproportionately on the shoulders of the poor.

And yet the irony is that, objectively, there were no scarcities. Outside of brief bouts of recession, the Western economies had been growing since the Great Depression, and per capita incomes had risen remarkably. Part of the difficulty, though, appears to have been that while the Western economies continued growing, from the 1970s they were growing at a slower rate than they had in the golden age. Consequently, the expectations of the babyboom generation, shaped as they were in a period of unprecedented bounty, outstripped the capacity of the economy to feed them. Such revolutions of rising expectations have been used to explain outbreaks of political violence and revolutionary activity.[13] In the industrial countries, the revolutions were not violent, but they were significant nonetheless. Added to this adjustment in the rate of growth is the paradox of prosperity, that rising income leads to even greater rises in demand. The privileged scions of the golden age would thus seek to maintain their standards of living. Groups that represented their interests would make it possible for them to get their demands heard, while the organizations intent on articulating broad societal interests—political parties—had diminished in their effectiveness.

The result, a political system that came to be seen as operating to the benefit of some more than others, was bound to produce a disaffection with politics. This was evident in a growing distrust of politicians, a development that appears to have been most acute among young people.[14] The babyboomers—who are now the older generation—grew up in history's most prosperous time and benefited greatly from the fruits of progress. They produced a culture of self-absorption and conspicuous consumption, and when recession hit in the 1970s, governments defended their gains with borrowed money. Yet when such policies impacted negatively upon inflation and interest rates, and thereby targeted the pocketbooks of the largest homeowning class in history, public sectors tended to shift the cost of retrenchment onto the shoulders of young people by, for example, freezing hiring. To this day, therefore, youth unemployment typically outstrips that of the population at large. In full-employment economies, like the United States in the late 1990s, young people landed jobs but were deprived of security and subject to inordinate amounts of stress. Even in Japan, the land famed for lifetime employment, firms kept their employees amid recession only by freezing hiring of new entrants to the job market. In the early 1990s, when the long Japanese recession began, overall unemployment remained low, officially at 3 percent, but among recent graduates it surpassed 15 percent.[15] One survey found that more young Americans believe in UFOs than believe social security will be available to them at retirement,[16] and unemployment may be the biggest fear among French youths.[17]

As noted in Chapter 3, young people everywhere have thus turned their backs on a system they see as serving someone else's benefit at their expense. Yet the younger generation did not produce a militancy that threatened the neoliberal regime, given that their preferred response was to retreat into solipsism. Still, at the margins, the cynicism turned into a hostility that at times threatened the harmony of liberal democracies. This was found particularly among the "angry white males," who often came from among the most marginalized segments of society and felt the most abandoned by the end of the postwar social compact. Unrepresented by the left, which in its appeals to the new left looked down on their social conservatism, the unskilled working class, hammered by the loss of employment from globalizing firms, looked to new patrons. They found them in a new right that blamed their fate on an obvious and, to them, omnipresent foe, namely immigrants. Their anger was misplaced, but it was not without a grain of truth. In addition to encouraging the sourcing of low-skilled jobs offshore, Western governments had devised immigration policies to attract unskilled labor from Third World countries. Typically, these immigrants moved into the same depressed communities where the working class lived. But with the decomposition of the working class, as the more skilled and prosperous elements moved to the suburbs, the inner city was left to the least-educated and least-employable remnants of the white working class. They now lived cheek by jowl with the very people with whom they were forced to compete for jobs.

Angry white males were frequently dismissed as selfish people who did not want to share the privileges they had inherited from their ancestors' sins. For example, they have tended to oppose affirmative action. In fact, those who had inherited these privileges were the "happy white males," who had already taken advantage of the preferential access to education and employment and only then turned around to close the door. Indeed, some left-leaning authors have argued that affirmative action has been a classic divide-and-rule strategy whereby existing elites have co-opted rising elites from marginalized groups, thereby separating the leadership of these groups from their mass base, but leaving the mass little better off than before.[18] In any event, being both economically marginalized and politically dismissed, they were bound to become angry. This anger manifested itself in the political domain in two ways. One was a slide into apathy and cynicism, the anger of Generation X. The other was the violent rage of the most deprived young men with the least advancement prospects, who saw all sorts of people traditionally lower than them advancing beyond their status. These manifestations provided the basis for a resurgence of fascism in Western Europe,[19] and of the less effective if more menacing militia movements in the United States.[20]

The decline of the left fed the rise of the far right. There was more involved than a shift in the ideological spectrum. Support for the far right seemed to have come not from a moderate right that had grown extreme, but from a leftist constituency that had grown disenchanted with the leftist parties, namely the increasingly decimated working class, who were generally white, male, and poorly educated.[21] One recalls that U.S. right-wing populist Pat Buchanan railed not only against foreigners, but against big business as well. In Germany, support for the Republican Party tended to come from working-class districts formerly supportive of the Social Democrats. In France, the Communist Party lost ground to the National Front, which became the favorite party of unemployed voters by the mid-1990s.[22] Moreover, fears of unemployment among young people not only bolstered the National Front—significantly, the party's youth wing was said to be more extremist than the party itself[23]—but even caused some young voters, traditionally leftist, to switch their allegiance to the moderate right.[24] In a similar vein, Belgium's Front National and Vlaams Blok capitalized on "concerns over unemployment and associated fears of losing jobs to immigrants,"[25] and ultranationalist parties in Central Europe tended to draw their support from among those most hurt by the region's economic transformation.[26] Austria's Freedom Party also won ground in working-class districts, draining support from the Social Democrats,[27] a pattern repeated in Scandinavia.[28] And in the 1996 Italian election, one activist for the Party of the Democratic Left (PDS, the successor to the Communist Party) complained that young people could be reached only by talk about jobs. But then, with youth unemployment running at 30 percent, this should have come as no surprise. The older generation on the left was willing to moralize from a position of relative comfort, just as babyboomers everywhere have bemoaned Generation X's loss of idealism. So one student complained that while young people wanted jobs, "the left still wants to give us lectures." That is why young voters were turning to the right, which seemed to talk the language of jobs that so concerned them: in 1994 they went heavily to Silvio Berlusconi before moving further to the right in 1996 and supporting Gianfranco Fini's National Alliance (successor to the Fascist Party).[29]

Not everywhere did significant far-right parties emerge. However, virtually everywhere the spectrum of politics moved to the right, and far-right sentiment rose. What united the far right was generally a strong opposition to immigration,[30] which often became outright racism. And anti-immigrant sentiment is on the rise virtually everywhere that employment is threatened. Nor is the problem likely to go away, since the new global economy demands cheap unskilled labor at rates below what domestic workers will accept, while at the same time declining population growth in the First World necessitates the supplementing of domestic labor forces by outside entrants if economic growth is to be maintained. Hence the need to depend on immigration, whether it be legal migration from Eastern Europe westward, or the illegal migration from Mexico into the United States. And since immigration is here to stay, politicians often find the political points scored by talking tough on foreigners too easy to resist.[31] Australia's loss of manufacturing operations to neighboring low-wage countries subsequent to its economic liberalization was believed to have been at the heart of the mercurial ascent of the country's One Nation Party.[32] This tribalism is a natural human response when one's access to resources is threatened, a sort of circling of the wagons in order to defend what one has against the perceived enemy outside. It may not produce the tribal barbarities we have recently seen in other societies, and which will be discussed below. But this is only because the wealth of the First World has lowered the stakes of the battle over resources. Nevertheless, violence against foreigners, whether guest workers in Germany or Gypsies in Austria and Czechoslovakia, is apparently on the increase.[33]

One is tempted to wish these extremists out of existence, to somehow hope they are a kind of millennial aberration that will eventually disappear, but their presence is deep-rooted. By and large they have not been old fascist and racist organizations whose ranks have been swelled by new entrants. In fact, long-established extremist movements remained marginal all along. The successful far-right groups have been new organizations,[34] often led by a young and media-savvy generation. They have drawn support not only from the marginalized traditional working class, but also from the rising new middle class of self-employed entrepreneurs who would have once found employment in the state but who have, in the age of leaner administration, been forced to fend for themselves.[35] Equally, far-right groups have filled a need among an alienated population to find a sense of belonging: in Eastern Europe, the collapse of a nurturing state provided a fertile recruiting ground for skinhead gangs, while weakened communities and families have allowed U.S. extremist groups to portray themselves as, in effect, virtual families for their members.[36]

If anything, these groups seem to be exploiting the new political and economic changes to foster their future development. The Southern Poverty Law Center has documented extensive communication by fax, Internet, and radio among U.S. extremist movements, while there is evidence that some of these movements have helped fund German neo-Nazi groups.[37] Glancing further afield, there has also been evidence that Belgian far-right groups funded Hutu extremist militias in Rwanda.[38] Such findings probably represent the tip of an iceberg of far-right linkages. That is not to mean we will ever witness a world revolution by the far right. Far-right parties scored only ephemeral successes in the 1990s and enjoy little real prospect of coming to power in any of the industrial liberal democracies. Even in France, where the far right perhaps went the furthest in establishing itself, a majority of voters opposed it all along.[39] By the late 1990s, the far right seemed to have reached something of a plateau, suffering disappointing results in a number of elections.

Yet the far right is probably not a spent force. To some extent the leveling-off resulted from the fact that more moderate parties had co-opted a good chunk of the far right's platform. For example, in the run-up to German Lander elections in 1996, both Christian Democrats and Social Democrats employed populist rhetoric that took a firm line against foreigners—they probably felt they had no choice, given Germany's unemployment rate of 11 percent, a postwar record-high at the time[40]—and in Denmark's 1998 election the Social Democrats borrowed the Popular Party's stand against immigration.[41] From California, where a referendum clamped down on Mexican immigrants, to Canberra, where Australian conservatives played to anti-immigrant sentiment, mainstream politicians have appropriated the language of the far right in order to preserve their share of the electorate. Similarly, the much vaunted return of the left toward the end of the 1990s was more apparent than real. It is true that by 1998, nominally leftist candidates were back in control of the governments of the United States, Canada, and most West European countries. Nevertheless, this was a new-look left, one that had adopted most of the ideology of its conservative predecessors and even, in the case of British immigration policies and U.S. welfare policies, took this ideology even further to the right. The far right has thus made its presence known. And as the sudden resurgence of the far right in Denmark's 2001 elections, the stunning first-round showing of Jean-Marie le Pen in France's 2002 presidential election, and the mercurial rise of Pim Fortuyn's List in the subsequent Dutch elections all testified, the far right was scarcely in abeyance.

One lesson of history is that the democratic pessimists of the early twentieth century turned out to be correct. By the time of World War II, democracy had been rolled back to a few Western bastions and was even there under threat. Of course, history need not repeat itself, and democracy is showing itself to be rather resilient in some places where it is threatened. However, a note of caution from one of the first generation of democratic pessimists is in order. Walter Lippmann suggested that the popular commitment to democracy was ever conditional on the regime's performance.[42] Evidence from some of the newer and more fragile democracies today seems to confirm this suspicion. Adam

Przeworski concludes that people will not support a democracy simply because it is a democracy but must have some "specific minimum probability of benefiting from it."[43] While Russians grew fonder of their newfound freedoms, they continued in the 1990s to pine for the old economic system[44] and to evince totalitarian leanings.[45] Their attachment to liberal democracy seems likely to weaken if the economy fails to regain its momentum in the twenty-first century (the same appears to hold true for Ukraine).[46]

However, these concerns aside, the real threat appears not to be that democracy is in retreat. As mentioned at the outset, setbacks must be set against advances, and not all the news as to the progress of democracy has been bad. The greater risk, rather, is that the rise of extremist movements is likely to fuel countertendencies that threaten to undermine regime stability. This is where the peculiar role of young people comes into play. Traditionally a natural support base for left-wing parties, their actions (or nonactions) have in recent years helped to fuel the rise of extremist political movements. First, as discussed above, they have tended to gravitate in disproportionate numbers toward movements of the far right in the liberal democracies. Second, their rates of nonparticipation tend to be higher than those for the population as a whole. As a result of this twin effect leading to the erosion of the left's support base, the far right has been able to surge, a phenomenon illustrated most dramatically in the 2002 French presidential election.[47] And while the far right is no longer committed to an antidemocratic agenda—meaning that democracy still looks safe, if less than abundantly healthy—its opposition to some elements of the globalization agenda, in particular immigration and regional integration, threaten to reverse the tide of globalization. At the same time, the growth of far-right political movements has prompted a move in immigrant communities toward political movements seen as likely to safeguard their interests. Ethnic politics and fundamentalism, which themselves have their problems with globalization, thus stand to gain from the rise of the far right. Add to all this the growth of the antiglobalization movement, which as noted in Chapter 3 has drawn important support from young people, not to mention the resurgence of populism in Latin America as citizenries protest the increasingly intolerable demands of neoliberal reform in the midst of economic contractions, and the tide against neoliberal globalization appears to have turned. In short, democracy, on balance, is probably not at risk. Neoliberalism may well be. More significantly, as we shall see, the 1990s produced a new form of politics in poorer regions that presented grave threats to global stability.

Postmodern Politics

In recent years it has become popular to speak of an impending resource struggle breaking out on an overpopulated planet, driving the world back into a tribal barbarism from which modernity has failed to free mankind. However, as we have seen, resource scarcities have not been ordained by nature, but rather have been created by humans themselves. In First World liberal democracies, growing fragmentation of the political universe, coupled with accelerated satisfaction of human wants by material consumption, has produced a subdued if occasionally still unpleasant battle among political networks over a resource pie that is, in spite of appearances, increasing.

However, such tribalism can produce different effects under different conditions. In situations where the "tribes" or political networks in question enjoy a territorial base, they can threaten not democracy but the territorial integrity and even the sovereignty of the nation-state. In effect, rival elites can emerge to challenge the authority of the nation-state and build mass networks within a fixed territory, spearheading what are de facto and even de jure secessionist movements. Rather than an apparently unending civil war within a state, one ends the conflict by, to put it simply, taking one's ball and going home. Some of the postmodern struggles that emerged in the 1990s have unleashed the worst barbarism the planet has seen since World War II.

It appears that both pull and push factors drive postmodern politics. In terms of pull factors, state retrenchment has weakened the resource-allocating power, and hence the influence, of national governments. This has given subnational elites a window of opportunity to assert their autonomy and try to pull partially if not entirely out of the dominant networks of politics. There are, of course, stages along a continuum that ends with secessionism. In Western Europe, municipal and regional governments expanded their budgets at times that national budgets were, in relative terms, stagnating or declining.[48] Secession has not always been on the cards, but given that some of these regions cross state boundaries, a change in citizen loyalties took place in many locales.

In terms of push factors—and this applies especially in the industrial democracies—the interest group politics identified earlier in the book pushed many people out of the distribution networks of the weakened nation-state. In some places, the fragmentation of the political universe coincided in part with regional divisions, with the elites of richer regions seeking to minimize their ties with poorer regions. Early in the book, it was suggested that postmodernism has become the ideology of the winners in the new global economy, fundamentalism that of its losers. One should not overstress the connection, which is at most a tendency and not a hard-and-fast rule. Still, one can say that in many and perhaps most instances, postmodern politics in industrial democracies begins as a revolt by the rich, who, seeking to preserve their share of resources, try to lessen their ties to nation-states that are seen to be redistributing resources from rich regions to poor regions. Poor regions seldom have cause to leave a political structure that is enriching them, unless they have already been pushed out, or if they see themselves facing a dangerous future if they stay in.[49] Rich regions that find themselves more heavily taxed to preserve the distributional programs of nation-states within the context of slowed growth will often want to preserve their share of the pie by pushing back the hand that wields the knife. Thus, just as the decline of the left and rise of the right and far right coincided with the move to slowed economic growth and widened income distribution in the First World, so too the outbreak of postmodern politics can be attributed to global economic trends. When growth slowed in the 1970s and 1980s, political elites developed an interest in challenging the nation-state. Hence the push for decentralization or outright secession in Europe was heard in the first instances in the more industrially advanced areas like the north of Italy,[50] Spain's Basque and Catalan regions, or the Croatian republic of the former Yugoslavia. In Belgium, the rich Flemish grew tired of subsidizing their poor cousins, the Walloons, through a single social security system,[51] just as western Canadians arguably stoked the rising anger of Quebec nationalists by their resistance to federal redistribution programs in the 1970s and 1980s. Animating subnational political elites was the complaint that poorer regions were draining resources from their territories. When those same elites found themselves largely excluded from positions of power in the central government, their desire to withdraw from the government became all the greater. From regions with populations in the millions down to the smallest condominium developments, scholars charted the revolt of the rich.[52]

The economic changes associated with globalization fed the rise of centrifugal tendencies in a number of societies. In democratic states, such decentralization took place peacefully, and was often legitimized with the argument that public administration would be made more efficient and flexible, and thus more responsive to the new economy, if more authority were given to subnational agencies. In the United States, congressional Republicans and governors, aided by a sympathetic Supreme Court, spearheaded a successful effort to devolve an increasing amount of federal authority to the states, while in Britain, Tony

Blair's communitarian ideology was invoked to justify the gradual devolution of power to Scotland and Wales, and further yet to municipal authorities. Such decentralization appeared eminently democratic, as it brought government closer to the people. However, when it involved changes in tax regimes that enhanced the revenue-generating capacity of subnational units, it heightened regional wealth and income differentials. Central governments everywhere found that the opportunity cost of equalization and federal programs was a loss of international competitiveness—in particular, their expenses driving up tax rates—so they began phasing them out. This weakened national glue, causing resentment among regions that lost prosperity and weakening the power of central authorities to discipline the constituent parts of a nation-state. The carrot was either gone or had become too withered to feed aggressive elites.

In fact, two processes coexisted. To hasten economic integration, national governments had to renounce a number of the economic levers they used to manage national economies. Monetary policy was tempered by international capital flows, taxes and regulations had to be kept in check to maintain competitiveness, standards had to be harmonized with those of dominant trading partners, trade policy had to become less protectionist. Thus national governments lost power above to regional trading blocs, and below to increasingly assertive subnational units. As noted earlier, regional elites anxious to emancipate themselves from the control of national ones were among the strongest proponents of accelerated economic integration.

The rule we can use is this: in times of resource scarcity—whether real or imagined, natural or human-made—politics tends to tribalize, and group leaders seek to reinforce the identities of followers in order to clarify who is in and who is out of their networks. This way they can defend and if possible expand their network's share of the available resources. The interest group politics of the First World societies can be seen as an instance of such tribalized politics. The greater the resource scarcity, the less civil the war. However, when a given group can claim exclusive or nearly exclusive control over a clearly demarcated territory, secession or at least some form of regional autonomy can forestall severe conflict. Few contested the secession of relatively homogeneous Slovenia from Yugoslavia, or the breakup of Czechoslovakia into its two constituent parts. On the other hand, when rival groups lay claim to the same territory, the conflict is bound to become severe as ethnic leaders seek to solidify their own territorial claims by purging their land of rival networks. Couple that with a resource scarcity that makes resource competition a struggle over life and death, as was the case in Rwanda in

1994, and the stage is set for a descent into the worst types of ethnic cleansing. In these circumstances the public becomes receptive to dangerous forms of racist ideology that justify one group excluding and even exterminating another.

Postmodern politics becomes most virulent in poor societies. But it is found everywhere, even among the world's richest lands, as the example of Canada illustrates. Canada owed its creation in 1867 to a pact among British colonies that wanted to withstand eventual integration into the United States. Essential to maintaining Canada's independence was an economic policy that limited trade south of the border and encouraged interprovincial trade. Given Canada's population distribution, this produced an economic structure that concentrated industry in southern Ontario and Quebec, with the remainder of the country being primarily sources of raw materials and markets for Canadian industrial goods. Essential to maintaining Canada's political stability—given that it was an uneasy pact between English-speaking provinces and one French-speaking one, Quebec—was a practice of giving Quebec's politicians privileged representation in the country's government, Supreme Court, and federal institutions. In the course of the twentieth century, successive federal governments sought to cement an already fragile federation with equalization payments that used the revenues of rich provinces to subsidize poor ones. On the one hand, this built up citizen loyalty by bringing the benefits of federation to a wider cross section of citizens. On the other, it afforded the federal government disciplinary powers over the provinces, as it could use payments or the threat of their withholding to pressure provincial governments to adopt federal standards.

Over time, though, western Canadians grew to resent this arrangement. In part, the opening of western Canada to European settlement brought waves of immigrants who were neither British nor French, and so had little invested in a compact between the two "founding nations." When in the 1970s the surge in the world price of oil, a resource in which western Canada is rich, created a situation in which the west was seen to be temporarily subsidizing the remainder of the federation, the resentment reached the boiling point.

By this time, the mood in Quebec had also tipped, but for different reasons. A nationalist intelligentsia had arisen from the French-speaking province in the postwar period, and in the 1960s it split in two. One faction, the separatists, who would come under the leadership of Rene Levesque, believed that Quebec could only preserve its distinct cultural identity by seceding from the federation. The other faction, the federalists, led by Pierre Trudeau, believed that Quebec could only retain its distinct identity, and English Canada its sovereignty from the United States, if the two founding nations drew closer together. Trudeau became the Canadian prime minister, and his government quickly implemented cultural policies to promote Canada's bilingual identity and economic policies to augment its separation from the United States. Western Canadians, unilingual and eager to lessen their dependence on the eastern Canadian axis, resented these policies and blamed them on French Canada. This hostility only fed the rise of the separatists. The separatists would go on to hold referenda in 1980, and again in 1995.

In no small part because their support base—descendants of the original French settlers—was contracting, the separatists lost both referenda. However, the de facto breakup of the country can already be seen. In 1988, Canada had created a free trade zone with the United States. The inevitable pressure to harmonize national standards and to improve the competitiveness of Canadian business, which paid higher taxes and faced more regulation than its counterpart south of the border, compelled the Canadian government to retreat from many of its social and equalization programs. As the federal government's relevance to people's lives receded, and as federal elites lost some of their disciplinary powers over the provinces, provincial elites became more assertive in their demands. Adding to this effect was a rise in north-south trade with a commensurate decline in east-west trade, attenuating the bonds among Canada's provinces.[53] As Canada rushes into the global age, by way of a regional trade agreement, it is becoming what Canadians now like to call the world's first postmodern state. As Pierre Trudeau lamented before his death, it may leave not with a bang but a whimper, going the way—as one commentator put it—of the Holy Roman Empire,[54] with the provinces gradually becoming sovereign within a shell of Canadian statehood. Were that to happen, it would be an inglorious ending. But at least it would be peaceful.

Such cannot be said for Yugoslavia, a country whose breakup was especially violent. Like Canada, Yugoslavia owed its creation to the shared desire of different nationalities—Serbs, Croats, Slovenes, and other Slavic peoples—to withstand foreign domination, whether of the Ottomans, Austro-Hungarians, or Russians. The union was not always an easy one, but it is probably reasonable to say that for a few decades after World War II, it brought peace and a modicum of prosperity to the bulk of the population.[55]

What changed everything was the economic crisis into which Yugoslavia found itself plunged in the 1980s. The effects of this crisis were bound to be exacerbated by the fact that since the mid-1970s, West European governments preoccupied with their own economic problems had begun reducing the number of Yugoslav guest workers they took in, depriving many Yugoslav families of this important income supplement.[56] To deal with the crisis, the Yugoslav leadership implemented liberalization and retrenchment policies that, coupled with the deteriorating economy, gravely eroded its resource-allocating power. Workers coping with eroded standards of living became restive and, in 1989, 1,900 strikes involving nearly half a million workers were reported.[57] This challenged political leaders to find new ways to solidify their support bases. It also created openings for rival elites, especially those who (like Boris Yeltsin in Russia) were marginalized in the national leadership, to build up their own power bases. Furthermore, constitutional changes in 1974 had sufficiently fragmented Yugoslavia to make it possible for elites to use the republics as power bases.[58] The focus of politics thereafter shifted away from the federal capital, Belgrade. Resource scarcity provoked tribalization, with leaders trying to secure or increase their share of the Yugoslav pie: Serbian nationalists wanted to expand their share by creating a Greater Serbia, and Croat nationalists wanted to withdraw from Yugoslavia in order to stem what they saw as the transfer of resources from their industrially developed region to the poorer south.[59] The Serbian communist leadership, led by Slobodan Milosevic, decided to co-opt nationalist ideology to shore up its authority in the late 1980s,[60] and in so doing provoked a defensive response in other republics. All the while, nationalist elites favored their own supporters when it came to resource allocation. When the nationalist Franjo Tudjman won the 1990 elections in Croatia, a year before the republic declared its independence, Croatian-controlled enterprises dismissed thousands of Serb workers.[61]

Where a territory was occupied by the support base of only one political elite, as in Slovenia, there was little if any fighting. But where two or more nationalities, with different leaderships, occupied the same land, war broke out. "Ethnic cleansing," designed to bring the territory into the regime of just one elite, then occurred. Only foreign occupation, by North Atlantic Treaty Organization and United Nations forces, succeeded in bringing an end to the fighting. And to this day, only foreign occupation appears to be keeping the peace.

However, the most violent incident of postmodern politics that the world saw in the 1990s took place in Rwanda. Unlike Canada and Yugoslavia, which were modern inventions, Rwanda's principal ethnic groups had a long history of coexistence in one political form or another. Although the Hutus were apparently the first to occupy what is today Rwanda, the Tutsis would later come to dominate the precolonial politics. Yet, as was the case in much of precolonial Africa, authority was decentralized and the Tutsi aristocracy's power was not absolute.[62] Moreover, the rigid distinction between Hutu and Tutsi had yet to emerge and, as in other African societies, ethnic identity remained fluid.[63] Though aware of their different ancestry, the Tutsis had adopted the language and customs of the Hutus and assimilated into their culture. In any event, attachment to other groups took precedence over allegiance based on ethnicity.[64]

Colonial rule altered this pattern, concentrating power at the center and thereby depriving not only Hutus but many ordinary Tutsis of access to power and privilege.[65] At independence in 1959, the Hutu majority, resentful of the weight of ethnic domination, overthrew the Tutsi monarchy. Subsequently, there were periods of conflict, but by and large Rwanda remained peaceful for the next few decades.

The peace began unraveling in the 1980s, though, as global recession and the spread of structural adjustment unleashed tensions throughout the region. When Yoweri Museveni overthrew the government of Ugandan dictator Milton Obote in the mid-1980s, he benefited greatly from his alliance with the Tutsi refugees who had provided much of the fighting force in his rebel movement. However, rather than integrating them into his government, Museveni found that the ethnic complexities of Ugandan politics made it necessary to gradually squeeze them out.[66] Meanwhile, in other African countries that harbored Tutsi refugees, economic decline had caused a turn against foreigners and Tutsis were targeted as scapegoats.[67] Faced with such pressures, the leadership of the exile Tutsi community pondered a return to Rwanda.

Yet the resources to absorb them were drying up, with government retrenchment exacerbating the economic recession. Beset by plunging coffee prices in the 1980s, the Rwandan accumulation regime was faltering, and in 1989 the budget was slashed by 40 percent. Social services bore the brunt of the cuts.[68] Drought then hit many areas of the country, while the government's structural adjustment program drove up prices for most Rwandans. Thus, as their revenue fell and state services were cut, living costs for most Rwandans rose.[69] Rwanda's governing Hutu elite insisted there was no empty land for the Tutsi refugees to settle. Furthermore, given the scarcity of resources in this small, crowded country, the ruling elite could not contemplate sharing power with the Tutsi elite, or with the Hutu opposition. The situation was getting desperate, as there was not enough pie to go around, let alone to accommodate new guests at the table. To force their way into government, therefore, Tutsi refugees (and a minority of Hutus) formed the Rwandan Patriotic Front, a guerrilla army that crossed the border from Uganda into Rwanda in 1990.

By 1994 the Tutsi advance was threatening the Hutu elite's hold on power. At this time, militants in the governing elite opted for a drastic solution. They purged the elite of its moderate elements, then laid the groundwork for a genocidal policy. The logic was simple: if, as Mao said, rebel armies were to swim among the peasantry like fish in a sea,[70] then the only solution was to drain the sea. All Tutsis and moderate Hutus would be eliminated, depriving the Tutsi elite of its support base. One thing scholars who have written about the Rwandan genocide agree about is that in contrast to portrayals of the genocide as an anarchic bloodbath, it was in fact meticulously planned and executed with bureaucratic efficiency.[71] Indeed, one commentator has noted that the killing rate of the Rwandan genocide was so high that it surpassed that of the Nazi Holocaust by a factor of five.[72]

However, most of the killings were not carried out by members of the elite. The militias that were organized by extremists to help carry out the task were recruited largely from among the urban poor,[73] but given the enormity of the task ahead of them the extremists depended on participation of Hutu peasants who swam in the same sea and therefore turned on their neighbors. Explaining what causes neighbors to turn on one another is always bewildering, but it helps to recall that this type of tragedy is not new. Germans in the 1930s did much the same sort of thing, as did the militias in Yugoslavia. What motivates people in such circumstances is partly the fear—exploited and manipulated by nationalist ideologues—that emerges in an uncertain environment, and partly concern with their own material well-being. Hutu peasants were persuaded of the reality of a Tutsi plot largely because their access to information was tightly controlled by the regime, making it possible for ideologues to feed them a diet of racism. Peasants thus had no evidence to the contrary and acted in self-defense. But they were also motivated by greed and desperation: murdered neighbors left behind land and cattle, and in the midst of deteriorating economic conditions that threatened life and well-being, the lure of these spoils frequently could not be resisted.[74] This is one of history's eternal and tragic recurrences. Many Germans gravitated to the Nazis for spoils,[75] Tutsis took advantage of massacres in Burundi in the 1970s with similar motives,[76] and, it has been suggested, some Algerians have taken part in massacres in their own recent civil war for much the same reason.[77] Nor can one attribute the savagery to ignorance: staff at the national university are reported to have aided the killers so as to eliminate rivals for promotion.[78] To outsiders, the behavior of ordinary Rwandans in 1994 may seem like a moment of insanity, as it probably does in hindsight to many of its participants. Yet within the context of the precarious state of the Rwandan economy in 1994 and the information famine, which always feeds rumor and wild speculation, it makes a perverse sort of sense.

As the twentieth century drew to a close, postmodern politics showed no signs of receding. Largely as a result of events in Rwanda, Zaire (renamed the Democratic Republic of Congo after the overthrow of Mobutu) virtually broke up into a series of autonomous fiefdoms. Ethnic tensions simmered in Nigeria and Côte d'Ivoire, dividing the countries along regional lines and threatening to split them open. East Timor finally seceded from Indonesia, sparking a resurgence of secessionism in other corners of the archipelago-country. There were coups in Fiji and the Solomon Islands that aimed to alter the balance between ethnic groups, while in faraway Trinidad and Tobago a growing ethnic polarity came to dominate that country's fragile democracy. Muslim rebels in the Philippines took Western tourists hostage and provoked open conflict with the government. Equally, in Latin America and the Caribbean, drug gangs have succeeded in carving out spaces in which they can operate free of the state, largely by providing citizens in ghettos, favelas, and barrios with access to resources—including security—that a retrenching state has been unable to provide.

Ever since Marx spoke of the withering away of the state in the mid–nineteenth century, theorists on the left have sometimes predicted the eventual collapse of the nation-state. In recent years, more conservative theorists have added their voices to this chorus by warning that globalization will, in creating a "borderless" world,[79] render the nation-state irrelevant. Yet for all the talk of states in crisis and of the breakup of nations, the nation-state looks surprisingly healthy and seems unlikely to disappear any time soon. Take Africa, for instance. One would expect that postmodern politics should, given the continent's complexity—over 1,000 spoken languages—yield a galaxy of new nation-states. It has not. Eritrea regained its sovereignty and Somaliland declared an independence that the international community refused to recognize. A few other countries, notably Sudan and Somalia, fragmented. Yet all in all the map of Africa, which has for so long been decried as irrelevant to African realities and so doomed to someday change, still looks remarkably intact.

Reports of the nation-state's demise have thus proved greatly exaggerated. And yet, over a million of the planet's citizens have died so far in these postmodern conflicts. In other words, while there is no crisis of the nation-state, there is undeniably a crisis. Given that the consequence of postmodern politics has been an increase in the numbers of those outside the distributional networks of politics, these are not tenable regimes. Looking back at Yugoslavia, it is revealing that the Serb nationalist leader Slobodan Milosevic, seemingly desperate to buy time for his regime when domestic opposition was burgeoning over the deepening economic crisis, looked farther afield to Kosovo to play the nationalist card.[80] But the writing was on the wall for his reign.

In the short term, postmodern politics may be more effective than the far-right politics of the industrial democracies, or the fundamentalist politics to be considered below, because by appropriating a resource base secessionist leaders are able to provide their regimes with the resources they need to become viable. An important proviso to this point is that identity politics of this sort can only succeed in its short-term objectives if the identity group in question can lay claim to a clearly demarcated territory. Otherwise the political elite cannot secure the resources it needs to build up distribution networks. This is why a group like the Nation of Islam, in the United States, is unlikely to ever pose the effective challenge to the U.S. government it seeks, because black Muslims, despite their call for a homeland, are unable to lay a claim to any piece of U.S. territory that would be widely accepted within the African American community, let alone within the wider American community as a whole. Desegregation has deprived the black bourgeoisie and petty bourgeoisie of the protected space they once enjoyed to sustain wholly separate cultural and political environments. The Nation of Islam has tried to build up its resource-distributing networks to enable its supporters to withdraw from the U.S. regime, but the business ventures created to fuel these have met with little success.[81] Just as globalization has opened up the space of national elites to outside penetration, so has integration in the United States opened up the hitherto sheltered space of the black bourgeoisie, foisting a punishing competition upon it.[82] Today the Nation of Islam depends for much of its revenue on security contracts with the federal government.[83] In other words, locked into a dependent relationship with the regime from which it seeks to withdraw, the Nation of Islam, lacking an autonomous resource base, cannot break from the federation.

However, even where postmodern political movements have laid claim to territory and secured control over it, their long-term survival depends on the elite expanding its resource base. This, in turn, depends on some form of economic integration. Postmodern politics does not merely coexist with regionalization and/or globalization, it depends upon it. This leads to an ironic outcome. Postmodern politics, which appears to increase fragmentation and the number of political units in the world, depends for its survival on the closer integration of nation-states and a reduction in the number of economic units in the world. It does not stem the tide of globalization. If anything, it hastens it.

Whether to resist postmodern politics, as South Africa did when it reined in centrifugal tendencies at the fall of apartheid, or to advance it, as in Quebec or Yugoslavia, political elites are finding it necessary to move their countries further down the road of globalization. So, while postmodern leaders sometimes base their ideological appeals on a call to resistance against domination by others, the players who are pushing globalization forward are strengthening their position. This, it seems reasonable to say, is the crux of the crisis. Those fractions of capital that, in alliance with the new global middle class, have benefited most from rolling back the nation-state have not sought to eliminate states, but to smash the regimes that underpinned the modern nation-state. Postmodern politics does not challenge the nation-state, but it does reinforce the dominance of the new elites who have enriched themselves by eroding their links to the remainder of the planet's population. When all is said and done, postmodern politics will do little to remedy the crisis. If anything, it is making matters worse. Those who seek to ameliorate the suffering of the millions squeezed out from the bottom of the hourglass will have to look to other ideological responses for solutions. Many believe they have found the answer in fundamentalism.

Fundamentalist Politics

Originally used to refer to a specific type of U.S. Protestantism, the term *fundamentalism* has in recent years been used to describe various types of religious movements that stress a return to the alleged fundamentals of a faith. As such, it has been applied to various types of Judaism, Buddhism, Hinduism, and, most commonly, Islam. Some dispute the applicability of the term, but in identifying the family resemblances among these various strains, it seems useful.[84] Fundamentalist ideologies have emerged as cultural critiques that respond to globalization, yet at the same time they exist in a symbiosis with globalization. However, while many find appeal in fundamentalist ideology, where such movements take root, it is primarily because they have exploited the gaps left by retrenching regimes in Third World countries. And, as we shall see, fundamentalism has arguably produced the most potent threat to neoliberal globalization, if in a roundabout way.

Nationalist elites at the time Muslim countries won their independence very often viewed their religious traditions with unsympathetic eyes: the power of religious authorities stood as a direct challenge both to the consolidation of their own rule and to the attainment of modernity. In the Persian Gulf states, oil wealth enabled traditional elites to solidify their hold on power and Islam retained a strong role in politics and society. In most other Muslim societies, though, nationalist intellectuals saw Islam, at worst, as a bastion of traditionalism and doubt and, at best, as a rival authority to that of the state. Equally, modernity implied that traditional religious elites had to submit to the authority of the state. Either their resource-generating and resource-allocating functions had to be taken over by the state, or they had to be brought under the supervision of the state. In many cases, the state broke up religious endowments and either nationalized or redistributed them.[85] Modern "protector" states, which assumed so many of the functions that mattered to important citizens, succeeded in attracting mass support in the days when economic prosperity vindicated their development strategies. Many states followed the Turkish model, whereby the state took over not only the resource-distributing powers but many of the economy's accumulation or resource-generating functions as well.

Problems began to surface in the 1970s, though, when these countries started facing the problems then emerging in the global economy. The Gulf states were awash with oil money, while Indonesia and Malaysia rode on the East Asian boom, but most Muslim countries suffered from the world recession and subsequent decade of austerity. By enriching oil exporters while creating difficulties for oil importers, one effect of the oil shocks may have been to tip the balance of power in the Muslim world away from modernizing states and toward conservative states, particularly those in the Persian Gulf, which would provide much of the patronage for Islamist groups. At a time when leftist movements threatened a number of Gulf states, the Saudi ruling elite found it opportune to patronize any groups that might neutralize the left,[86] just as the Israeli government would later find it opportune to encourage Palestinian Islamists as a counterweight to the nationalist Palestine Liberation Organization. Furthermore, the rapid growth in the Gulf-state economies attracted migrant labor both from the rural areas of these countries and from other Muslim countries. Several scholars have traced the reawakening of Muslim consciousness to the experience of alienation and search for identity that occurred in these exile communities. Mosques, surrounded by charitable and educational organizations, frequently preceded the arrival of state agencies in these burgeoning suburbs and shantytowns. To the extent it was able, through its labor, to secure a share of the benefits of the oil economy, this population enjoyed the financial resources needed to patronize newly forming Islamist groups.[87] In India, returning Muslims awash with cash and wedded to Islamist ideas stoked fear among Hindu intellectuals and so probably helped contribute to the rise of Hindu fundamentalism as a response.[88]

Although Islamic fundamentalism dates back to the 1920s, it gained salience with the crisis of Arab nationalism after the Arab defeat in the 1967 war with Israel. Opposed both to the constituted authorities and to the left, Islamic fundamentalism had become the dominant opposition movement by the 1980s.[89] The year 1979 turned out to be a watershed in the rise of the movement, if such it can be called. In that year the Shah of Iran was overthrown in a revolution that, following a period of uncertainty, brought to power an Islamist leadership who created a theocracy. In some countries, conservative elements who had seen their interests threatened by the changes brought on by secular modernizing states allied themselves to Islamic fundamentalists in an attempt to reassert their control.[90] The year 1979, of course, was also the year that—owing to the withdrawal of Iranian production during the revolution—saw the second oil shock and the beginning of the recession in much of the global economy. And, of course, it saw the spread of structural adjustment in the Third World (though adjustment would become most pronounced in Arab countries only after the Gulf War in the early 1990s). Western economic and social models were increasingly imposed on Third World societies, and the pain of adjustment fell heavily on ordinary people who had less and less reason to remain loyal to the elites who had governed them. In this context, Islamic fundamentalism appeared to a great many people to offer a more effective challenge to Western imperialism than nationalism once did. As important, though, and perhaps even more important, Islamic fundamentalist movements often proved to be very effective at taking on resource allocation tasks abandoned by retrenching states.

There are thus two distinct sources of support for Islamic fundamentalism, one coming from the elites driving these organizations, the other from the mass bases underpinning them. Speaking of the first group, Islamic fundamentalism has attracted highly educated people with its ideology of resistance to imperialism and Western domination. Gilles Kepel has noted a heavy representation of people with scientific and technical training among all fundamentalist movements, including those of Islam.[91] Active support has also come from traditional middle-class or petty bourgeois elements, such as merchants, traders, small-business people, and *bazaaris*.[92] However, this ideological support base, the most devoted component, usually accounts for a small share of a movement's base. In Turkey, for example, it is estimated that no more than a third, and perhaps less than a tenth, of support for the chief

Islamist party has come from people who share its religious ideology.[93]

If rebels need a sea of support in which to swim, the Islamists, as they are also known, have created one through good works among those who have been marginalized by the changes in the global economy and consequent experiences with structural adjustment. Economic liberalization has increased the wealth of a minority without a corresponding gain for the majority. Hence, secular nationalist states that gained their legitimacy as protector states have now largely lost this status.[94] Rival elites to those of the secular nationalists have frequently filled the vacuum.

All over the Arab world, in the midst of growing shortages of jobs, housing, education, and services, not to mention a widening pattern of income distribution that is fueling a resentment of the privileged classes, many people—particularly young men, who are left idle and without appreciable prospects—have gravitated to the support networks of Islamist organizations, be they clinics, schools, daycare centers, welfare distribution programs, investment companies, or even banks.[95] In the 1992 Cairo earthquake, unofficial Islamist groups rather than the state were the first to provide shelter and medical relief. In Palestine and Lebanon they have provided basic social services, such as medical assistance, education, an alternative legal system, and low-priced or free basic goods.[96] In southern Lebanon, the Islamist movement Hizbollah, created in the early 1980s, built up its popular support not only because of its fight against Israeli occupation but because of the social services it offered the poor. Financed by the Iranian government, Hizbollah built up a complex of social institutions, which included schools, orphanages, and religious study circles. Given the virtual disappearance of the Lebanese state in the civil war, this network attracted war-displaced and rural migrant Shi'ites to Hizbollah.[97] After Israel's "Grapes of Wrath" onslaught in 1996, Hizbollah claimed credibly to have repaired 5,000 Lebanese homes, rebuilt many roads, and paid compensation to 2,300 farmers.[98] In Pakistan, where deep budget cuts worsened the public education system, Islamists stepped into the breach and now educate between 2.5 million and 3.5 million students in their own schools and academies.[99] In Jordan, the Muslim Brotherhood has similarly devoted itself to developing the social and cultural infrastructure of an Islamic republic. In Indonesia, Islamic organizations grew throughout the 1970s and 1980s and the largest, the Muhhammadijah, eventually created a virtual welfare state with cradle-to-grave services offered through a network of schools, clinics, hospitals, and university-level institutions.[100]

Most of these organizations were formed in the 1970s and 1980s, but one of the earliest ones emerged in Turkey. There an Islamist party appeared as early as the late 1960s, though it was reborn in a couple of guises before rising to the heights of power in the 1990s under the name of the Refah (Welfare) Party. In Turkey, the once-predominant state suffered one setback after another, leaving many of its poorest citizens outside its once wide skirts. Refah, reborn yet again as the Virtue Party after the former was outlawed in 1998, has acted as much as a social welfare agency as a political party, obtaining appointments for people at hospitals and other public agencies. In the municipalities it has controlled, it has distributed coal, clothing, soup, and food to the needy.[101] It appeals to recent migrants from the countryside who have come to the city in search of better accommodation, and helps them find both housing and, very importantly, friends. It even arranges for children to be assisted with their homework, and maintains a well-organized network of activists, including women who can arrange home visits at any time.[102] Needless to say, this provides Islamist elites with close links to a growing support base that is being fed to them by economic liberalization.

In the wake of the 1979 Iranian revolution, there were hopes (and fears) that an Islamic tide would sweep through the Middle East, installing theocracies in all Muslim countries. By the 1990s, though, the fundamentalists seemed to be on the defensive. Only in Iran, Afghanistan, and Sudan did they take power; in the latter two, the governments were not secure, while in the first, it presided over a feeble economy. The disappointed hopes of the Islamists led some scholars to declare the movement all but dead by the end of the 1990s.[103] Turning to the grassroots, though, the picture looks different. All over the Muslim world fundamentalist movements have emerged to unnerve and challenge the legal authorities. In some countries, like Tajikistan and Algeria, they include guerrilla armies that have at times posed a serious threat to the state. In others, like Turkey, Palestine, and Bangladesh, their effectiveness is as rivals to the state that may, in time, capture state power through democratic means (Turkey's Islamists are ascendant in this respect). Their ideologies typically are anti-Western, and their leaders seek to resist globalization by breaking with the West and forging an Islamic trade bloc. Most important, as the tragic events of 11 September 2001 revealed, they need little in the way of state patronage to make their force felt. In fact, it appears they can thrive in contexts in which the state's authority has collapsed: postmodern politics feeds fundamentalist politics.

Hindu fundamentalism differs in some respects from Islamic fundamentalism. To begin with, it is not a transnational movement, in that it does not seek to transcend or replace the nation-state. Focused on one country, it seeks instead to protect India from outside influences and therefore is often referred to as Hindu nationalism. Given the primary (though hardly the only) religious divide between Muslims and Hindus in Indian politics, Hindu fundamentalism can also be seen as a sort of tribal politics, a means of securing privileged access to resources for members of the political networks affiliated to Hindu organizations. Still, in other respects, Hindu fundamentalism bears a resemblance to other varieties of fundamentalism. Christophe Jaffrelot notes how Hindu nationalists copied Western missionaries in forming their ideology. Anxious to have some fundamentals that they could impart to their flock, they virtually created a canon out of the plethora of sacred Hindu texts.[104] This stress on fundamentals was then coupled with a call for a return to the glories of the past, although modern fundamentalists do not renounce the tools of modernity in the pursuit of this goal. Indeed, the Hindu nationalist Bharatiya Janata Party (BJP) was proud to declare itself the first Indian party with an Internet website. Like Islamic fundamentalists, Hindu nationalists stress the preservation and even restoration of cultural purity, rejecting Western, Christian, and Muslim cultural influences. They seek to import religion into politics and to build a society more consonant with Hindu traditions. They also see much of the secular modernist project of contemporary India's founding fathers as morally bankrupt and, today, a spent force. The support bases of Hindu fundamentalism also resemble those of Islamic fundamentalist movements, and in both cases these support bases have emerged as a result of global economic changes. Hence, like Islamic fundamentalism, Hindu fundamentalism has grown dramatically since the 1970s.

Two political parties in particular have embodied Hindu fundamentalism in India. These are the BJP, which has an almost nationwide profile, and Shiv Sena, its more militant coalition partner in the populous industrial state of Maharashtra. Shiv Sena was formed in 1966 and the BJP in 1980. Yet despite its recent creation, the BJP has deep roots, following in a long line of organizations that, dating back to the nineteenth century, sought to resist the corrupting effects of British colonialism.

In the decades following India's independence from Britain, Hindu fundamentalists enjoyed little political success. This was because, as was then the case in the Arab world, nationalism had won many adherents. From the 1930s the ruling Congress Party, through its control of regional councils,[105] had forged alliances with rural elites, whom it brought into its distributional networks. Once it declared independence, the Congress Party set about creating a large state industrial sector and assumed direction of the economy. While it borrowed the idea of the five-year plan from communist states, the Indian government nurtured the development of a private sector. Still, by retaining control of so much of the country's resource-generating and resource-allocating powers, the Congress Party managed, by drawing powerful elites into its patronage network, to build up its networks of support and draw most Indians into the developmentalist regime it had created. In the early years of independence, India's economy grew quickly, making the fruits of modernity gradually apparent to ordinary Indians, particularly in the cities. From independence in 1947 to 1967, the governing Congress Party used transfer payments and state employment to draw support from most sectors of society.[106] Interestingly, not only traditionalists but radicals too found themselves increasingly edged out by a regime that was winning the adherence of more and more people. In Bombay, for example, India's leading industrial city, rapid industrialization from 1955 to 1965 created so much employment and helped drive wages up so far that communist militancy seemed futile. In the words of one unionist, "the tribunals and courts granted almost every wage demand, and the feeling that the mill owner and the government were friends of the working class grew strong."[107]

However, the regime began to descend into crisis in the 1960s. Indira Gandhi inherited the mantle of leadership from her father, Jawaharlal Nehru, and turned the Congress Party away from its elite accommodationist practices and toward the left. She adopted a populist strategy in which the state took over many of the resource-distributing functions previously performed by local elites. By this time, the power of local elites was weakening in many places: capitalism was penetrating more deeply into the countryside, replacing traditional relationships with contractual ones and thereby attenuating the authority that went along with the traditional relationship.[108] This reinforced the position of national elites. But the strategy also coincided with a time of economic crisis. By the mid-1960s, India's economic growth was slowing. Buoyed by new Green Revolution technologies, agriculture managed to maintain its vigor until the end of the decade, but industry was running into problems. Meanwhile, the failure of India's nationalist leaders to seriously challenge the power of landowning elites at the time of independence came back to haunt them. The concentration of land and industrial assets in a relatively small number of hands meant that a small, privileged part of the population experienced very large income gains, while the mass of the urban population saw conditions stay much the same or even worsen.[109] To make matters worse, distributional problems intensified the impact of the economic downturn in many areas. From the point of view of many Indians, a crisis had emerged.[110]

It was in this climate of rising unemployment and growing economic deprivation that Shiv Sena was born. From its inception it was led by Bal Thackeray, by profession a political cartoonist. Unabashedly nationalistic and militantly Hindu, Thackeray's primary appeal seems never to have been religious or even, it would seem, cultural. Since independence, Maharashtrians tended to be less educated and literate than migrants from elsewhere in India, and the Bombay business community came to be dominated by outsiders. Hence, Maharashtrians were especially hard hit by the economic downturn. Thackeray's call to limit migration and favor native Maharastrians in employment touched a sympathetic chord. In some cases, Shiv Sena gangs got involved in communal violence with the aim of discouraging further migration to Bombay. But Shiv Sena did more than just echo the anger of Maharashtrians. The organization built up an elaborate network of services that dealt with everything from domestic quarrels to leaking pipes, helped Shiv Sena's supporters find jobs, provided legal services to members in trouble with the law, and organized cultural festivals and theaters that charged nominal admission prices.[111] With economic circumstances leaving many Maharashtrians in Bombay feeling vulnerable, Shiv Sena emerged to pick up followers with its program of distribution.

On the national level, the Hindu fundamentalists had tried creating several parties and organizations over the decades, but none of them attained anything close to Shiv Sena's success in Bombay. Things changed in the 1980s, though. The BJP came into being but at first enjoyed little electoral success. However, as the 1980s went on, it shifted further to the right.[112] As part of its rightward shift, the BJP also adopted a neoliberal economic agenda, yet coupled it to a program of economic nationalism that favored the protection and promotion of Indian firms against foreign competition. The strategy seemed to work, for in election after election the BJP augmented its parliamentary representation. By the 1990s it was knocking down one Congress Party government after another in state elections. Finally, in the 1996 nationwide election, it replaced the Congress Party as the leading parliamentary bloc, a position it solidified in the 1998 polls.

The phoenix-like rise of the BJP did not result simply from its ideological repackaging, though. It had positioned itself very well to fill the void left by the atrophy of the developmentalist regime that the Congress Party had created and tried to maintain since India's independence. The erosion in the Congress Party's distributional networks accelerated in the mid-1980s, when India began its first, tentative efforts at economic reform and liberalization. The 1980s were not bad years for India's economy, all things considered, and enabled the government to postpone the dismantling of much of its state economic apparatus. But that all changed in 1991. For in that year India ran into a balance-of-payments crisis, whereupon the government opted for shock therapy. India began structural adjustment in earnest. In so doing the government renounced many of the levers it had used to manage the economy and control resource distribution.

As everywhere, structural adjustment wrought profound changes in Indian society. Growth resumed and some businesses began to thrive, but the wealth gap widened and many Indians were left more exposed to the changing winds of a harsh economic climate than before. At the same time, structural adjustment intensified a process under way for some time: the rise of a middle class who saw themselves as increasingly self-reliant and less respectful of state elites. These Indians had gradually moved from an acceptance of traditional authority structures toward a belief that they themselves could effect change, and this new self-consciousness made them receptive to the BJP's stress on identity issues.[113] Believing that the Congress Party, allied as it was to powerful landed and industrial interests, no longer served their interests, they began switching to the BJP.[114] The party's principles spoke to the typical middle-class concerns of this India: people who were comfortable but not rich—shopkeepers, owners of small businesses, school and college teachers, and junior civil servants—while the party also attracted considerable support in rural areas.[115] As the state retreated from economic life, the BJP may also have benefited from its organizational structure to pick up support. After some relatively fruitless experiments at elite accommodation, the BJP in the late 1980s renewed its emphasis on grassroots organization and social work among the poor.[116] Opening its doors to Indians excluded from the heights of political networks, the BJP found a large and rapidly expanding political market.

The dangers of this fundamentalism became apparent in late 2001, when Hindu fundamentalism and Islamic fundamentalism effectively came face-to-face in Kashmir. As Islamist militants, some connected to the Pakistani state, launched attacks on India, a government committed to the "Hinduness" of India—so much so that it was accused of turning a blind eye to anti-Muslim riots within India in the months that followed—came under pressure from its constituents to take a firm line against a Muslim enemy. For their part, the Islamic militants behind the attack on the Indian parliament at the end of 2001 were suspected in some quarters of being connected to the Al-Qaida network, and of seeking to open another front in their war against the United States by diverting Pakistani troops from the Afghan border to the increasingly militarized frontier with India. This, and the fact that both India and Pakistan were by now nuclear-armed, gave a regional struggle global dimensions. Once again, globalization and localization fed off one another.

What conclusions can be drawn from this comparison of fundamentalisms? The first thing that can be said is that in some respects fundamentalism represents the Third World version of the same trends in the industrial democracies that were discussed earlier. There, economic changes, and in particular the growth of a middle class alongside widening income disparities, gave rise to the new right and far right respectively. The far right, in turn, was being fed a support base largely by an imploding left. There are broad parallels to this in some of the societies just mentioned. There is not a new right and far right, but there are moderate and extreme fundamentalists. The moderates, like the BJP in India or the Islamic Salvation Front in Algeria, draw support from a middle class increasingly angry with the excesses of a privileged political-economic elite. The extremists, like India's Shiv Sena or Algeria's Armed Islamic Group, the latter a shadowy army of savage guerrillas composed mainly of unemployed young men[117]—the same profile, one recalls, of the typical far-right supporter in a First World country—draw support from those who feel themselves to have been pushed out of the regime. In those countries where the left had once been strong, its own weakness has in part accounted for a rise of extreme fundamentalists. For instance, Dipankar Gupta has connected the rise of Shiv Sena to a crisis of the left in Maharashtra state;[118] indeed, in most of India, the left and its working-class support base became largely demobilized in the postindependence period.[119] In Turkey, meanwhile, the Welfare Party has largely replaced the leftist parties, which shun populism, in addressing such matters as equality, social security, welfare, and social justice.[120]

The role of middle classes in undermining the developmentalist regimes of Third World nation-states deserves special mention. Long derided by fashionable opinion for being the sociocultural equivalent of white bread, the middle class may now be entering its own in Third World politics. As this class has grown in size, so it has augmented its political influence. Samuel Huntington has identified the growth of the middle class as a key factor in the push for democratization in a number of Third World countries.[121] In Asia at the end of the 1990s, governments in Thailand and, in some respects, Indonesia were brought down by middle-class revolts against unpopular leaders. One can include, along with these, the drive against corruption in South

Korea. In all these cases, the revolt targeted corruption and state excess and demanded political reform. In all countries, state-led development strategies had, in more prosperous days, enabled political elites to favor some clients with huge amounts of public money. Corruption was a way of life, but most citizens tolerated it since they were not prevented from getting their share of the spoils. But in the era of structural adjustment, citizens cut off from access to public largesse have demanded the same probity of their leaders. Where the constituency cutoff is primarily the poor, riots have often resulted. But where a large middle class exists, the push has been for reform and liberalization.

If one were to draw a profile of this new middle-class citizen in the Third World, it would be of a person who sees him- or herself standing somewhere between the ignorance of the rural poor and the cosmopolitanism of the urban elite.[122] This citizen is independent, but not as rich and worldly as the member of what earlier in the book was called the new global middle class. Therefore, this new middle-class citizen neither clings to tradition nor fawns at Westernization. Bound to the state neither as patron nor client, this person seeks autonomy and a space in which to accomplish his or her own resource accumulation. Even if this person's ideological orientation seems profoundly different from that of a First World petty bourgeois voter, in fact the new middle-class citizen reflects similar concerns and his or her rise to prominence has occurred at much the same time.

Earlier, we saw the way in which the rise of the middle class has permanently altered the politics of the First World, providing a support base for the new right and weakening the old left. The support of "petty bourgeois" voters for parties of the right and at times the far right is an ongoing source of interest for political scientists. The tendency of the emerging middle classes in many Third World countries to back fundamentalist organizations finds an interesting parallel in France in the 1950s, when people of similar class backgrounds—shopkeepers and small farmers—supported the far right *poujadiste* movement.[123] But there is one fundamental difference between the *poujadiste* middle-class revolt and that underlying support for fundamentalism. *Poujadisme* represented a last-gasp effort by a declining class to cling to a fast-disappearing way of life. In contrast, the middle-class constituency underlying fundamentalism in the Third World is growing, and the changes that brought it into existence will be around for some time. Combine this with the fact that the conditions of the Third World poor show few signs of improving, and that their ranks show few signs of thinning anytime soon, and this other constituency for fundamentalism remains solid. Fundamentalism in the Third World will be anything but ephemeral.

Yet while often interpreted as a manifestation of cultural resistance to globalization, fundamentalism is locked in a paradoxical symbiosis with the latter. For example, Islamic fundamentalism sees the U.S. presence in and support for regimes in the Middle East as a form of neoimperialism revolving around control of the region's oil supply. Fundamentalists want Muslim states to retake control of this commodity. The United States wants to keep the supply open at all costs, fundamentalists want to close or at least control it. Yet the financial resources that support many Islamist movements come largely from oil revenues, such that Islamists depend on continued oil sales to the West for their existence. Thus fundamentalism cannot effectively resist globalization, for it depends upon it. However, as we shall see, it may all the same be deepening the crisis of neoliberalism, rendering the regime increasingly fragile.

Conclusion

What, then, are the key conclusions to be reached from this discussion? Over the past twenty years or so, neoliberal regimes have replaced the Keynesian welfare state, the developmentalist state, and communism in most of the world. The result was a period of high growth but increased marginalization, or put differently, a period characterized by effective accumulation regimes but ineffective distribution regimes. The outcome was unstable political conditions and the emergence of antisystemic tendencies that, in threatening political stability, heralded a possible crisis of neoliberalism.

As has been argued, the crisis of neoliberalism has given rise to various improvisations and attempts at resolution. Nonetheless, the symptoms persist and, indeed, worsen. Nor do any of the attempts at resolution look likely to provide viable alternative regimes. If they try various ad hoc approaches to tackle the distributional crisis, they fail to effectively challenge the neoliberal accumulation regime that lies at its heart. Indeed, as the 1990s drew to a close, neoliberalism appeared more solidly entrenched than ever.

However, neoliberalism appeared to be undermining itself, as the next chapter will show. The symptoms of crisis that first became manifest in the Third World began to have profound repercussions in the First World. And by the end of the twentieth century, the crisis had come home to the neoliberal heartland.

Notes

1. See, for instance, Gilles Kepel, *Jihad: Expansion et déclin de l'Islamisme* (Paris: Gallimard, 2000).

2. See, for instance, Samuel Huntington, *The Third Wave: Democratization in the Late Twentieth Century* (Norman: University of Oklahoma Press, 1991); and Francis Fukuyama, *The End of History and the Last Man* (New York: Free Press, 1992).

3. Arthur Schlesinger Jr., "Has Democracy a Future?" *Foreign Affairs* 76, no. 5 (September–October 1997): 2–12. See also Larry Diamond, "Is the Third Wave Over?" *Journal of Democracy,* July 1996, pp. 20–37; and Fareed Zakaria, "The Rise of Illiberal Democracy," *Foreign Affairs* (November–December 1997): 22–43.

4. For a fuller discussion, see the United Nations Development Programme's 2002 Human Development Report, titled *Deepening Democracy in a Fragmented World* (New York: Oxford University Press, 2002).

5. In survey responses, "Don't know" was the most common answer given as to why workers supported Labour. See Mark Abrams, "Social Class and British Politics," *Public Opinion Quarterly* 25, no. 3 (1961): 342–350.

6. In elections in 1995, 40 percent of Belgian voters were still undecided shortly before the election. William M. Downs, "Federalism Achieved: The Belgian Elections of May 1995," *West European Politics* 19 (1996): 171–172. Whereas in France, most voters in the first round of the presidential election did not even have preferred candidates but voted against those they disliked. Radio France Internationale 23 April 1995.

7. *Financial Times* (London), 29 June 1995.

8. Benjamin Radcliff and Patricia Davis, "Labor Organization and Electoral Participation in Industrial Democracies," *American Journal of Political Science* 44, no. 1 (January 2000): 132–141, finds that the strength of the labor movement has a strong impact on aggregate rates of voter turnout.

9. For examples of this line of reasoning, see Ernesto Laclau and Chantal Mouffe, "Hegemony and Radical Democracy," in Ernesto Laclau and Chantal Mouffe, trans. Winston Moore and Paul Cammack, *Hegemony and Socialist Strategy* (London: Verso, 1985); and Chantal Mouffe, "Working-Class Hegemony and the Struggle for Socialism," *Studies in Political Economy* 12 (Fall 1983).

10. Ronald Inglehart, *The Silent Revolution* (Princeton: Princeton University Press, 1977). See also Ronald Inglehart and Paul R. Abramson, "Economic Security and Value Change," *American Political Science Review* 88 (1994): 336–354, in which the thesis is reaffirmed for the 1990s, but with the caveat that postmaterialism may decline in times of economic insecurity.

11. Jeremy Richardson, "The Market for Political Activism: Interest Groups as a Challenge to Political Parties," *West European Politics* 18, no. 1 (1995): 116–139. Compare Ruud Koopmans, "New Social Movements and Changes in Political Participation in Western Europe," *West European Politics* 19, no. 1 (January 1996): 28–50.

12. See Mancur Olson Jr., *The Logic of Collective Action* (Cambridge: Harvard University Press, 1965). As E. E. Schattschneider put it, "The flaw in

the pluralist heaven is that the heavenly chorus sings with a strong upper class accent." E. E. Schattschneider, *The Semisovereign People* (New York: Holt, 1960), p. 35.

13. For discussion on this, see Samuel Huntington, *Political Order in Changing Societies* (New Haven: Yale University Press, 1968); Daniel Lerner, "Toward a Communication Theory of Modernization," in *Communications and Political Development,* edited by Lucian Pye (Princeton: Princeton University Press, 1963); and Ted Robert Gurr, *Why Men Rebel* (Princeton: Princeton University Press, 1970).

14. While distrust of politicians has been rising in most of the industrial democracies over the past few decades, the causes remain uncertain and complex. See Joseph S. Nye, Philip D. Zelikow, and David C. King, eds., *Why People Don't Trust Government* (Cambridge: Harvard University Press, 1997). However, among young people, evidence of a turning away from a political system seen to be neglecting their concerns seems less ambiguous. See, for example, Mark Strama, "Overcoming Cynicism: Youth Participation and Electoral Politics," *National Civic Review* 87, no. 1 (Spring 1998): 71–77, which ascribes growing youth cynicism to a revulsion at the role of money in politics; and W. Lance Bennett, "The Uncivic Culture: Communication, Identity, and the Rise of Lifestyle Politics," *PS: Political Science and Politics* 31, no. 4 (December 1998): 741–761.

15. *Financial Times* (London), 5 July 1995.

16. *Monitor Radio International,* 15 August 1995.

17. See the report in *Le Nouvel Observateur* (Paris), 2 November 1995.

18. See, for instance, Michael Lind, *The Next American Nation* (New York: Free Press, 1996). Lind's thesis apparently finds empirical support in W. Avon Drake and Robert D. Holsworth, *Affirmative Action and the Stalled Quest for Black Progress* (Urbana: University of Illinois Press, 1996).

19. Evidence suggests that support for far-right political parties in Western Europe tends to come disproportionately from among young voters. See Hans-Georg Betz and Stefan Immerfall, eds., *The New Politics of the Right* (New York: St. Martin's Press, 1998), esp. pp. 19, 35, 70; Paul Hainsworth and Paul Mitchell, "France: The Front National from Crossroads to Crossroads?" *Parliamentary Affairs* 53 (2000): 443–456, and esp. p. 447; and Anders Widfeldt, "Scandinavia: Mixed Success for the Populist Right," *Parliamentary Affairs* 53 (2000): 486–500, and esp. p. 497.

20. Daniel Junas, "The Rise of the Citizen Militias," *Covert Action Quarterly,* Spring 1995.

21. Hans-Georg Betz, *Radical Right-Wing Populism in Western Europe* (London: Macmillan, 1994), chap. 5.

22. Jonathan Marcus, "Advance or Consolidation? The French National Front and the 1995 Elections," *West European Politics* 19 (1996): 303–320; Hainsworth and Mitchell, "France."

23. Marcus, "Advance or Consolidation?"

24. Joseph Szarka, "The Winning of the 1995 French Presidential Election," *West European Politics* 19 (1996): 151–167.

25. Downs, "Federalism Achieved," p. 171.

26. Thomas S. Szayna, "Ultra-Nationalism in Central Europe," *Orbis* 37 (1993): 527–550.

27. By 1996, more than 50 percent of Austria's working-class voters, the traditional backbone of the Socialists, had switched allegiance to the Freedom Party in European elections. Reuters, 19 October 1996.

28. Widfeldt, "Scandinavia."

29. *Financial Times* (London), 13–14 April 1996, p. 2.

30. Roger Karapin, "Radical-Right and Neo-Fascist Political Parties in Western Europe," *Comparative Politics* 30 (1998): 213–234, identifies immigration as the main focus of the most successful far-right parties in Europe.

31. For example, in September 1996 the French interior minister's popularity soared after he ordered police to raid a Paris church and evict African immigrants seeking legal residence. Reuters, 7 September 1996.

32. *Financial Times* (London), 7 June 1997.

33. Take, for instance, the Czech Republic, where in 1992 there were 160 racist attacks, mainly against Gypsies, a big increase over the previous year. CET Online (Internet newsletter), 17 May 1995.

34. Karapin, "Radical-Right."

35. Karapin, "Radical-Right," p. 223; Hans-Georg Betz, "The New Politics of Resentment: Radical Right-Wing Populist Parties in Western Europe," *Comparative Politics* 25 (1993): 413–427.

36. For a detailed look, see Raphael S. Ezekiel, *The Racist Mind: Portraits of American Neo-Nazis and Klansmen* (New York: Penguin Books, 1995).

37. In *Fuhrer-Ex: Memoirs of a Former Neo-Nazi* (London: Chatto and Windus, 1996), Ingo Hasselbach noted in particular the role of Garry Lauck, an American who in 1996 was sentenced in a German court to four years imprisonment for his neo-Nazi activities.

38. *Le Soir* (Brussels), 20 December 1994.

39. See, for example, the poll in *Le Nouvel Observateur* (Paris), 2–8 February 1995, in the run-up to that year's French presidential election.

40. Radio Deutsche Welle, 19 March 1996.

41. BBC World Service, 11 March 1998.

42. "Men do not long desire self-government for its own sake. They desire it for the sake of results. That is why the impulse to self-government is always strongest as a protest against bad conditions." See Walter Lippman, *Public Opinion* (New York: Harcourt, Brace, 1922), p. 312.

43. Adam Przeworski, *Democracy and the Market: Political and Economic Reforms in Eastern Europe and Latin America* (Cambridge: Cambridge University Press, 1991), p. 30. See also Adam Przeworski, Michael Alvarez, José Antonio Cheibub, and Fernando Limongi, "What Makes Democracies Endure," *Journal of Democracy* 7, no. 1 (1996): 39–56; and Huntington, *Third Wave.*

44. Richard Rose, "Ex-Communists in Post-Communist Societies," *The Political Quarterly* 67, no. 1 (1996): 14–25; Iurii Levada, "'Homo Sovieticus' Five Years Later: 1989–1994," *Russian Social Science Review* 37, no. 4 (1996): 3–17.

45. Grigory Vainshtein, "Totalitarian Public Consciousness in a Post-Totalitarian Society: The Russian Case in the General Context of Post-Communist Developments," *Communist and Post-Communist Studies* 27 (1994): 247–259; Susan Rose-Ackerman, "Trust and Honesty in Post-Socialist Societies," *Kyklos* 54 (2001): 415–444.

46. James L. Gibson, "A Mile Wide but an Inch Deep (?): The Structure of Democratic Commitments in the Former USSR," *American Journal of Political Science* 40 (1996): 396–420.

47. In terms of votes, the showing of the National Front candidate scarcely improved over the 1995 election, but the decline in voter turnout meant that the National Front's static vote tally became a proportionate gain. Although young voters, apparently repentant that their abstention had aided the rise of Jean-Marie le Pen, turned out in sufficient numbers for the second round of voting to trounce the far-right candidate, they returned to their sluggish habits when the parliamentary elections came around a month later.

48. John Newhouse, "Europe's Rising Regionalism," *Foreign Affairs* 76, no. 1 (January–February 1997): 67–84.

49. Pranab Bardhan, "Method in the Madness? A Political-Economy Analysis of the Ethnic Conflicts in Less Developed Countries," *World Development* 25, no. 9 (1997): 1381–1398.

50. Treviso, in the north of Italy, is one of the country's fastest-growing districts, but its infrastructure remains poor. In the 1996 general elections, 42 percent of its votes went to the Northern League, well above the national average and apparently motivated by a perception that "Treviso gives a lot to Rome, and gets very little back." *The Economist* (London), 25 May 1996, p. 35.

51. As *The Economist* (London), 22–28 February 1997, put it, the Flemish wanted more autonomy from the Walloons, "whom they regard as addicts of public aid to crumbling industries."

52. See Christopher Lasch, *The Revolt of the Elites and the Betrayal of Democracy* (New York: W. W. Norton, 1995). Evan McKenzie, in *Privatopia: Homeowner Associations and the Rise of Residential Private Government* (New Haven: Yale University Press, 1994), points out that over one-tenth of Americans now live in common-interest developments (e.g., condominiums). Boosted by demand coming from these developments, private security guards now outnumber police in the United States. This has resulted in what Robert B. Reich, in *The Work of Nations* (New York: Alfred A. Knopf, 1991), has called the secession of the successful, manifested in such things as condominium owners opposing double taxation—paying municipal taxes for the services they get from paying condominium fees—and lessening their participation in municipal politics. Some scholars believe that this is worsening class divisions, which take this added geographical shape.

53. Tom Courchene with Colin R. Telmer, *From the Heartland to North American Region State: The Social, Fiscal, and Federal Evolution of Ontario* (Toronto: Centre for Public Management, Faculty of Management, University of Toronto, 1998).

54. *Ottawa Citizen*, 25 September 1997.

55. Mihailo Crnobrnja, *The Yugoslav Drama*, 2nd ed. (Montreal: McGill-Queen's Press, 1996).

56. Robert J. Donia and John V. A. Fine Jr., *Bosnia and Hercegovina: A Tradition Betrayed* (New York: Columbia University Press, 1994), pp. 188–189.

57. Ibid., p. 199.

58. Ibid., pp. 190–191.

59. Bruno Dallago and Milica Uvalic, "The Distributive Consequences of Nationalism: The Case of Former Yugoslavia," *Europe-Asia Studies* 50, no. 1 (1998): 71–90.

60. See Laura Silber and Allan Little, *The Death of Yugoslavia,* rev. ed. (London: Penguin, 1996), chaps. 1–2. See also Bardhan, "Method in the Madness?"

61. Donia and Fine, *Bosnia and Hercegovina,* p. 223.

62. For details, see Gérard Prunier, *The Rwanda Crisis* (London: Hurst, 1995), pp. 11–12.

63. Colette Braeckman, *Rwanda: Histoire d'un génocide* (Paris: Fayard, 1994), pp. 35–36. Compare René Lemarchand, *Burundi: Ethnic Conflict and Genocide* (New York: Woodrow Wilson Center Press, 1996), pp. 9–10.

64. Claudine Vidal, "Les politiques de la haine," *Les Temps Modernes* 583 (1995): 6–33.

65. As Gérard Prunier says, the centralization was originally a "centre versus periphery affair and not one of Tutsi versus Hutu." Prunier, *Rwanda Crisis,* p. 21.

66. See Prunier, *Rwanda Crisis,* pp. 67–74.

67. Braeckman, *Rwanda,* p. 58.

68. Prunier, *Rwanda Crisis,* p. 87.

69. David Newbury, "Understanding Genocide," *African Studies Review* 41, no. 1 (April 1998): 73–97.

70. "The people are water, the Eighth Route Army are fish; without water the fish will die." The slogan has also been attributed to Chu Te and P'eng Te-huai. See Geoffrey Fairbairn, *Revolutionary Guerrilla Warfare* (London: Penguin, 1974), p. 99.

71. For closer looks at the Rwandan genocide, see Prunier, *Rwanda Crisis;* Braeckman, *Rwanda;* Vidal, "Les politiques de la haine"; Newbury, "Understanding Genocide"; and Alex De Waal and Rakiya Omaar, "The Genocide in Rwanda and the International Response," *Current History,* April 1995, pp. 156–161.

72. Prunier, *Rwanda Crisis,* p. 261.

73. Ibid., pp. 231–232, 242–243.

74. Ibid., p. 142.

75. William Brustein, *The Logic of Evil: The Social Origins of the Nazi Party, 1925–1933* (New Haven: Yale University Press, 1996).

76. Lemarchand, *Burundi,* p. 102.

77. Algeria's daily *L'Authentique,* reporting on a massacre attributed to the government by the Armed Islamic Group (GIA) and carried out in late 1997, said that at least some of the GIA militants were former neighbors who were motivated not by ideology but by a desire to capture their neighbors' property. *Mail and Guardian* (Johannesburg), 6 January 1998. Given Algeria's

own government-imposed information famine, it is usually impossible to verify such claims.

78. Braeckman, *Rwanda*, pp. 228–229.

79. "Borderless World" is the title of an essay by Kenichi Ohmae. Kenichi Ohmae, *The Borderless World: Power and Strategy in the Interlinked Economy*, rev. ed. (New York: HarperBusiness, 1999).

80. The Zajedno opposition, whose tenacity and popularity shook the Milosevic-led elite, suggested that Kosovo was used by Milosevic to detract attention from the failures of his own policies.

81. See Mattias Gardell, *Countdown to Armageddon: Louis Farrakhan and the Nation of Islam* (London: Hurst, 1996), chap. 10.

82. For a case study of the way in which integration has affected the black bourgeoisie, see Robert E. Weems Jr., *Black Business in the Black Metropolis: The Chicago Metropolitan Assurance Company, 1925–1985* (Bloomington: Indiana University Press, 1996).

83. Ernest Allen Jr., "Religious Heterodoxy and Nationalist Tradition: The Continuing Evolution of the Nation of Islam," *Black Scholar* 26, nos. 3–4 (1996): 19.

84. As noted by Martin E. Marty and R. Scott Appleby, the fundamentals upon which such movements found themselves typically emerge from a "selective retrieval of doctrines, beliefs, and practices from a sacred past," which are then altered to suit contemporary circumstances. See the foreword by Martin E. Marty and R. Scott Appleby in *Islamic Fundamentalisms and the Gulf Crisis*, edited by James Piscatori (Chicago: Fundamentalism Project, American Academy of Arts and Sciences, 1991), p. xii. Sadik J. al-Azm argues that some Islamic fundamentalists drew their ideas or inspiration directly from U.S. Protestant fundamentalists. See Sadik J. al-Azm, "Islamic Fundamentalism Reconsidered: A Critical Outline of Problems, Ideas, and Approaches," *South Asia Bulletin* 13, nos. 1–2 (1993): 93–121; and 14, no. 1 (1994): 73–98.

85. Gilles Kepel, *The Revenge of God*, translated by Alan Braley (Cambridge: Polity Press, 1994), p. 31.

86. For an idea of the threat posed by left-wing Arab groups to conservative regimes in the 1960s and early 1970s, see Fred Halliday, *Arabia Without Sultans* (New York: Vintage Books, 1975).

87. Kepel, *Revenge of God;* Arjun Appadurai, *Modernity at Large: Cultural Dimensions of Globalization* (Minneapolis: University of Minnesota Press, 1996), pp. 37–39. See also Christophe Jaffrelot, *Les nationalistes hindous* (Paris: Presses de la Fondation Nationale des Sciences Politiques, 1993), pp. 406–407.

88. See Jaffrelot, *Les nationalistes hindous,* chap. 10.

89. Kepel, *Revenge of God,* chap. 1.

90. See, for example, M. Rashiduzzaman, "The Liberals and the Religious Right in Bangladesh," *Asian Survey* 34, no. 11 (1994): 974–990; and David Gibbs, "The Peasant as Counter-Revolutionary: The Rural Origins of the Afghan Insurgency," *Studies in Comparative International Development* 21, no. 1 (Spring 1986): 36–59.

91. Kepel, *Revenge of God.*

92. See Samuel Huntington, *The Clash of Civilizations and the Remaking of World Order* (New York: Simon and Schuster, 1996), p. 113; Ilkay Sunar and Binnaz Toprak, "Islam in Politics: The Case of Turkey," *Government and Opposition* 18 (1983): 421–441; and Nitish Dutt and Eddie J. Girdner, "Challenging the Rise of Nationalist-Religious Parties in India and Turkey," *Contemporary South Asia* 9, no. 1 (2000): 7–24.

93. Metin Heper, "Islam and Democracy in Turkey: Toward a Reconciliation?" *Middle East Journal* 51, no. 1 (Winter 1997): 32–45.

94. Jeremy Salt, "Nationalism and the Rise of Muslim Sentiment in Turkey," *Middle Eastern Studies* 31, no. 1 (1995): 13–27.

95. Mark Tessler, "The Origins of Popular Support for Islamist Movements: A Political Economy Analysis," in *Islam, Democracy, and the State in North Africa,* edited by John P. Entelis (Bloomington: Indiana University Press, 1997).

96. Fred Halliday, "The Politics of 'Islam': A Second Look," *British Journal of Political Science* 25 (1995): 399–417; Erika G. Alin, "Dynamics of the Palestinian Uprising: An Assessment of Causes, Character, and Consequences," *Comparative Politics* 26 (1994): 479–498.

97. Rosemary Sayigh, *Too Many Enemies: The Palestinian Experience in Lebanon* (London: Zed Books, 1994), p. 183.

98. *The Economist* (London), 7 September 1996.

99. Ahmed Rashid, "Pakistan: Trouble Ahead, Trouble Behind," *Current History* 95, no. 600 (April 1996): 160.

100. Huntington, *Clash of Civilizations,* p. 112.

101. Heper, "Islam and Democracy in Turkey."

102. Sencer Ayata, "Patronage, Party, and State: The Politicization of Islam in Turkey," *Middle East Journal* 50, no. 1 (1996): 40–56.

103. See, for example, Kepel, *Jihad.*

104. Jaffrelot, *Les nationalistes hindous;* Christophe Jaffrelot, "Le syncrétisme stratégique et la construction de l'identité nationaliste hindoue: L'identité comme produit de synthèse," *Revue Française de Science Politique* 42, no. 4 (August 1992): 594–617.

105. James Manor, "Anomie in Indian Politics: Origins and Potential Wider Impact," *Economic and Political Weekly,* annual no. 1983.

106. Pradeep Chhibber, "Who Voted for the Bharatiya Janata Party?" *British Journal of Political Science* 27, no. 4 (October 1997): 631–639.

107. Dipankar Gupta, *Nativism in a Metropolis: The Shiv Sena in Bombay* (New Delhi: Manohar, 1982), p. 59.

108. André Béteille, "The Indian Village Past and Present," in *Peasants in History: Essays in Honour of Daniel Thorner,* edited by E. J. Hobsbawm et al. (Bombay: Oxford University Press, 1980).

109. Francine Frankel, *India's Political Economy, 1947–1977: The Gradual Revolution* (Princeton: Princeton University Press, 1978), chap. 10.

110. Sudipta Kaviraj, "Indira Gandhi and Indian Politics," *Economic and Political Weekly* 19, nos. 38–39 (20–27 September 1986): 1697–1708.

111. See Gupta, *Nativism in a Metropolis,* for a detailed look at Shiv Sena. See also Sikata Banerjee, "The Feminization of Violence in Bombay: Women in the Politics of Shiv Sena," *Asian Survey* 36, no. 2 (1996): 1213–1225.

112. Manini Chatterjee, "The BJP: Political Mobilization for Hindutva," *South Asia Bulletin* 14, no. 1 (1994): 14–23.

113. Dennis Austin and Peter Lyon, "The Bharatiya Janata Party of India," *Government and Opposition* 28, no. 1 (Winter 1993): 36–50.

114. Chhibber, "Who Voted for the Bharatiya Janata Party?"

115. Chatterjee, "The BJP"; Dutt and Girdner, "Challenging the Rise of Nationalist-Religious Parties."

116. Jaffrelot, *Les nationalistes hindous,* pp. 475–484.

117. Barbara Smith, "Algeria: The Horror," *New York Review of Books,* 23 April 1998.

118. Gupta, *Nativism in a Metropolis.*

119. A. R. Kamat, "The Emerging Situation," *Economic and Political Weekly* 14, nos. 7–8 (February 1979): 349–354.

120. Ayata, "Patronage, Party, and State," p. 54.

121. See Huntington, *Third Wave.*

122. Compare Sunar and Toprak, "Islam in Politics," which speaks of the "townstyle" of the Turkish petty bourgeoisie, with Chatterjee, "The BJP," which speaks of an Indian middle class who are jealous of the cosmopolitan English-speaking elite while also fearful of a mass upsurge.

123. See Phillip M. Williams, *Crisis and Compromise: Politics in the Fourth Republic* (London: Longman, 1964), chap. 12.

6

The Crisis Comes Home

Regime crises produce the symptoms of disease discussed in the previous chapter. However, as with any illness, the symptoms are manifestations of the disease. In and of themselves, they do not bring about their own resolution, just as revolutionary situations do not in themselves produce revolutions. Early theorists of revolution like Lenin or Gramsci learned from experience what later, often less sympathetic students of revolution learned from their observation, namely that it takes a revolutionary action to tip a regime from crisis to collapse.

Equally, as we have seen, the symptoms of a crisis do not necessarily emerge at the point where they originated. Whereas much of the crisis of neoliberalism can be said to have originated in the First World, its symptoms have frequently first appeared in the Third World. Nevertheless, in time, the symptoms can create chain reactions that work their way back up the chain and ultimately show up close to their point of origin. At this stage, they may be misdiagnosed and assigned local causes. This, as we shall see, was the case with the economic downturn that took hold in the Western economies in 2000. From the outset, economists and analysts attributed the downturn to domestic factors, and thus predicted a short slowdown. In fact, the tensions began far away. Being thus far less easy to manage with traditional policy tools, they would render the slowdown not only a recession, but a recession of long duration.

Let us remember a basic thesis being used throughout this book: when pushed out of a regime, citizens will use whatever means they have at their disposal to obtain those resources they feel are rightly theirs. Sometimes this leads to a violent turn against the governing elite,

147

other times the behavior will be more peaceful and, on the surface at least, not obviously antisystemic. In this case, the reaction turned violent in the Third World, and would thus jeopardize the health of the U.S. economy, which had come to depend on the stability of Third World markets for much of its prosperity. At the same time, the bust in the United States would stand in direct proportion to the boom, because of tensions that accumulated in the U.S. economy as the U.S. regime crisis sought to resolve itself (apparently successfully, since tensions were all but absent in the United States in the 1990s; but as we shall see, the success was indeed *apparent*). Thus neoliberalism fueled the boom, creating a highly effective accumulation regime. Yet by building its accumulation regime on the ashes of the distribution regime it had dismantled, it sowed the seeds of its own eventual demise.

The Asian Crisis: The Zenith of Neoliberalism

In 1997, instability in East Asian financial markets both caused a global financial crisis and brought an end to the Asian economic boom. Although neoliberal policy reforms had caused the financial crisis in the first place, the irony is that the same crisis created an opportunity for the forces driving neoliberalism—spearheaded by the U.S. Treasury Department—to consolidate the hegemony of neoliberalism on a global scale. As the crisis worsened, the contagion spread beyond East and Southeast Asia. Third World governments that had benefited from the emerging-markets craze of the 1990s, when Western fund managers sought fast gains, found themselves tarred with the brush of risk. Capital began rushing out of the Third World and into "safe havens," particularly U.S. Treasury paper. Faced with a sudden loss of the investor confidence that had driven the boom, Third World governments were forced to turn to international financial agencies, and in particular the International Monetary Fund (IMF), for assistance. Desperate for capital to shore up beleaguered currencies and plunging stock and real estate markets, these governments could ill-resist the conditions that were being attached to financial aid. In particular, they were compelled to respond to the economic crisis by accelerating neoliberal reforms, further reducing the state's involvement in the economy and society (a role that had been quite ambitious in the case of the East Asian governments).

The long-celebrated East Asian boom had come thudding to a halt when the Thai bhat crashed in the summer of 1997, initiating a wave of financial crises that swept through East Asia. To some degree, both the boom and its bust can be seen as having been produced by neoliberalism. The initial phase of postwar rapid growth in East Asia arose mainly from domestic conditions and policies, but with the liberalization of capital markets from the 1980s, money rushed in to exploit the opportunities that were then seen to abound in these dynamic economies. This drove up asset and property values and, by strengthening the value of local currencies and thus raising the export prices of their goods, ate into the competitive edge that had been enjoyed by East Asian manufacturers. Consequently, over time, the underlying economic conditions started looking less promising. Consequently, money began to flow out and, in turn, asset and property values declined, as did the value of the currencies, which created a crisis of confidence and brought the region crashing down.[1] Given the globalized nature of capital markets, the contagion spread through the Third World as money flowed out of so-called emerging markets and into the perceived safe havens in Europe and North America.

The flight of capital from the world's equity markets provoked a global downturn. As a result, the world economy was teetering dangerously on the brink of crisis. Even the booming U.S. economy was not immune. By the autumn of 1998 the New York stock market had begun a seemingly inexorable slide that threatened a global recession. So, led by the U.S. administration, Western governments responded with a series of interest rate cuts and an infusion of capital into the Third World, which aimed to restore stability to markets and confidence in emerging economies. Despite the fact that he was facing impeachment by the U.S. Congress, President Bill Clinton persuaded the Republican leadership, which may have been tempted to pull up the drawbridges and create a fire wall between their country and the rest of the world, to inject tens of billions of dollars into the coffers of the IMF. These funds were then made available to embattled countries. It was hoped that the promise of a ready injection of hard currency would deter panicked investors from their course. In any event, the strategy worked, at least for a time, as stock markets rebounded and the outflow of capital from the Third World slowed. However, the price tag of assistance was high. Governments that were bailed out had to agree to accelerate neoliberal reforms, and the U.S. Treasury Department began to micromanage some of the economies to whose rescue it claimed to be coming. Even those governments that were not forced to turn to the IMF for assistance found their fiscal position strained by the global slowdown, and thus had to further tighten their belts.

In the short term, the U.S.-led bailout appeared to have worked so marvelously that many commentators were quick to dismiss the Asian crisis as a hiccup. Certainly from a U.S. vantage point, the times that followed had never been better. The massive flow of funds into the U.S. market actually fueled a powerful rebound in the stock market, which was further strengthened by the interest rate cuts, while global deflation took the sting out of any building inflationary pressures. Yet the relief would prove temporary.

Though the spending cuts of austerity packages were not supposed to target the poor, the fact that policy reforms were designed to preserve the asset values of mostly rich investors could scarcely have been lost on poor people, who experienced the backwash of the crisis in higher costs for basic goods in the midst of an economic recession. A rebellion against neoliberalism began to take hold.

The year 1999 seemed to be the pivotal point. In the spring of that year, for instance, the Jamaican government, desperate to raise revenue to plug its growing fiscal gap, raised the tax on petroleum. In so doing it had overlooked what might have seemed an obvious lesson of history: not only had gas price rises led to rioting in Jamaica a decade earlier, but the hike in the price of cooking oil had helped bring down the Indonesian government the year before. Within a day of the government's announcement, roadblocks cropped up at a few Kingston intersections as commuters in crowded transit areas, their anger fueled by the rising heat, broke into spontaneous protests. Within days these protests spread, and by the following week they had broken into a full-scale frenzy of rioting that shut down the island. Eventually the government was forced to back down from its proposed gas tax.

Jamaica hardly stood alone that spring. Around the world, similar events were taking place as mass protests demanded an attenuation or end to neoliberal reforms. There were nationwide strikes in Colombia and Ecuador as workers protested the impact of government cutbacks. Doctors in the Dominican Republic went on strike over unpaid wages, and teachers in Haiti rioted over pay. South Korea's Confederation of Trade Unions waged an "all-out" struggle against the government's plans to restructure the economy. Romanian miners marched on Bucharest, demanding pay raises and an end to pit closures. The Ford Motor Company suspended operations at its Brazil plant because workers sacked before Christmas returned to occupy it. Rioting in Indonesia, spurred by the uneven distribution of gains across ethnic groups, continued without letup. Meanwhile in China, Argentina, Mexico, and South Africa, slowing economies, rising unemployment, and widening incomes gaps gave rise to sharp increases in the crime rate.

As the year progressed, there were national strikes in Bangladesh,

Peru, the Dominican Republic, El Salvador, Colombia, Burkina Faso, Pakistan, and Romania. Student demonstrations protesting cuts in education spending turned violent in Chile and Côte d'Ivoire. Farmers in Argentina, Brazil, and Poland took to the streets, demanding more government assistance in dealing with low commodity prices, and cane workers began burning fields in Brazil. There were major public-sector strikes in Brazil, Honduras, Jamaica, Guyana, and Zimbabwe. Workers and students marched on La Paz, Bolivia, to protest their government's austerity program, and there were transportation shutdowns in Argentina, Ecuador, and Nicaragua. Venezuela's government placed military guards at oil installations in the east of the country, where demonstrations by the unemployed turned violent. In Croatia, public-sector workers put down their tools in protest at government plans for privatization, while in Romania metalworkers anxious over possible job losses besieged government offices.

A year of protests climaxed symbolically—but did not end—in Seattle, when street demonstrations brought the meetings of the World Trade Organization to a halt. It is quite likely not coincidental that after the Asian crisis, international financial gatherings were constantly dogged by huge and at times violent protests. What appears to have happened is that a motley international alliance came into being, uniting First World activists who recoiled at the U.S.-led attempt to extend the market to every sphere of the planet's life, with Third World activists who were more preoccupied with the debilitating economic effects neoliberalism was having on their societies. Thus, cultural and material critiques blended into an emergent radical discourse that, at first, knew less what it stood for than what it stood against. All the same, that confusion did not dampen the cry of "Enough!" that was heard in the streets.

Although the protesters in the Third World were, more often than not, motivated by local concerns, what their actions served to do was globalize the crisis of neoliberalism. In its very heartland, the regime was now crumbling. The truth was that the Asian crisis was but the first intimation of the climax of the neoliberal regime. As far removed from New York and Washington as the riots and demonstrations seemed to be, they were actually bringing the crisis home to its heartland. The wave of neoliberalism first exported from there across the globe a generation before was now washing back up. But this time, it came with an angry and destructive vigor.

For the tensions erupting in the Third World were not confined there. They were simmering in the rich countries as well, and the same globalization that had made it possible for the First World to exploit new opportunities in the poor countries made it inevitable that events in the poor countries would work their way back up the global chain.

The Shaky Foundation of U.S. Neoliberalism

Late in his term of office, President Clinton embarked on a symbolic tour of some of his country's poorest areas in an attempt to draw attention to the fact that the great boom of the 1990s had bypassed many people. By now, it was clear to most people that the great prosperity of the decade coexisted with great poverty. What is perhaps less commonly known is that the great prosperity was in fact founded on this very poverty. Those who saw their relative and often absolute standard of living falling were not so much denied the fruits of neoliberalism, as they were yielding them.

Labor market reforms and technological changes during the 1980s and 1990s put the U.S. labor movement, like most of those in the Western world, on the defensive. Central banks, which forged close ties with financial communities and targeted inflation by raising unemployment, were given more freedom by their governments; social safety nets were pared back, since rising unemployment raised government social expenditure, which monetary authorities would not tolerate; labor laws were interpreted more restrictively and in some cases governments waged war on unions (as in the U.S. PATCO strike or the British coal miners' strike).[2] In consequence, wages remained low and employment less secure, as was recorded earlier in the book. New forms of management also reorganized the labor process, shifting employment to smaller firms and moving the assembly process of some subsectors to low-wage zones overseas.

To be able to exploit these new opportunities, though, firm managers needed access to foreign labor supplies. History offered some lessons in this regard. In the early twentieth century, immigration had provided the burgeoning U.S. economy with an abundance of cheap labor, making it possible to keep costs low and profits high. This arrangement was captured by Upton Sinclair in his classic book *The Jungle:*

> People said that old man Durham himself was responsible for these immigrations; he had sworn that he would fix the people of Packingtown so that they would never again call a strike on him, and so he had sent his agents into every city and village in Europe to spread the tale of the chances of work and high wages at the stockyards. The people had come in hordes, and old Durham had squeezed

them tighter and tighter, speeding them up and grinding them to pieces and sending for new ones. The Poles, who had come by tens of thousands, had been driven to the wall by the Lithuanians, and now the Lithuanians were giving way to the Slovaks. . . . It was easy to bring them, for wages were really much higher, and it was only when it was too late that the poor people found out that everything else was higher too. They were like rats in a trap, that was the truth; and more of them were piling in every day.[3]

In the late twentieth century, though, new information and communications technologies made it unnecessary to bring workers to the factory, since the factory, in effect, could now go to the workers. The low cost of air transport, rapid increases in computing power and in information-management software, faxes, e-mail, and the Internet, all made it possible for firms in some subsectors—most notably durable goods manufacturing—to move parts of their operations offshore. Typically, what managers did was to keep design, marketing, and skill-intensive assembly at home, but shift low-skilled assembly tasks to low-wage zones where labor was plentiful. As discussed earlier in the book, this aggravated the worsening income distribution picture by eliminating low-end jobs while maintaining or swelling demand for high-end ones.

Still, this kind of globalization was only possible if firm managers could shift their operations offshore and gain duty-free or at least relatively inexpensive access to the U.S. market for their reexported products. Only if the U.S. government pursued an aggressive strategy of trade and financial liberalization would this come to pass. Fortunately for U.S. capital, it enjoyed a strong ally in the 1990s in President Clinton, who inherited his predecessor's North American Free Trade Agreement and ran with it. As a result, firm managers were able to wield the threat of globalization to keep a lid on wage demands. That is to say, they could threaten to move their operations to low-wage zones. The threat was typically more apparent than real, because the actual amount of "world sourcing" that took place in the 1990s was a good deal more modest than what some neoliberal dogmatists, enamored of the idea of a global market, suggested. In the 1990s, for instance, U.S. foreign direct investment in durable goods manufacturing in Third World countries seldom surpassed more than 1 percent of total gross fixed private investment.[4] Nonetheless, in a context in which organized labor was still very weak, the rate of unionization continued to decline throughout the decade—firm managers were able not only to keep labor costs down, but also to demand more work from labor, resulting in a rise in productivity that further kept manufacturing employment receding. Throughout most of the decade, while productivity in the service

sector remained more or less flat and employment thus rose—most
service-producing firms had to locate close to their consumers rather
than their producers, and so could not globalize their operations in this
way—productivity in durable goods manufacturing rose and employment, consequently, declined.[5]

Low wages meant low inflation. Low inflation, in turn, allowed
nominal interest rates to fall. By reducing borrowing costs and keeping inflation low, this virtuous combination allowed ordinary
Americans to experience a modest improvement in their standard of
living. But it also gave rise to another phenomenon, which would
come to characterize the 1990s boom. Cheap credit fueled the huge
run-up in stock prices from 1995 to 2000. Throughout the decade, privately held debt, and especially consumer credit, grew at a rate far
faster than both nominal incomes and the economy.[6] What appears to
have happened is that Americans used their own money to buy shares,
but then used credit to fuel their purchases, the idea being that at a
later date they could draw upon their capital gains to pay off their
debts. Were this so, one would expect that when the cost of credit
resumed rising, the flow of funds into the stock market would slow,
causing gains to taper and leading eventually to a liquidation of positions as Americans paid off their debts, resulting in a stock market
crash. This, as we shall see, is what happened beginning in late 1999.
Market analysts dismissed the possibility of there ever being another
1929-style crash on the grounds that rules on margin lending had been
tightened since then. This was true, and consequently margin lending
was much less of a factor in the 1990s than it had been seventy years
before. However, what such analysts did not reckon with was the
growth of the consumer credit industry in the post–World War II period, and the possibility that consumer credit could, in a roundabout
way, be used to fuel a stock market bubble.

Meanwhile, the number of Americans who held stock had surged in
the 1990s. At the start of the 1980s, when the postwar compact came
under attack, shareholding was still generally the business of the rich.
By the mid-1990s, though, it had become a Main Street activity, with
roughly half of Americans owning shares. Similarly, the amount of
money flowing into stock market mutual funds—where retail investors
put their money—was relatively modest at the start of the decade: in
1990, Americans lodged some $13 billion in stock mutual funds; by
decade's end, that figure had risen more than twenty times over.[7] But as
interest rates came down, the flow into all types of mutual funds went
up, as Graph 6.1 shows (note that the interest-rate axis is a descending
scale).

Graph 6.1 Interest Rates and Mutual Fund Inflows

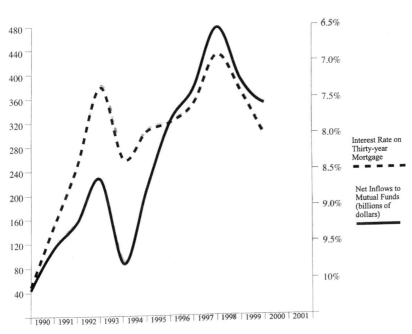

Interest Rate on
Thirty-year
Mortgage

Net Inflows to
Mutual Funds
(billions of
dollars)

Sources: U.S. Federal Reserve Board, Investment Company Institute.

Stocks absorbed an increasing share of Americans' savings: in 1990, stock funds attracted 29 percent of the new money retail investors put into their mutual funds, but by 2000 they were absorbing just short of 80 percent of this flow; in 1990, stocks accounted for 23 percent of the total mutual fund holdings of Americans, but by the end of the decade nearly 60 percent of total fund assets were held in equity.[8] Given that the number of Americans who owned stock exploded at the same time that their stock market assets swelled, this meant that many people were feeling the wealth effects of the extraordinary growth in asset values. This in turn boosted incomes. A virtuous but potentially dangerous cycle then emerged. Flush with paper wealth, Americans went on a spending spree that drove the economy, and thus stock prices, higher yet. It would appear that at least some of this spending was done on credit, as the savings rate dropped below zero by the end of the decade and debt levels reached record heights. In fact, the situation may not have been as dire as it appeared, for if capital gains are added to income, Americans were in fact living within their means.[9] Save for one small matter: if they were in fact borrowing against unrealized capital gains to do their spending—which would explain the run-up in debt—it meant that a debt overhang would eventually pull the stock market into a bear phase.

It is important to note what was in play here. I have argued that in the United States, as on the rest of the planet, the distributional crisis of the neoliberal regime worsened throughout the decade. The dismantling of the distributional regime, I have argued, served the accumulation regime, with the result being what was apparently the biggest economic boom in history. However, the theory put forth in this book is that a distributional crisis will manifest itself politically, and cannot simply be obscured by a functional accumulation regime. In lay terms, rising employment, and even rising wages, will not obscure the discontent that accompanies a breakdown of the social compact manifested by widening income and wealth distribution patterns.

The reasoning put forth by the myriad neoliberal apologists, including the U.S. administration, for the growing wealth gap in the 1990s, was that while some were benefiting more than others, all were better off. And on the face of it, the supposition appeared correct. The previous chapter noted some evidence of discontent in the 1990s among marginalized groups—especially the unskilled working class and African Americans— but by late in the decade any evidence of U.S. discontent seemed to have evaporated. The president's poll approval ratings were high, surveys of contentment found positive results, and the indicators of antisystemic tendencies seen earlier in the decade—crime, antisocial behavior, the growth of antisystemic movements like the militia movements, millenarian cults, and the Nation of Islam—had all gone into reverse. On the face of it, therefore, U.S. exceptionalism ruled once again.

In fact, it appears it did not. Instead, with the retreat from the already-weak social compact in the United States, Americans turned from redistributing wealth via the public sector, to redistributing it via the market. When credit was employed to come into the stock market, the resulting bubble drove up capital gains. These gains could be borrowed against to fuel additional consumption, while still leaving enough in asset portfolios to pay off the accumulated debt at a later date. One must remember that with interest rates dropping throughout the decade, the cost of carrying debt was falling just as returns on stock market investments were rising. From a neoliberal vantage point, this was, if anything, a testament to the superiority of the neoliberal regime. In effect, it could be reasoned, Americans were making sacrifices at the workplace to improve their efficiency and reduce their costs, thereby swelling profits, but they were reaping the gains of these sacrifices by buying shares of those same firms. Indeed, not a few commentators would remark that this development had fundamentally remade U.S. capitalism for the better: by buying shares in the firms in which they worked, U.S. laborers had given themselves a vested interest in keeping the cost of those firms down and their productivity high. Gone were the days of union strife and conflictual labor relations.

In fact, this conclusion was hasty. Had workers been buying shares with their own income, the thesis might have held. But because they were apparently buying them on credit, they were essentially gambling that they could augment their income. As suggested above, once credit costs rose, the stock market bubble would stop inflating, and would soon begin deflating as retail investors liquidated their assets to settle their bills. This is where events in the Third World came into play.

As has been posited, productivity gains resulted from a shift in the balance of power away from labor and toward capital: firm managers in the durable goods subsector could, by threatening to globalize production, extract concessions from labor in the form of both restrained wage gains and greater workplace productivity. But this bargaining power depended on the reality of a reserve labor army—a large mass of cheap, available labor that could be brandished by managers to extract concessions from workers ("If you won't, someone else will"). If capital lost access to this reserve labor army in the Third World, it would have to fall back on its domestic supply, which was constrained by the late 1990s by the rising demand for labor coming from the burgeoning and relatively unproductive (hence labor-intensive) service sector. The wave of protests, strikes, and riots that began sweeping across the Third World in 1999 had just this effect. Under pressure, many governments began reorienting their politics and policies away from neoliberalism; where they did so, foreign direct investment tended to contract (see the Appendix).

If the Asian crisis signaled the end of a globalization wave—the flow of capital into emerging economies slowed abruptly—the resistance kept any further waves at bay. Capital flowed back into the Third World, but precrisis levels did not return.[10] Given that the threat of globalization was a pressure release valve on U.S. wages, the tightening of this valve could be expected to have lessened disinflationary effects. This appears to have happened starting in late 1999. Apparently emboldened by the weakening in the bargaining position of globalized fractions of U.S. capital, not to mention tight labor markets, organized labor began something of an advance. In 1999 the U.S. labor movement's long decline in membership bottomed out. The following year, as the wave of antigovernment protests continued around the world, a number of important strikes reinjected a hint of militancy back into U.S. labor markets. In particular, major strikes at Boeing, U.S. Airways, and Verizon not only raised the wage bar in their industries, but also signaled that organized labor was penetrating the so-called new economy. The idea that the mushrooming services sector would avoid unionization and thus be able to keep its labor costs down was drawn sharply into question. The year 2000 saw a degree of labor militancy never witnessed in the 1990s: the number of days lost to industrial action in the United States shot up tenfold over the previous year, and the percentage of working time lost to strikes was triple that of the next worst year of the decade.[11] As if encouraged by the militancy in the Third World, U.S. labor appeared to crawl back from its sickbed in 2000. In response, wages began climbing and productivity gains bought at the expense of labor began slowing.

Graph 6.2 illustrates this relationship between globalization and the cost of labor to U.S. firms. The left-hand axis is an index of globalization—determined as a percentage of total U.S. investment accounted for by outsourcing of manufacturing to low-wage zones[12]—on a descending scale. The right-hand axis measures unit labor costs in U.S. manu-

Graph 6.2   Globalization and Unit Labor Costs in Manufacturing

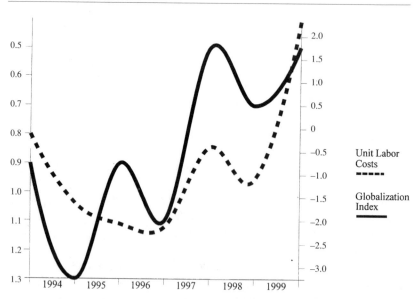

Sources: U.S. Department of Labor, Bureau of Labor Statistics; U.S. Department of Commerce, Bureau of Economic Analysis.

facturing, which is arguably the best measure of the strength of labor:[13] as the bargaining power of labor rises, so too will unit labor costs, thereby eroding profits and shifting income from capital-owners to workers. The use of an inverted left-hand scale reflects the hypothesis that as globalization declines, labor costs rise. What the graph illustrates is that the reversal in globalization provoked by the Asian crisis—hence the dividing-line drawn in 1997, when the Asian crisis began—apparently caused unit labor costs, which had been declining, to begin rising sharply (in line with the sudden reversal in globalization). The result was price inflation, which first appeared in early 2000. By forcing the U.S. Federal Reserve to raise interest rates, these inflationary pressures rattled investors, resulting in the mini–market crash in April 2000.

Once the bear market took hold, the economy slid into recession as households pulled back on spending and increased their conventional saving. At this point, the Federal Reserve was able to prevent the economy from going into free fall with an ultraloose monetary policy of lowering interest rates to levels not seen in two generations. This massive influx of liquidity into the economy shored up asset values, on both shares and real estate, thereby stanching the implosion of consumer spending. Nonetheless, serious problems persisted, mirrored in the sluggish response of the economy to this fresh wave of stimulus. In part, the economy was beset with the excess capacity built up during the boom days, when financial speculation, egged on by an administration that was talking up the virtues of the endless-growth new economy, led to overinvestment in several industries.

Yet lying at the heart of the slow rebound were the problems inherent in the neoliberal regime. For example, the political instability discussed earlier in the book, in places like Nigeria, Indonesia, Venezuela, and eventually Iraq, put a crimp on oil exports and thereby kept energy prices from falling in a way that would assist an economic rebound. But even if these problems could have been resolved, the deeper problems discussed in this chapter would have remained. At the root of the U.S. productivity revolution that justified the speculative wealth creation of the 1990s was the globalization of corporate America; to the extent that the political reaction against neoliberalism persisted in the Third World, this was restrained. So too, then, was any rebound in productivity. In other words, the U.S. economy had shifted to a lower growth path, ensuring that the distribution crises of neoliberalism would become more acute.

By the autumn of 2001, the New York stock market was sliding, dragging the economy into recession. Then, during rush hour on the morning of 11 September, two planes hijacked by Islamists slammed into the World Trade Center, another struck the Pentagon, and a fourth crashed in Pennsylvania. The antisystemic forces unleashed by neoliberal globalization had come crashing home to roost. Conservative commentators were quick to denounce any purported link between poverty and terrorism, but voices from the Third World, whence emanated the threat, differed. Chilean intellectuals reminded those who would listen that 11 September 2001 also marked the twenty-eighth anniversary of the overthrow of Salvador Allende, initiating the world's first thoroughgoing experiment with neoliberalism, while a Catholic priest from a ghetto in Kingston, Jamaica, wrote a newspaper column in which he said the collapse of the Twin Towers represented an assault on global neoliberalism. Whether or not it was construed in that way, the crisis of neoliberalism had nonetheless become acute, setting the stage for a precarious and uncertain future.

Conclusion

How much closer to the home of neoliberalism could its crisis have struck? The forces unleashed by this regime crisis came home to exacerbate the economic malaise that had also resulted from this same crisis, converging on that fateful day. As the World Trade Center came crashing down, so too, in a metaphorical sense, did neoliberalism. By year's end, the world economy was in its first coordinated recession since the 1970s. And with globalization now in reverse—tighter border controls, brought on by the war on terrorism, raised import costs and so further dampened investment flows—the virtuous cycle of the 1990s went into reverse: even as prices fell during the recession, labor costs rose and productivity growth slowed. This ate into profits. The vast amounts of liquidity unleashed by the Federal Reserve, along with the stimulus of the federal government, supported asset prices for a while, but did not lead to wholesale rises in demand. Even were the economy to bounce back, the crisis at its core was bound to reemerge, making any future recovery tentative while intensifying future risks. Already by the middle of 2002, the U.S. economic rebound—and with it the global economy—had slowed back into a low-growth phase. The neoliberal age had apparently exhausted itself.

What had happened? The success of the neoliberal accumulation regime in the United States depended on the dismantling of the Keynesian distribution regime. By concentrating wealth, this drove up share values. By restraining the bargaining power of labor, it kept inflation low. Low inflation meant that credit costs could fall, at least in the short term. This allowed ordinary Americans to apparently resolve the distributional crisis by crowding into the stock market and borrowing against unrealized capital gains, thereby swelling their income. Yet it also created a debt overhang that would hinder any recovery when the stock market went into reverse. Meanwhile, the whole edifice was ultimately built upon the cheap labor of the Third World. When access to this was threatened by the rebellion against neoliberalism in the Third World, the distribution crisis provoked an accumulation crisis. The distribution crisis remained unresolved. Moreover, the temporary resolution option, a credit-fed stock market bubble, was no longer available: the reduction in the effective reserve labor army, by boosting labor's bargaining power, meant that—all things being equal—profit rates would not return to levels seen in the 1990s. The stock market ceased to be the income supplement it had formerly been. Not surprisingly, therefore, as the stock market fell, conventional savings rates rose. In effect, since the total income of Americans had come down, there was a rise in the non–capital gains portion of their regular income devoted to saving, which thus conspired to limit the resurgence of demand the Federal Reserve had hoped to engineer through its loose monetary policy. So, with the distribution crisis unresolved, and with the means used to temporarily resolve it in the 1990s no longer available, it was bound to persist. And to the extent it drove the accumulation crisis, the accumulation crisis would persist. Whatever temporary resolutions governing elites could find to manage it in the short term, the fundamental problems remained, enfeebling the neoliberal regime. Cycles of growth and recovery would return to the U.S. economy, but the underlying trend, of low long-term growth amid a widened wealth gap, had settled in.

Notes

1. For more on the Asian crisis, see Peter G. Warr, *Macroeconomic Origins of the Korean Crisis,* Working Paper in Trade and Development no. 00/04 (Canberra: Australian National University, 2000); Giancarlo Corsetti, "Interpreting the Asian Financial Crisis: Open Issues in Theory and Policy," *Asian Development Review* 16, no. 2 (1998): 18–63; Yung Chul Park and Chi-Young Song, "The East Asian Financial Crisis: A Year Later," *IDS Bulletin* 30, no. 1 (January 1999): 93–107; and Laurids S. Lauridsen, "The Financial Crisis in Thailand: Causes, Conduct, and Consequences," *World Development* 26, no. 8 (1998): 1575–1591. Compare Nurhan Yentürk, "Short-Term Capital Inflows and Their Impact on Macroeconomic Structure: Turkey in the 1990s," *Developing Economies* 37, no. 1 (March 1999): 89–113; and Stephany Griffith-Jones, *Causes and Lessons of the Mexican Peso Crisis,* Working Paper no. 132 (Helsinki: World Institute for Development Economics Research, 1997).

Yentürk and Griffith-Jones show how similar causes—rapid liberalization of capital accounts—gave rise to similar crises in other settings.

2. Michele I. Naples, "Industrial Conflict, the Quality of Worklife, and the Productivity Slowdown in U.S. Manufacturing," *Eastern Economic Journal* 15, no. 2 (1988): 157–166.

3. Upton Sinclair, *The Jungle* (New York: Signet Classic Edition, [1906]), p. 70.

4. U.S. Department of Commerce figures.

5. See Robert J. Gordon, "Has the 'New Economy' Rendered the Productivity Slowdown Obsolete?" June 1999, available at http://faculty-web.at.nwu.edu/economics/gordon/researchhome.html.

6. This ratio is compiled by comparing U.S. Department of Commerce figures on income and output growth with U.S. Federal Reserve Board figures on privately held debt.

7. Investment Company Institute.

8. Ibid.

9. Richard Peach and Charles Steindel, "A Nation of Spendthrifts? An Analysis of Trends in Personal and Gross Spending," *Current Issues in Economics and Finance* 6, no. 10 (September 2000): 1–6.

10. See U.S. Department of Commerce for figures.

11. U.S. Department of Labor, Bureau of Labor Statistics.

12. The actual formula used to calculate the index is $G = m/I$, where G is an index of corporate globalization, m is U.S. foreign direct investment in Third World countries by manufacturers of durable goods, and I is gross fixed private investment in the United States. U.S. Department of Commerce, Bureau of Economic Analysis; U.S. Department of Labor, Bureau of Labor Statistics.

13. This is because unit labor costs take into account two factors, compensation and productivity, both of which reveal the strength of labor. If labor's bargaining power is strong vis-à-vis capital, one would expect, *ceteris paribus,* that compensation would increase while productivity would grow more slowly or even diminish. Both trends would raise unit labor costs. Furthermore, the use of unit labor costs as a measure has the added advantage that it helps smooth the effect of recessions, when diminishing labor costs might mask a situation in which labor's fundamental bargaining power is obscured by cyclical economic weaknesses: because productivity generally slows during recessions, this would offset declines in compensation due to a temporary feature in the business cycle.

7

Epilogue

The message of the previous chapter could well be that in contemporary politics, by severing their ties to the poor, the rich can allow themselves a good party. But sooner or later those they have locked out in the cold and left to press on the windowpanes will crash the door and come rushing in. The stock market collapse was like the mirror ball that comes smashing to the floor: it silences the revelers quite abruptly, but it is only the start of what will follow. Come the morning, a few disheveled revelers will be left to survey a smoking, littered ballroom, and while they may blame the envy of the gate-crashers for ruining their fun, they would do better to look at how they contributed to the mess in the first place.

In this case, the reaction to the celebrations began in the neighborhoods of the poor, in the Third World and depressed communities of the First World. In earlier times, dominant elites and classes might have sealed off these neighborhoods and confined the carnage. This, in a microcosm, was what the apartheid government in South Africa used to do to protect the prosperity and privilege of the white minority: seal the violent reaction to its oppression into black communities. And on a global scale, First World governments used to be able to protect themselves similarly, keeping out undesired immigrants or severing ties to troubled countries. But the lessons of apartheid are instructive: as the regime came to depend more and more on black labor, it became increasingly difficult and ultimately impossible to isolate political instability in the black townships.[1] In the same way, globalization has so intertwined the economies of most of the planet that events in faraway corners of the globe reverberate close to one's home, brought there by trade, financial, information, and demographic flows. To a considerable extent, the planet was bound to rise and fall as one. Thus the widening divergence between rich and poor could only be temporary: sooner or later, the rich would get pulled back down, and like two spheres joined by an elastic band, the farther they flew away from each other, the harder would be the impact of their eventual collision. So it has come to pass.

To recapitulate the argument of this book, stable polities rely on stable regimes, which include both accumulation and distribution regimes. Neoliberalism is an inherently unstable regime, because it is rooted in a tension, namely that the functioning of its accumulation regime depends on a dysfunctional distribution regime (this arises from an apparent error at the heart of neoliberal theory, namely the idea that human contentment is directly related to absolute rather than relative changes in material well-being). As a result of this inherent instability, neoliberal regimes everywhere gave rise to symptoms of crisis, which generally manifested a growing fragmentation—social, political, and cultural. But while these symptoms have helped to deepen the crisis of neoliberalism, in themselves they offer no resolution. And efforts by rival elites to construct viable alternatives to the neoliberal regime have foundered on the fact that they have failed to challenge—indeed, in some cases, they have reinforced—the hegemony of the neoliberal accumulation regime.

Crises can be managed within a dysfunctional regime, but never resolved. They will continue to multiply and deepen. This does not mean the neoliberal regime is about to come to an end. As Lenin argued, crises can fester indefinitely. It takes a viable alternative regime, put into action by a political elite, to bring about the transformation. If we have entered a revolutionary phase, we have yet to begin a revolution (in the Kuhnian, paradigmatic sense),[2] and there is no telling how long we will wait for the next regime transformation to take place. And as to the alternative to neoliberalism, as yet we can only talk in terms of general outlines. What does seem evident, though, is that in the global age, a viable regime will need to rectify the distributional crisis both locally and globally. In consequence, a return to the Keynesian welfare state, whatever its many virtues, is no longer an option, because Keynesianism presumes the existence of essentially national economies governed by essentially autonomous states. However, when France experimented with Keynesianism in the early 1980s, it both drove French investment abroad and boosted imports, since the stimulus did not benefit French industry so much as that of its neighbors (whose costs remained lower). Therefore, transnational solutions will have to be found. The idea that growth itself, prompted by neoliberal reforms, will suffice to distribute income gains to the Third World is itself dubious.[3] What does seem clear is that a major infusion of capital—on a scale that would dwarf the Marshall Plan reconstruction of Western Europe and surpass anything ever seen before—will be necessary if the Third World is to lift itself from crisis and get onto a sustainable growth path. Failing that, the citizens of the rich countries will either have to resign themselves to a world of worsening instability, or find a way to raise the drawbridges and isolate themselves from the troubles of the Third World. But reversing globalization will probably have negative effects on productivity, while slowing immigration would almost certainly affect growth negatively. What was said of South Africa's white population in the dying years of apartheid, that it must adapt or die,[4] can be said today of the world's most privileged citizens.

Yet the fact that the transition from apartheid has not been painless for South Africa's white minority may perhaps be instructive as to what lies ahead in the global political economy. For the same may be the case for a permanent correction to the global distributional crisis. An apparently fundamental problem in neoliberalism lies in the inherent difficulty of relying upon the accumulation regime to itself resolve crises of the distribution regime. At its heart, neoliberalism in all its avatars treats accumulation as primary: once the neoliberal accumulation regime is functioning, distribution looks after itself. An example of this premise is convergence theory. Neoliberals have long argued that in a fully globalized, liberalized world economy, capital will naturally flow from rich to poor regions as firms seek to lower their costs by employing cheap labor. It was this logic that in the 1990s led several Western governments, especially that of the United States, to cut their aid budgets while pushing a free trade agenda: since globalization would make poor countries—and by extension poor people—rich, aid would no longer be necessary. As Chapter 6 pointed out, this much-anticipated gush of investment benefited only a few countries. In point of fact, the gap between rich and poor countries widened, just as it had between rich and poor people. And today, few economists still believe that liberalization alone will bring about a narrowing of the gap between rich and poor.[5]

Yet even if it could, problems would remain. If the rich countries continue growing as they have done, and the poor countries eventually converge with them, then global output at the end of the twenty-first century will end up being roughly 140 times what it is today. While efficiency gains will occur, if the past record is anything to go by, they will not increase in an order of similar magnitude.[6] In short, given that many environmental scientists are saying that, for example, current levels of planetary pollution output are unsustainable, those that will result from the future growth of the Third World will likely be unbearable.

Thus two scenarios, both troubling, come into sight. One is that the Third World will have to be prevented from developing to the level of the First World. The other is that rich countries may have to contemplate slowed growth or even reverses in their levels of output. If the second option seems politically implausible, the first would simply perpetuate the current crisis of global politics. And over time, the cost of that crisis may become too great for even the rich countries to bear. If the ground is to be prepared for a transformation on this scale, though, it seems likely that a cultural critique—one that questions both the possibility and, if need be, the desirability of the neoliberal belief in the virtues and possibilities of endless growth—will have to accompany the material critique of neoliberalism. That process seems to have started already and, not surprisingly, much of its impetus is coming from the Third World.

One of the interesting upshots of the events of the past few years is that they illustrate the stubbornness of humans when it comes to learning the lessons of the past. In the twentieth century, socialism rose and fell with the rage of the working class, and with its fall toward the end of the century a great many neoliberal historians consigned it to the dustbins of history. Yet even if socialism as we know it has died its unceremonious death, populism will return in some form or another unless a viable regime that rebuilds the bonds linking the powerful and the powerless is devised. Already, we are seeing the rising ground swell of what is likely to be the new opposition movement of the new century.

*   *   *

One hot summer afternoon I squeezed myself into a turtleneck and jacket and drove into Kingston to attend a farewell service for a friend of mine. He had served for six years as a pastor at a church in one of the city's roughest neighborhoods, sandwiched as it was between the turfs of rival gangs. Now he was leaving to go to another church overseas. The time had come to say good-bye to a community that had fallen deeply in love with him and could not imagine how it would survive without him.

Jamaican churches seem to judge a man's faith by the level of discomfort he is willing to bear, and the heavier the suit, the quicker your ascent to heaven would seem to be. "Make sure you dress well," my friend had said, knowing my penchant for jeans and loose shirts. I took a seat on a hard wooden bench under a dusty old fan, soaking as I was in the still, sultry heat and anxious to snatch at what air currents could be had. It was a stately if austere old red-brick church, built by Scottish Presbyterians in the nineteenth century when Kingston was a colonial town, and since then surrounded by the zinc roofs and breeze-block walls and clapboard rum-bars and throbbing boom-boxes that had grown up with the city. Because he had given so much of himself to this community—helping to build a nursery, bakery, and skills training center, intervening on behalf of people in trouble with the law, helping them to find homes when they were evicted from their premises, visiting the sick even when the worst of the violence was breaking out and he had to conduct telephone calls over the racket of automatic gunfire in the streets or hide under his desk as bullets whizzed by, imploring people in moving sermons to never let go of their trust that there can be a better tomorrow—news of his departure was greeted with anger at first by a people who felt abandoned. Having had a few months to digest the news, they had now come to accept that all things must end. But he had injected a glorious joy into their lives, and now he was leaving, and no words of reassurance could bring them to believe that they would ever again taste happiness as they had during their time with him. People were sad, some convulsed with sobs in the course of the three-hour service, like a lover who cannot let go of one who they know must leave. No sooner was a little hope injected into their lives than it was taken away again. No words, I was certain, could reassure them that there really would be a better tomorrow.

After tributes in dance, song, and words, tear-filled thank-yous, gift presentations, and long embraces in which people seemed determined not to let go, a minister was invited to the platform to deliver the message. A pastor from another inner-city church, he seemed to approach the platform reluctantly and confessed, in a low and formal voice, that he had been given all of two days' notice to put together a sermon for the occasion. He seemed bored, as if preoccupied by other matters, but then he paused, and began. He spoke about hope. Hope as a choice, as a revolutionary option, as a defiant refusal to purchase the wares of the peddlers of despair and resignation, as the strongest weapon against injustice, the power to never submit and accept the world as it is, but to shout to a world that sometimes does not want to listen that there is another way, and as he charged deeper into his message his voice rose, and with it his passions. As if the building, weighed down by the sorrows of its occupants, were itself rising with his call, clapping began, people yelled their amens, and the spirit seemed to come back to them. "In every gesture," he called out to them, "from building a nursery to visiting the sick to caring for our families to feeding the hungry, we proclaim hope as a testament of all we hold dear. And it is not something which is given to and taken away from us. It is a choice we make, every day of our lives, whatever the sorrows it causes us, because we know it is right." My departing friend had grounded his ministry in this explicit resistance to neoliberalism and a determination to proclaim a different way forward—"I beg to differ!" he would often thunder when decrying the resignation and legitimation of poverty, suffering, and inequality, and the so-called inevitability of the emerging global order. Then–U.S. president Bill Clinton had recently called it a force of nature, and one is not supposed to get into the habit of resisting forces of nature, but my friend had.

Whether from the pulpits of inner-city churches, at the barricades of Third World riots, in Brazilian farms occupied by landless peasants, in the voting booths of those countries where there is a rising populist tide, or in the streets outside the gatherings of the world's political and financial leaders, there is a growing chorus of people who are saying that they beg to differ. They may not yet know what it is they seek, but they do know what they refuse. And, sometimes in the most unlikely places, the search for alternatives is under way.

Notes

1. P. Maylam, "The Rise and Decline of Urban Apartheid," *African Affairs* 89, no. 354 (1990): 57–84.

2. As opposed to a radical revolution in the social or political sense, though as noted earlier in the book, this is one of many possible resolutions to a regime crisis.

3. See John Rapley, "Convergence: Myths and Reality," *Progress in Development Studies* 1, no. 4 (2001): 295–308.

4. Robert A. Schrire, *Adapt or Die* (New York: Ford Foundation, 1971).

5. Rapley, "Convergence."

6. For a discussion, see John Rapley, *Understanding Development*, 2nd ed. (Boulder: Lynne Rienner, 2002), pp. 169–170.

Appendix:
Neoliberalism and
Corporate Globalization

The 1990s saw a surge in U.S. foreign direct investment (FDI) destined toward outsourcing the manufacturing of durable goods to low-cost zones. The vast bulk of it, however, went into a mere twelve countries. To attract it, this book has argued, countries had to maintain neoliberal regimes that allowed firms to import inputs and export their finished products with a minimum of duties and bureaucratic delay and, very importantly, to repatriate their profits freely. If and when governments began retreating from neoliberalism, one would expect this type of FDI to reverse as well. Table A.1 lists the Third World countries that figured most prominently in the globalization of U.S. durable goods manufacturing, and correlates the behavior of inward U.S. FDI in durable goods manufacturing with the political environment, to ascertain the impact of the latter on the former. The hypothesis is as follows: in those countries that turned against neoliberalism in the wake of the Asian financial crisis, U.S. FDI in durable goods manufacturing can be expected to have gone into reverse.

The political environment is determined by reference to the databases of Oxford Analytica and the Economist Intelligence Unit. Each of the twelve countries in question was monitored in order to determine if after 1998 its political and policy orientation turned against neoliberalism; the methodology involved qualitative assessments drawing upon correspondents in the countries in question, as well as expert analyses, to produce periodic reports on the political and economic situation of each country. Each of them entered the Asian crisis with a policy regime that was broadly favorable to neoliberalism. So the task is to separate those countries in which policy continuity remained the order of the day from those in which the tide turned against neoliberalism. Of the twelve countries in question, those in which there was policy continuity included Venezuela, Singapore, China, Mexico, Hong Kong, Chile, South Korea, and Thailand, for the following reasons:

Venezuela. Although President Hugo Chavez came to power in December 1998 on a populist platform, his government's economic policies remained prudent; for example, rises in minimum wage were kept below the inflation rate.

Singapore. Sometimes said to have its region's dullest politics, Singapore experienced continuity throughout the Asian crisis and thereafter. Liberalization policies designed to deepen integration into the global economy—such as financial reforms and further openings to foreign investment in telecommunications—continued, while the government responded to the Asian crisis by freezing wages and slashing labor costs. Owing to the weakness of the opposition, public discontent over rising inequality found little voice, and the ruling party's hold on power was actually tightened.

China. Reform in China continued throughout the Asian crisis and its aftermath. The privatization of state-owned enterprises, financial liberalization, and accession to the World Trade Organization reinforced this process. Changes in the Communist Party leadership signaled continued commitment to reform along the lines of the Chinese model, whereby the economy would be liberalized while calls for political liberalization would be quelled.

Mexico. The country weathered the Asian crisis much better than most, and so austerity measures were never so severe. Throughout, wage growth continued, so the pain of adjustment did not turn the country against neoliberalism.

Hong Kong. While the Beijing-appointed administration that took control when Britain withdrew from Hong Kong in 1997 clamped down on some political freedoms, it did not tamper with Hong Kong's liberal economic model. The labor movement was weak and there was little in the way of political instability.

Chile. The paradigmatic case of neoliberal adjustment in the Third World, Chile's political parties shared a broad consensus in favor of continuity. Despite their commitment to welfare spending, Chile's politicians adhered to the goal of fiscal prudence. After 1998 the country also increased the competitiveness of the banking sector, introduced a capital gains tax exemption, and reformed its labor laws, which, although they raised business costs, also benefited business by augmenting market flexibility. Importantly, Chile was spared the political instability of some of its neighbors; there was little evidence of populism, while the political spectrum, if anything, tipped further to the right.

South Korea.   Although the unions were militant in rejecting neoliberal reforms imposed in the wake of the Asian crisis, only 10 percent of the workers belonged to them and they were seen by ordinary Koreans as being privileged.

Thailand.   There was broad continuity in government policies, which entailed a blend of state-led growth and structural adjustment. Following the prodemocracy movement, there was little restiveness, and the working class was seen as conservative even by Asian standards.

Conversely, those countries that saw a turn against neoliberalism included Malaysia, Argentina, and Brazil, for the following reasons:

Malaysia.   After the Asian crisis, populism began rising, with discontented Malays gravitating toward the Parti Islam sa-Malaysia (PAS). The PAS received a considerable boost in the 1999 elections. To shore up his support base in the face of some of the worst demonstrations in thirty years, Prime Minister Mahathir Mohammed employed more anti-Western rhetoric and loosened the purse strings, allowing the fiscal deficit to rise. The United Malays National Organization (UMNO), the ruling elite, saw a power struggle between neoliberals, led by Anwar Ibrahim, and Malay nationalists, led by Mahathir, with victory going firmly to the latter.

Argentina.   Argentina's currency board led to an overvalued peso, which hurt exports and so worsened the recession. The result was a descending spiral of fiscal adjustments, which worsened the recession, which eroded revenues and necessitated further fiscal adjustments. Popular anger rose as a result. Provincial governments balked at federal attempts to limit spending.

Brazil.   After President Cardoso's second term of office began in 1998, land occupations by the Landless Rural Workers Movement (MST) increased. After the 2000 municipal elections, the Workers Party (PT) consistently rose in the polls, culminating in the 2002 election victory of PT presidential candidate Lula Ignacio da Silva. State governors then began threatening to default on their debt payments, frustrating the federal government's efforts to maintain fiscal austerity.

Finally there is *Taiwan,* which has been left out of Table A.1 on the grounds that it is a special case. With the opening of mainland China to foreign investment, it has surpassed its island neighbor (and, officially, province) as a target for FDI. As a result, the principal factor governing FDI flows into Taiwan in recent years has been less its economic policy regime and more its policy toward China, which veers between the poles of isolationism and reunification. Given that the pattern of investment flows into Taiwan is governed by this overriding influence, it has been omitted from the table for the purposes of testing the hypothesis, as its presence would skew any results. The table looks simply at whether the government retreated from neoliberal policies (represented by "anti"), or remained committed to them (represented by "pro") in the country in question after the Asian financial crisis.

There appears to be a clear connection between policy orientation and the behavior of FDI. Of the three countries that turned against

Table A.1   Policy Orientation and Inflows of Foreign Direct Investment

Country	Policy Orientation	% Change in FDI Inflows (1998–2000 average versus 1997)
Malaysia	anti	−146
Venezuela	pro	−116
Argentina	anti	−89
Brazil	anti	−84
Singapore	pro	−37
China	pro	+6
Mexico	pro	+22
Hong Kong	pro	+119
Chile	pro	+151
South Korea	pro	+575
Thailand	pro	+1,165

Sources: U.S. Department of Commerce, Bureau of Economic Analysis; Economist Intelligence Unit; Oxford Analytica.

Note: "Pro" represents continuity of neoliberalism; "anti" represents reversal of neoliberalism.

neoliberalism, all three suffered a reversal in inflows of FDI. Of the eight countries that maintained their neoliberal orientation, all but two saw FDI augment; further, Venezuela may present a special case, as the actual policy regime was clashing with what one might call the rhetorical one, leading investors to anticipate the reversals that would later come. During the 1998–2000 period, U.S. FDI in durable goods manufacturing in the Third World as a whole declined, on average, 34 percent from 1997, the peak year. All three of the "non-neoliberal" countries in the above survey group saw even greater outflows than this; all but two of the "neoliberal" countries experienced a better performance. In other words, what seems evident is that as some countries in the Third World began turning against the neoliberal model, U.S. FDI began moving around and chasing a smaller set of destinations.

Bibliography

Abrams, Mark. "Social Class and British Politics." *Public Opinion Quarterly* 25, no. 3 (1961): 342–350.

al-Azm, Sadik J. "Islamic Fundamentalism Reconsidered: A Critical Outline of Problems, Ideas, and Approaches." *South Asia Bulletin* 13, nos. 1–2 (1993): 93–121; and 14, no. 1 (1994): 73–98.

Alin, Erika G. "Dynamics of the Palestinian Uprising: An Assessment of Causes, Character, and Consequences." *Comparative Politics* 26 (1994): 479–498.

Allen, Ernest, Jr. "Religious Heterodoxy and Nationalist Tradition: The Continuing Evolution of the Nation of Islam." *Black Scholar* 26, nos. 3–4 (1996): 2–25.

Anderson, Benedict. *Imagined Communities.* London: Verso, 1983.

Anderson, Perry. *Lineages of the Absolutist State.* London: Routledge, 1974.

Appadurai, Arjun. *Modernity at Large: Cultural Dimensions of Globalization.* Minneapolis: University of Minnesota Press, 1996.

Austin, Dennis, and Peter Lyon. "The Bharatiya Janata Party of India." *Government and Opposition* 28, no. 1 (Winter 1993): 36–50.

Ayata, Sencer. "Patronage, Party, and State: The Politicization of Islam in Turkey." *Middle East Journal* 50, no. 1 (1996): 40–56.

Balassa, Bela, et al. *The Structure of Protection in Developing Countries.* Baltimore: Johns Hopkins University Press for the World Bank and Inter-American Development Bank, 1971.

Baker, Russ. "The Squeeze." *Columbia Journalism Review,* September–October 1997.

Banerjee, Sikata. "The Feminization of Violence in Bombay: Women in the Politics of Shiv Sena." *Asian Survey* 36, no. 2 (1996): 1213–1225.

Barber, Benjamin. *Jihad vs. McWorld.* New York: Ballantine Books, 1996.

Bardhan, Pranab. "Method in the Madness? A Political-Economy Analysis of the Ethnic Conflicts in Less Developed Countries." *World Development* 25, no. 9 (1997): 1381–1398.

Bauer, P. T. *The Rubber Industry: A Study in Competition and Monopoly.* Cambridge: Harvard University Press, 1948.

———. *West African Trade: A Study of Competition, Oligopoly, and Monopoly in a Changing Economy.* Cambridge: Cambridge University Press, 1954.

Bennett, W. Lance. "The Uncivic Culture: Communication, Identity, and the Rise of Lifestyle Politics." *PS: Political Science and Politics* 31, no. 4 (December 1998): 741–761.

Berman, Sheri. "Civil Society and the Collapse of the Weimar Republic." *World Politics* 49, no. 3 (1997): 401–429.

Besley, Tim. "Decentralising Governance." *Risk and Regulation,* Spring 2002.

Béteille, André. "The Indian Village Past and Present." In *Peasants in History: Essays in Honour of Daniel Thorner,* edited by E. J. Hobsbawm et al. Bombay: Oxford University Press, 1980.

Betz, Hans-Georg. "The New Politics of Resentment: Radical Right-Wing Populist Parties in Western Europe." *Comparative Politics* 25 (1993): 413–427.

———. *Radical Right-Wing Populism in Western Europe.* London: Macmillan, 1994.

Betz, Hans-Georg, and Stefan Immerfall, eds. *The New Politics of the Right.* New York: St. Martin's Press, 1998.

Bhagwati, Jagdish. "Directly Unproductive, Profit-Seeking (DUP) Activities." *Journal of Political Economy* 90 (1982): 988–1002.

Braeckman, Collette. *Rwanda: Histoire d'un génocide.* Paris: Fayard, 1994.

Brustein, William. *The Logic of Evil: The Social Origins of the Nazi Party, 1925–1933.* New Haven: Yale University Press, 1996.

Brysk, Alison, and Carol Wise. "Liberalization and Ethnic Conflict in Latin America." *Studies in Comparative International Development* 32, no. 2 (1997): 76–104.

Chatterjee, Manini. "The BJP: Political Mobilization for Hindutva." *South Asia Bulletin* 14, no. 1 (1994): 14–23.

Chazan, Naomi, et al. *Politics and Society in Contemporary Africa.* 2nd ed. Boulder: Lynne Rienner, 1992.

Chhibber, Pradeep. "Who Voted for the Bharatiya Janata Party?" *British Journal of Political Science* 27, no. 4 (October 1987): 631–639.

Clement, Wallace. *The Canadian Corporate Elite.* Ottawa: Carleton University Press, 1986.

Cohen, Robin. *Global Diasporas: An Introduction.* London: UCL Press, 1997.

Colley, Linda. *Britons: Forging the Nation, 1701–1837.* New Haven: Yale University Press, 1992.

Commerzbank. *Sector Report: Forecast for German Industry 1996/97.* Frankfurt am Main: Commerzbank, February 1996.

Connors, Michael. *The Race to the Intelligent State.* Oxford: Capstone, 1997.

Corsetti, Giancarlo. "Interpreting the Asian Financial Crisis: Open Issues in Theory and Policy." *Asian Development Review* 16, no. 2 (1998): 18–63.

Courchene, Tom, with Colin R. Telmer. *From the Heartland to North American Region State: The Social, Fiscal, and Federal Evolution of Ontario.* Toronto: Centre for Public Management, Faculty of Management, University of Toronto, 1998.

Crnobrnja, Mihailo. *The Yugoslav Drama*. 2nd ed. Montreal: McGill-Queen's Press, 1996.

Dahl, Robert A. *Democracy and Its Critics*. New Haven: Yale University Press, 1989.

———. *Polyarchy*. New Haven: Yale University Press, 1971.

Dallago, Bruno, and Milica Uvalic. "The Distributive Consequences of Nationalism: The Case of Former Yugoslavia." *Europe-Asia Studies* 50, no. 1 (1998): 71–90.

Daniels, Robert V. *The End of the Communist Revolution*. London: Routledge, 1993.

Devonish, Hubert. "Walking Around the Language Barrier: A Caribbean View of the Ebonics Controversy." *Small Axe* 2 (September 1997): 63–76.

De Waal, Alex, and Rakiya Omaar. "The Genocide in Rwanda and the International Response." *Current History,* April 1995.

Diamond, Larry. "Is the Third Wave Over?" *Journal of Democracy,* July 1996.

Donia, Robert J., and John V. A. Fine Jr. *Bosnia and Hercegovina: A Tradition Betrayed*. New York: Columbia University Press, 1994.

Downs, William M. "Federalism Achieved: The Belgian Elections of May 1995." *West European Politics* 19 (1996): 171–172.

Drake, W. Avon, and Robert D. Holsworth. *Affirmative Action and the Stalled Quest for Black Progress*. Urbana: University of Illinois Press, 1996.

Drogus, Carol Ann. "The Rise and Decline of Liberation Theology: Churches, Faith, and Political Change in Latin America." *Comparative Politics* 27 (1995): 465–477.

Drucker, Peter F. "The Changed World Economy." *Foreign Affairs* 64, no. 4 (Spring 1986): 768–791.

Dutt, Nitish, and Eddie J. Girdner. "Challenging the Rise of Nationalist-Religious Parties in India and Turkey." *Contemporary South Asia* 9, no. 1 (2000): 7–24.

Easterlin, Richard. *Growth Triumphant: The Twenty-First Century in Historical Perspective*. Ann Arbor: University of Michigan Press, 1996.

———. "Income and Happiness: Towards a Unified Theory." *Economic Journal* 111 (July 2001): 465–484.

Ezekiel, Raphael S. *The Racist Mind: Portraits of American Neo-Nazis and Klansmen*. New York: Penguin Books, 1995.

Fairbairn, Geoffrey. *Revolutionary Guerrilla Warfare*. London: Penguin, 1974.

Fairbank, John King. *China: A New History*. Cambridge: Harvard Belknap, 1992.

Feenstra, Robert C., and Gordon H. Hansen. "Globalization, Outsourcing, and Wage Inequality." *American Economic Review* 86, no. 2 (1996): 234–239.

Finer, S. E. *The History of Government*. Oxford: Oxford University Press, 1997.

Flora, Peter, and Jens Alber. "Modernization, Democratization, and the Development of Welfare States in Western Europe." In *The Development of Welfare States in Europe and America,* edited by P. Flora and A. J. Heidenheimer. New Brunswick, N.J.: Transaction, 1984.

Forcese, Dennis. "Elites and Classes: The Structure of Inequality." In *Politics*

Canada, 6th ed., edited by Paul W. Fox and Graham White. Toronto: McGraw-Hill Ryerson, 1987.

Frank, Thomas. *The Conquest of Cool: Business Culture, Counterculture, and the Rise of Hip Consumerism.* Chicago: University of Chicago Press, 1997.

Frankel, Francine. *India's Political Economy, 1947–1977: The Gradual Revolution.* Princeton: Princeton University Press, 1978.

Friedman, Milton. "The Role of Monetary Policy." *American Economic Review* 58 (1968): 1–17.

Frisby, Tanya. "The Rise of Organised Crime in Russia: Its Roots and Social Significance." *Europe-Asia Studies* 50, no. 1 (1998): 27–49.

Fukuyama, Francis. *The End of History and the Last Man.* New York: Free Press, 1992.

Gaidar, Egor. "How the Nomenklatura 'Privatized' Its Own Power." *Russian Social Science Review* 37, no. 3 (1996): 23–34.

Gardell, Mattias. *Countdown to Armageddon: Louis Farrakhan and the Nation of Islam.* London: Hurst, 1996.

Gerlach, Allen. "Economic Decline and the Crisis of American Liberalism." *Contemporary Review* 270, no. 1572 (January 1997): 1–7.

Gibbs, David. "The Peasant as Counter-Revolutionary: The Rural Origins of the Afghan Insurgency." *Studies in Comparative International Development* 21, no. 1 (Spring 1986): 36–59.

Gibson, James L. "A Mile Wide but an Inch Deep (?): The Structure of Democratic Commitments in the Former USSR." *American Journal of Political Science* 40 (1996): 396–420.

Giddens, Anthony. *The Class Structure of the Advanced Societies.* London: Hutchinson University Library, 1973.

Gifford, Paul. *African Christianity.* Bloomington: Indiana University Press, 1998.

Giles, Michael W., and Melanie A. Buckner. "David Duke and Black Threat: An Old Hypothesis Revisited." *Journal of Politics* 55 (1993): 702–713.

Gordon, Robert J. "Has the 'New Economy' Rendered the Productivity Slowdown Obsolete?" June 1999. Available at http://faculty-web.at.nwu.edu/economics/gordon/researchhome.html.

Gottschalk, Peter, and Timoth M. Smeeding. "Cross-National Comparisons of Earnings and Income Inequality." *Journal of Economic Literature* 35 (1997): 633–687.

Gough, Ian. *The Political Economy of the Welfare State.* London: Macmillan, 1979.

Greenberg, Edward S. *The American Political System: A Radical Approach.* 5th ed. Boston: Scott, Foresman, 1989.

Griffith-Jones, Stephany. *Causes and Lessons of the Mexican Peso Crisis.* Working Paper no. 132. Helsinki: World Institute for Development Economics Research, 1997.

Gupta, Dipankar. *Nativism in a Metropolis: The Shiv Sena in Bombay.* New Delhi: Manohar, 1982.

Gurr, Ted Robert. *Why Men Rebel.* Princeton: Princeton University Press, 1970.

Hackett, Robert A. "For a Socialist Perspective on the News Media." *Studies in Political Economy* 19 (Spring 1986): 141–156.

Hainsworth, Paul, and Paul Mitchell. "France: The Front National from Crossroads to Crossroads?" *Parliamentary Affairs* 53 (2000): 443–456.

Hall, Stuart. "The Question of Cultural Identity." In *Modernity and Its Futures,* edited by Stuart Hall, David Held, and Tony McGrew. Cambridge: Polity Press in association with the Open University, 1992.

Halliday, Fred. *Arabia Without Sultans.* New York: Vintage Books, 1975.

———. "The Politics of 'Islam': A Second Look." *British Journal of Political Science* 25 (1995): 399–417.

Hardt, Michael, and Antonio Negri. *Empire.* Cambridge: Harvard University Press, 2000.

Harriott, Anthony. *Police and Crime Control in Jamaica.* Kingston: University of the West Indies Press, 2000.

Hartz, Louis, et al. *The Founding of New Societies.* New York: Harcourt and Brace, 1964.

Harvey, David. *The Condition of Postmodernity: An Enquiry into the Origins of Cultural Change.* Oxford: Blackwell, 1990.

Harvey, Neil. *The Chiapas Rebellion: The Struggle for Land and Democracy.* Durham, N.C.: Duke University Press, 1998.

Hayek, Friedrich. *The Constitution of Liberty.* London: Routledge, 1960.

———. *The Fatal Conceit: The Errors of Socialism.* London: Routledge 1988.

Heidenheimer, Arnold J., Hugh Heclo, and Carolyn Teich Adams. *Comparative Public Policy.* New York: St. Martin's Press, 1983.

Helleiner, Eric. *States and the Re-emergence of Global Finance.* New York: Cornell University Press, 1994.

Hellman, Judith Adler. Lecture at the University of the West Indies, Mona, Jamaica, 19 February 1998.

Heper, Metin. "Islam and Democracy in Turkey: Toward a Reconciliation?" *Middle East Journal* 51, no. 1 (Winter 1997): 32–45.

Heredia, Blanca. "Prosper or Perish? Development in the Age of Global Capital." *Current History* 96, no. 613 (November 1997): 383–388.

Hinkson Craig, Barbara, and David M. O'Brien. *Abortion and American Politics.* Chatham, N.J.: Chatham House, 1993.

Hirst, Paul. "The Global Economy: Myths and Realities." *International Affairs* 73, no. 3 (1997): 409–426.

Hirst, Paul, and Grahame Thompson. *Globalization in Question: The International Economy and the Possibilities of Governance.* Cambridge: Polity Press, 1996.

Hobhouse, L. T. *Liberalism.* New York: Henry Holt, 1911.

Hochschild, Jennifer L. *Facing Up to the American Dream: Race, Class, and the Soul of the Nation.* Princeton: Princeton University Press, 1996.

Hood, Christopher. *Explaining Economic Policy Reversals.* Philadelphia: Open University Press, 1994.

Hoogvelt, Ankie. *Globalisation and the Postcolonial World.* London: Macmillan, 1997.

Hough, Jerry F. *Democratization and Revolution in the USSR, 1985–1991.* Washington, D.C.: Brookings Institution, 1997.

Hourani, Albert. *A History of the Arab Peoples.* London: Faber and Faber, 1991.

Huntington, Samuel. *The Clash of Civilizations and the Remaking of World Order.* New York: Simon and Schuster, 1996.

———. *Political Order in Changing Societies.* New Haven: Yale University Press, 1968.

———. *The Third Wave: Democratization in the Late Twentieth Century.* Norman: University of Oklahoma Press, 1991.

Hyden, Goran. *Beyond Ujamaa in Tanzania.* London: Heinemann, 1980.

Hyslop, Jonathan. "Problems of Explanation in the Study of Afrikaner Nationalism: A Case Study of the West Rand." *Journal of Southern African Studies* 22 (1996): 373–385.

Ingham, Barbara, and A. K. M. Kalam. "Decentralization and Development: Theory and Evidence from Bangladesh." *Public Administration and Development* 12 (1992): 373–385.

Inglehart, Ronald. *The Silent Revolution.* Princeton: Princeton University Press, 1977.

Inglehart, Ronald, and Paul R. Abramson. "Economic Security and Value Change." *American Political Science Review* 88 (1994): 336–354.

Jacoby, Henry. *The Bureaucratization of the World.* Translated by Eveline L. Kanes. Berkeley: University of California Press, 1973.

Jaffrelot, Christophe. "Le syncrétisme stratégique et la construction de l'identité nationaliste hindoue: L'identité comme produit de synthèse." *Revue Française de Science Politique* 42, no. 4 (August 1992): 594–617.

———. *Les nationalistes hindous.* Paris: Presses de la Fondation Nationale des Sciences Politiques, 1993.

Johnson, Harry G. *Money, Trade, and Economic Growth.* London: George Allen and Unwin, 1964.

Junas, Daniel. "The Rise of the Citizen Militias." *Covert Action Quarterly,* Spring 1995.

Kamat, A. R. "The Emerging Situation." *Economic and Political Weekly* 14, nos. 7–8 (February 1979): 349–354.

Karapin, Roger. "Radical-Right and Neo-Fascist Political Parties in Western Europe." *Comparative Politics* 30 (1998): 213–234.

Kaviraj, Sudipta. "Indira Gandhi and Indian Politics." *Economic and Political Weekly* 19, nos. 38–39 (20–27 September 1986): 1697–1708.

Kepel, Gilles. *Jihad: Expansion et déclin de l'islamisme.* Paris: Gallimard, 2000.

———. *The Revenge of God.* Translated by Alan Braley. Cambridge: Polity Press, 1994.

Kohli, Atul, et al. "The Role of Theory in Comparative Politics: A Symposium." *World Politics* 48, no. 1 (1996): 1–49.

Koopmans, Ruud. "New Social Movements and Changes in Political Participation in Western Europe." *West European Politics* 19, no. 1 (January 1996): 28–50.

Kössler, Reinhart, and Henning Melber. "The Concept of Civil Society and the Process of Nation-Building in Africa." *Internationale Politik und Gesellschaft [International Politics and Society]* 1 (1996): 69–80.

Kotlikoff, Laurence J., and Lawrence H. Summers. "The Role of

Intergenerational Transfers in Aggregate Capital Formation." *Journal of Political Economy* 89 (1981): 706–732.

Krueger, Anne O. "The Political Economy of the Rent-Seeking Society." *American Economic Review* 64 (June 1974): 291–303.

———. "Trade Strategies and Employment in Developing Countries." *Finance and Development* 21, no. 4 (June 1984): 23–26.

Krugman, Paul. *The Age of Diminished Expectations*. Rev. and updated ed. Cambridge: MIT Press, 1994.

Kryshtanovskaia, Ol'ga V. "Transformation of the Old Nomenklatura into a New Russian Elite." *Russian Social Science Review* 37, no. 4 (1996): 18–40.

Kuhn, Thomas S. *The Structure of Scientific Revolutions*. Chicago: University of Chicago Press, 1970.

Laclau, Ernesto, and Chantal Mouffe. "Hegemony and Radical Democracy." In Ernesto Laclau and Chantal Mouffe, trans. Winston Moore and Paul Cammack, *Hegemony and Socialist Strategy*. London: Verso, 1985.

Lasch, Christopher. *The Revolt of the Elites and the Betrayal of Democracy*. New York: W. W. Norton, 1995.

Lauridsen, Laurids S. "The Financial Crisis in Thailand: Causes, Conduct, and Consequences." *World Development* 26, no. 8 (1998): 1575–1591.

Le Roy Ladurie, Emmanuel. *The Peasants of Languedoc*. Translated by John Day. Urbana: University of Illinois Press, 1974.

Lemarchand, René. *Burundi: Ethnic Conflict and Genocide*. New York: Woodrow Wilson Center Press, 1996.

Lerner, Daniel. "Toward a Communication Theory of Modernization." In *Communications and Political Development*, edited by Lucian Pye. Princeton: Princeton University Press, 1963.

Levada, Iurii. "'Homo Sovieticus' Five Years Later: 1989–1994." *Russian Social Science Review* 37, no. 4 (1996): 3–17.

Lind, Michael. *The Next American Nation*. New York: Free Press, 1996.

Lippmann, Walter. *Public Opinion*. New York: Harcourt, Brace, 1922.

Lipset, S. M. *Revolution and Counter-Revolution*. New York: Anchor Books, 1970.

Losson, Christian, and Paul Quinio. *Génération Seattle*. Paris: Grasset, 2002.

Lucas, John. "The Politics of Business Associations in the Developing World." *Journal of Developing Areas* 32, no. 1 (Fall 1997): 71–96.

Majone, Giandomenico, ed. *Deregulation or Re-regulation?* London: Pinter, 1990.

Mann, Sheilah. "What the Survey of American College Freshmen Tells Us About Their Interest in Politics and Political Science." *PS: Political Science and Politics* 32, no. 2 (June 1999): 263–268.

Manor, James. "Anomie in Indian Politics: Origins and Potential Wider Impact." *Economic and Political Weekly*, annual no. 1983.

Manzo, Kathryn. *Creating Boundaries: The Politics of Race and Nation*. Boulder: Lynne Rienner, 1996.

Marcus, Jonathan. "Advance or Consolidation? The French National Front and the 1995 Elections." *West European Politics* 19 (1996): 303–320.

Maylam, P. "The Rise and Decline of Urban Apartheid." *African Affairs* 89, no. 354 (1990): 57–84.

McKenzie, Evan. *Privatopia: Homeowner Associations and the Rise of Residential Private Government.* New Haven: Yale University Press, 1994.

McNeill, W. *The Pursuit of Power.* Chicago: University of Chicago Press, 1982.

Michels, Robert. *Political Parties.* New York: Free Press, 1962.

Miliband, Ralph. *The State in Capitalist Society.* London: Weidenfeld and Nicolson, 1973.

Mills, C. Wright. *The Power Elite.* New York: Oxford University Press, 1957.

Monroe, Kristin Renwick, ed. *The Economic Approach to Politics.* New York: HarperCollins, 1991.

Moore, Barrington. *Social Origins of Dictatorship and Democracy.* London: Penguin, 1966.

Mouffe, Chantal. "Working-Class Hegemony and the Struggle for Socialism." *Studies in Political Economy* 12 (Fall 1983).

Muller, Edward N., and Mitchell A. Seligson. "Inequality and Insurgency." *American Political Science Review* 81, no. 2 (1987): 425–450.

Munroe, Trevor, and Ivelaw L. Griffith. "Drugs and Democratic Governance in the Caribbean." In *Democracy and Human Rights in the Caribbean,* edited by Ivelaw L. Griffith and Betty N. Sedoc-Dahlberg. Boulder: Westview Press, 1997.

Myint, Hla. "Economic Theory and the Underdeveloped Countries." *Journal of Political Economy* 73 (1965): 477–491.

Naples, Michele I. "Industrial Conflict, the Quality of Worklife, and the Productivity Slowdown in U.S. Manufacturing." *Eastern Economic Journal* 15, no. 2 (1988): 157–166.

Newbury, David. "Understanding Genocide." *African Studies Review* 41, no. 1 (April 1998): 73–97.

Newhouse, John. "Europe's Rising Regionalism." *Foreign Affairs* 76, no. 1 (January–February 1997): 67–84.

North, Douglas C., and Robert Paul Thomas. *The Rise of the Western World.* Cambridge: Cambridge University Press, 1973.

Nozick, Robert. *Anarchy, State, and Utopia.* Oxford: Blackwell, 1974.

Nye, Joseph S., Philip D. Zelikow, and David C. King, eds. *Why People Don't Trust Government.* Cambridge: Harvard University Press, 1997.

Obi, Cyril I. *Structural Adjustment, Oil, and Popular Struggles: The Deepening Crisis of State Legitimacy in Nigeria.* Monograph Series no. 1/97. Dakar: Codesria, 1997.

O'Connor, James. *The Fiscal Crisis of the State.* New York: St. Martin's Press, 1973.

Offe, Claus. *Contradictions of the Welfare State.* Edited by John Keane. Cambridge: MIT Press, 1984.

Ohmae, Kenichi. "The Rise of the Region State." *Foreign Affairs* 72, no. 2 (Spring 1993): 78–87.

Olson, Mancur, Jr. *The Logic of Collective Action.* Cambridge: Harvard University Press, 1965.

Ortega y Gasset, José. *The Revolt of the Masses.* Authorized translation. London: George Allen and Unwin, 1951.

Paige, Jeffery M. *Agrarian Revolution.* New York: Free Press, 1975.

Park, Yung Chul, and Chi-Young Song. "The East Asian Financial Crisis: A Year Later." *IDS Bulletin* 30, no. 1 (January 1999): 93–107.

Peach, Richard, and Charles Steindel. "A Nation of Spendthrifts? An Analysis of Trends in Personal and Gross Spending." *Current Issues in Economics and Finance* 6, no. 10 (September 2000): 1–6.

Persson, Torsten, and Guido Tabellini. "Is Inequality Harmful for Growth?" *American Economic Review* 84 (1994): 600–621.

Piscatori, James, ed. *Islamic Fundamentalisms and the Gulf Crisis.* Chicago: Fundamentalism Project, American Academy of Arts and Sciences, 1991.

Polanyi, Karl. *The Great Transformation.* New York: Rinehart, 1944.

Popkin, Samuel. *The Rational Peasant.* Berkeley: University of California Press, 1979.

Popov, Vladimir. "Emerging Structure of Russian Capitalism." *Development* 40, no. 3 (1997): 37–45.

Prunier, Gérard. *The Rwanda Crisis.* London: Hurst, 1995.

Przeworski, Adam. *Democracy and the Market: Political and Economic Reforms in Eastern Europe and Latin America.* Cambridge: Cambridge University Press, 1991.

Przeworski, Adam, Michael Alvarez, José Antonio Cheibub, and Fernando Limongi. "What Makes Democracies Endure." *Journal of Democracy* 7, no. 1 (1996): 39–56.

Putnam, Robert. "Bowling Alone: America's Declining Social Capital." *Journal of Democracy* 6, no. 1 (1995): 65–78.

———. "Tuning In, Tuning Out: The Strange Disappearance of Social Capital in America." *PS: Political Science and Politics* 28, no. 4 (December 1995): 664–683.

Radcliff, Benjamin, and Patricia Davis. "Labor Organization and Electoral Participation in Industrial Democracies." *American Journal of Political Science* 44, no. 1 (January 2000): 132–141.

Rand, Ayn. *The Virtue of Selfishness.* New York: New American Library, 1964.

Rapley, John. "Convergence: Myths and Reality." *Progress in Development Studies* 1, no. 4 (2001): 295–308.

———. *Understanding Development.* 2nd ed. Boulder: Lynne Rienner, 2002.

Rashid, Ahmed. "Pakistan: Trouble Ahead, Trouble Behind." *Current History* 95, no. 600 (April 1996): 158–164.

Rashiduzzaman, M. "The Liberals and the Religious Right in Bangladesh." *Asian Survey* 34, no. 11 (1994): 974–990.

Rawls, John. *A Theory of Justice.* Cambridge: Harvard Belknap, 1971.

Reich, Robert B. *The Work of Nations.* New York: Alfred A. Knopf, 1991.

Reinicke, Wolfgang H. "Global Public Policy." *Foreign Affairs* (November–December 1997): 127–138.

Richardson, Jeremy. "The Market for Political Activism: Interest Groups as a Challenge to Political Parties." *West European Politics* 18, no. 1 (1995): 116–139.

Roosens, E. *Creating Ethnicity.* London: Sage, 1989.

Rose, Richard. "Ex-Communists in Post-Communist Societies." *The Political Quarterly* 67, no. 1 (1996): 14–25.

Rose-Ackerman, Susan. "Trust and Honesty in Post-Socialist Societies." *Kyklos* 54 (2001): 415–444.

Rueschmeyer, Dietrich, Evelyn Huber Stephens, and John D. Stephens. *Capitalist Development and Democracy.* Chicago: University of Chicago Press, 1992.

Runciman, W. G. *Relative Deprivation and Social Justice.* Berkeley: University of California Press, 1966.

Russell, Bertrand. *A History of Western Philosophy.* London: Unwin, 1984.

Sachs, Jeffrey D., and Howard J. Shatz. "U.S. Trade with Developing Countries and Wage Inequality." *American Economic Review* 86, no. 2 (1996): 234–239.

Salt, Jeremy. "Nationalism and the Rise of Muslim Sentiment in Turkey." *Middle Eastern Studies* 31, no. 1 (1995): 13–27.

Sassen, Saskia. "Cities and Communities in the Global Economy." *American Behavioural Scientist* 39 (1996): 629–639.

Sayigh, Rosemary. *Too Many Enemies: The Palestinian Experience in Lebanon.* London: Zed Books, 1994.

Schattschneider, E. E. *The Semisovereign People.* New York: Holt, 1960.

Schatzberg, Michael G. "Ethnicity and Class at the Local Levels: Bars and Bureaucrats in Lisala, Zaire." *Comparative Politics* 13 (1981): 461–478.

Schlesinger, Arthur, Jr. "Has Democracy a Future?" *Foreign Affairs* 76, no. 5 (September–October 1997): 2–12.

Scholte, Jan Aart. "Global Capitalism and the State." *International Affairs* 73, no. 3 (1997): 427–452.

Schor, Juliet B. *The Overspent American: Upscaling, Downshifting, and the New Consumer.* New York: Basic Books, 1998.

Schwartz, Shalom H., Anat Bardi, and Gabriel Bianchi. "Value Adaptation to the Imposition and Collapse of Communist Regimes in East-Central Europe." In *Political Psychology,* edited by Stanley A. Renshon and John Duckitt. New York: New York University Press, 2000.

Scitovsky, Tibor. *The Joyless Economy: An Inquiry into Human Satisfaction and Consumer Dissatisfaction.* New York: Oxford University Press, 1976.

Scott, James C. *The Moral Economy of the Peasant.* New Haven: Yale University Press, 1976.

Seligson, Mitchell A., and John T. Passé-Smith, eds. *Development and Underdevelopment: The Political Economy of Global Inequality.* 2nd ed. Boulder: Lynne Rienner, 1998.

Shane, Scott. *Dismantling Utopia.* Chicago: Ivan R. Dee, 1995.

Sherman, Paul W., and Jennifer Billing. "Antimicrobial Functions of Spices: Why Some Like It Hot." *Quarterly Review of Biology* 73, no. 1 (March 1998).

Silber, Laura, and Allan Little. *The Death of Yugoslavia.* Rev. ed. London: Penguin, 1996.

Sklair, Leslie. *Sociology of the Global System.* Baltimore: Johns Hopkins University Press, 1991.

Smith, Barbara. "Algeria: The Horror." *New York Review of Books,* 23 April 1998.

Sorel, Georges. *Réflexions sur la violence.* 11th ed. Paris: Librairie Marcel Rivière et Cie., 1950.

Stark, Rodney. *The Rise of Christianity.* San Francisco: HarperCollins, 1997.

Strama, Mark. "Overcoming Cynicism: Youth Participation and Electoral Politics." *National Civic Review* 87, no. 1 (Spring 1988): 71–77.

Strange, Susan. *The Retreat of the State: The Diffusion of Power in the World Economy.* Cambridge: Cambridge University Press, 1997.

Sunar, Ilkay, and Binnaz Toprak. "Islam in Politics: The Case of Turkey." *Government and Opposition* 18 (1983): 421–441.

Szarka, Joseph. "The Winning of the 1995 French Presidential Election." *West European Politics* 19 (1996): 151–167.

Szayna, Thomas S. "Ultra-Nationalism in Central Europe." *Orbis* 37 (1993): 527–550.

Taylor, Charles. "Atomism." In Charles Taylor, *Philosophy and the Human Sciences.* Cambridge: Cambridge University Press, 1985.

Tessler, Mark. "The Origins of Popular Support for Islamist Movements: A Political Economy Analysis." In *Islam, Democracy, and the State in North Africa,* edited by John P. Entelis. Bloomington: Indiana University Press, 1997.

Therborn, Goran. "Classes and States: Welfare State Developments, 1881–1981." *Studies in Political Economy* 14 (1984): 7–42.

Turton, David. "War and Ethnicity: Global Connections and Local Violence in Northeast Africa and Former Yugoslavia." *Oxford Development Studies* 25, no. 1 (1997): 77–94.

United Nations Development Programme. *Human Development Report.* New York: United Nations, 1998.

United Nations Economic Commission for Africa. *Transforming Africa's Economies.* Addis Ababa: United Nations, 2001.

Vainshtein, Grigory. "Totalitarian Public Consciousness in a Post-Totalitarian Society: The Russian Case in the General Context of Post-Communist Developments." *Communist and Post-Communist Studies* 27 (1994): 247–259.

Vidal, Claudine. "Les politiques de la haine." *Les Temps Modernes* 583 (1995): 6–33.

Voss, D. Stephen. "Beyond Racial Threat: Failure of an Old Hypothesis in the New South." *Journal of Politics* 58 (1996): 1156–1170.

Walton, John, and David Seddon. *Free Markets and Food Riots: The Politics of Global Adjustment.* Oxford: Blackwell, 1994.

Warr, Peter G. *Macroeconomic Origins of the Korean Crisis.* Working Paper in Trade and Development no. 00/04. Canberra: Australian National University, 2000.

Waters, Malcolm. *Globalization.* London: Routledge, 1995.

Weems, Robert E., Jr. *Black Business in the Black Metropolis: The Chicago Metropolitan Assurance Company, 1925–1985.* Bloomington: Indiana University Press, 1996.

White, Gordon. *Riding the Tiger: The Politics of Economic Reform in Post-Mao China.* Stanford, Calif.: Stanford University Press, 1993.

Widfeldt, Anders. "Scandinavia: Mixed Success for the Populist Right." *Parliamentary Affairs* 53 (2000): 486–500.

Wiebe, Gerhardt D. "The Social Effects of Broadcasting." In *Mass Culture Revisited,* edited by Bernard Rosenberg and David Manning White. New York: Van Nostrand Reinhold, 1971.

Williams, Phillip M. *Crisis and Compromise: Politics in the Fourth Republic.* London: Longman, 1964.

Wilson, Bryan R. *Magic and the Millennium.* London: Heinemann, 1973.

Wolf, Eric. R. *Peasant Wars of the Twentieth Century.* New York: Harper and Row, 1969.

World Bank. *World Development Indicators 2002.* Baltimore: Johns Hopkins University Press, 2002.

Wright, Gavin. *Old South, New South: Revolutions in the Southern Economy Since the Civil War.* New York: Basic Books, 1986.

Yentürk, Nurhan. "Short-Term Capital Inflows and Their Impact on Macroeconomic Structure: Turkey in the 1990s." *Developing Economies* 37, no. 1 (March 1999): 89–113.

Zakaria, Fareed. "The Rise of Illiberal Democracy." *Foreign Affairs* (November–December 1997): 22–43.

Databases

Center on Budget Policy and Priorities (www.cbpp.org).

Investment Company Institute (www.ici.org).

U.S. Census Bureau (www.census.gov).

U.S. Department of Commerce, Bureau of Economic Analysis (www.bea.gov).

U.S. Department of Labor, Bureau of Labor Statistics (www.bls.gov).

U.S. Federal Reserve Board (www.federalreserve.gov).

News Sources

BBC World Service
Canadian Press News Agency
CET Online (Internet newsletter)
cnnfn.com
The Economist (London)
Far Eastern Economic Review
Financial Times (London)
Forbes
Ha'aretz (Jerusalem)
The Independent (London)
Le Nouvel Observateur (Paris)

Le Soir (Brussels)
Maclean's Magazine (Toronto)
Mail and Guardian (Johannesburg)
Middle East Economic Survey
Monitor Radio International
Ottawa Citizen (Ottawa)
Radio Deutsche Welle
Radio France Internationale
Reuters News Agency
Times of India (Delhi)

Index

About the Book

Has the far-reaching experiment in creating a new world order along neoliberal lines succeeded? John Rapley answers with an emphatic no, contending that the rosy picture painted by neoliberal proponents of globalization was based on false assumptions.

True, Rapley acknowledges, neoliberal reforms often did generate economic growth—but at a price. The resulting increase in inequality led to political instability and spawned tendencies ranging from right-wing populism to renewed ethnic and Islamic militancy.

Rapley offers a range of cases to illustrate how neoliberal globalization has helped to destroy regimes in the developing world by profoundly altering patterns of income distribution and resource allocation. The political tensions unleashed by these regime crises, he argues, are now being manifested around the globe, with the negative consequences still to be fully realized.

John Rapley is senior lecturer in the Department of Government at the University of the West Indies, Mona. He is author of *Understanding Development: Theory and Practice in the Third World* (now in its second edition) and *Ivoirien Capitalism: African Entrepreneurs in Côte d'Ivoire*.